AMERICAN WRITERS AND RADICAL POLITICS, 1900–39

AMERICAN WRITERS AND RADICAL POLITICS, 1900-39

EQUIVOCAL COMMITMENTS

ERIC HOMBERGER

Lecturer in American Studies, University of East Anglia

St. Martin's Press   New York

First published in the United States of America in 1986

Printed in Hong Kong

ISBN 0–312–02792–3

Library of Congress Cataloging-in-Publication Data

Homberger, Eric.
   American writers and radical politics, 1900–39.

   Bibliography: p.
   Includes index.
   1. American literature—20th century—History and
criticism. 2. Radicalism in literature. 3. Politics
in literature. 4. Authors, American—20th century—
Political and social views.   I. Title.
PS228.R34H65   1986   810′.9′0052   86–1760
ISBN 0–312–02792–3

To Paul Kennedy

Contents

Preface

There was no shortage of events in the nineteenth century which dragged American writers to the centre stage of political controversy. The abolition of slavery and the rise of American imperialism were such issues, but it was not until the twentieth century that the forms of radicalism shifted away from an *ad hoc* preoccupation with specific issues to a more general sense that the system itself was wrong, and that far-reaching changes were needed.

The following studies describe three 'generations' within the literary radicalism of the period between 1900 and 1939. The experience of each 'generation' was shaped by different political environments, and by dramatically different ideological aspirations. The generation which came of age in 1900, which is represented in Chapters 1 and 2 by Jack London and Upton Sinclair, was shaped by the struggle to create a Socialist Party. In *The Jungle* and *The Iron Heel*, the ambiguities of conversion to socialism, and some of the tensions of Socialist Party policy of 1900–10, are revealed. The third and fourth chapters concentrate on the generation which came of age with *The Masses*, Max Eastman's magazine, which got into its stride in 1914. John Reed was the chief discovery of *The Masses* and has come to stand for a larger group of writers, artists and thinkers who were increasingly drawn to left-wing political commitments. Reed's career, from Harvard College to the Kremlin, was given important direction by the bitter industrial dispute in Colorado in 1914. The events in Colorado brought together divergent strands of socialism: Reed and Eastman visited the scene of the worst violence in Ludlow, as did Upton Sinclair, whose *King Coal* (1917) attempted to reinterpret the causes of the strike. The *dramatis personae* of Colorado in 1914 stirred the nation: there was an exploiting capitalist, John D. Rockefeller, Jr; a brilliant liberal journalist, Walter Lippmann; a clever and forceful lawyer, Frank P. Walsh, to put the people's case; and a well-meaning but seemingly ineffectual President in Washington. The Colorado strike and its aftermath provide a microcosm of the interplay of personality, economic interest, political ideals and intense commitments which marks the transition from the 'socialist' generation of writers to the 'Communist' generation symbolized by John Reed.

The period of Communist predominance remains in certain key respects ill-understood. The more obvious manifestations of the 'literary class war' in the 1930s have received some attention. The careers of Dos Passos, Hemingway, Farrell and Steinbeck have been exhaustively studied. It is equally possible, and perhaps even more illuminating, to watch the commitments and ambivalences of the decade as they appear in less familiar institutions, such as the John Reed Clubs, and groups such as the Objectivists. The John Reed Clubs enable us to understand the impact of Soviet Marxist theories of proletarian culture upon the American literary left. And the fate of the Objectivists is one of the most revealing facets of the encounter between literary modernism and the Communist Party. The Objectivists were a small group of radical Jewish poets in New York in the late 1920s. They attempted to hold together divergent commitments to modern poetry, which derived from Ezra Pound and William Carlos Williams, and a growing involvement with the Communist Party. In the end, the taste of Communist Party reviewers, editors and writers could not be reconciled with high modernism. The Objectivists dispersed: George Oppen ceased to write poetry, and devoted himself to party work among the unemployed in Brooklyn. Others withdrew into personal life: Carl Rakosi pursued his career as a therapist and social worker; Charles Reznikoff turned to a Jewish subject-matter for his writing, thus condemning himself to bourgeois nationalism in party eyes, and resumed the printing of small editions of his own work. Louis Zukofsky found it easier to print his essays than his difficult poems in the aftermath of his *An Objectivists' Anthology* (1932). There was no precise equivalent to John Reed's role in the 1930s, but one figure, Edmund Wilson, seemed to represent many liberal intellectuals in America who were drawn to the Communist Party. His subsequent disillusionment with the party, and with Marxism as a theoretical system, anticipates yet another period, another generation, in which the ex-Communist emerges as culture hero.

It has often seemed to me that feelings matter more than ideas, and ideas more than economic forces, in the making of radicals. Socialism and Communism are intellectually complex systems of thought. Few imaginative writers have attempted to master the intricacies of Marxian economic doctrine, and fewer still in America were familiar with the philosophic thought on which Marxism rests. But of course the mastery of economic theories is not a prerequisite to political commitment. If anything, it comes later, providing something of an intellectual rationale for emotional commitments already made. It is even possible that the usual concerns of politics have little or nothing to do with the making of radicals. Such people find themselves in sensitivities suddenly aroused, in a range of human sympathies discovered by a process analogous to religious conversion. It all sounds like something out of George Eliot or Mrs Gaskell, but the premiss of many a hopeful Victorian novel, in which everything depends upon a turn of heart, is not so very remote from the experience of socialists and even some Communists in the period from 1900 to 1939. There is no Marxist theory for the psychology of conversion, and in the face of rigorous materialism there is little room for psychology at all. There was a sometimes bitter debate within the Socialist Party, and then within the Communist Party, about whether bourgeois converts to socialism (or Communism) could or should be accepted into the party and be allowed to play a full role. The suspicion that they would shape the party into something congenial to their class values, a process that would inevitably lead to reformism and accommodation with capitalism, was frequently voiced. Men of letters generally fell into this category of well-meaning bourgeois converts. There is no simple equation between class background and ideological affiliation within socialism; however often, like Eastman and Reed, they shared the perspectives of the left wing of the Socialist Party, or were involved in any of the sectarian groupings within the Communist Party, they could regularly expect to have their accent, table manners, social life, mode of dress and family background thrown back at them. The cult of proletarianism in the left was often the vehicle for older American hostilities towards intellectuals, whose books never quite seemed truly socialist or Communist. A bourgeois social background was a kind of original sin, endlessly to be expiated. Intellectuals, especially those within the Communist Party, soon learned to talk and dress, and then to write, as they imagined proletarians would do. There were many ways to respond to this pressure: Mike Gold kept carefully hidden the fact that he had, briefly, attended Harvard College. Few writers seem to have been very satisfied with the resulting compromises. It was hard to abandon bourgeois notions of artistic autonomy, individualism. Such was the social crisis in America that the demand that writers throw themselves into the class struggle (which mainly meant party assignments) did not seem ridiculous. Many young writers did their best, for a time, to fulfil them. As policy shifted across a spectrum of issues, writers struggled to translate sympathies into assent to policies. It was a situation richly productive of misgivings and inner conflict. When examined in detail, the political commitments of American writers often seem equivocal. Their commitments are a manuscript which they are endlessly revising. It is precisely in the space where ideological certainties and emotional desires come into conflict that the most interesting stories and essays, novels and poems, emerge.

E. H.
Norwich

Acknowledgements

Several trips to the United States have incurred debts of hospitality which are a pleasure to acknowledge: to Bill Janeway and Wesley Resnick in New York, Scott and Ruthie Sanders in Bloomington, Norman and Bici Pettit in Cambridge, Paul and Cath Kennedy in New Haven, and Barbara Ruland in Charlottesville. Several of my colleagues have shared my interest in the fate of the American radical spirit, and have read drafts of the manuscript: Bill Albert and Richard Crockatt. Alan Wald, Malcolm Sylvers, Mark Krupnick and Lawrence Schwartz have, in their own work, sharpened my sense of the issues at stake; as have the late Ella Winter, A. B. Magil and Sender Garlin. Robert Gorham Davis, who was willing to write frankly and at length about the 1930s in correspondence, has a balance of personal experience and scholarly integrity which I admire. Professor Daniel Aaron was kind enough to encourage my interest in radicalism at a particularly helpful point. Mrs Ann C. Wood and the staff of the Inter-Library Loan Office in the University of East Anglia have been endlessly resourceful. Research for this book was at several stages aided by the School of English and American Studies, University of East Anglia.

Certain chapters have previously appeared in print, and appear here with the editor's or publisher's permission. Chapter 5 was originally presented to the University of Essex conference on the Sociology of Literature in July 1978. It was revised and published in the *Journal of American Studies* in 1979; Chapter 6 began life as a long book review in the *Times Higher Education Supplement*, 5 December 1980, and appears here by permission; Chapter 7 (i) was first published in *George Oppen: Man and Poet*, ed. Burton Hatlen (National Poetry Foundation, 1981), and (ii) in Duncan Glen's periodical *Akros* in April 1982. In each case there has been significant revision of the text and notes in the light of further research, new publications and rethinking the argument. In only one instance has this resulted in an overturned judgement. The idea, as I suggested in *Akros*, that Louis Zukofsky would not in 1931 have been aware of the political implications of the term 'objectivist' does not give sufficient credit to the author of 'Memory of V. I. Ulianov', 'During the Passaic Strike of 1926' and other expressions of a political sensibility. Zukofsky was a knowledgeable and committed Marxist by the late 1920s. This view is considerably supported by a recent article by Burton Hatlen in the summer 1984 issue of *Contemporary Literature* in which he argues that Zukofsky in the first ten sections of *A* was 'explicitly and consistently a political poet'. But even in Hatlen's sympathetic presentation, Zukofsky's politics are still too abstract, theoretical and remote. In Chapter 7 I have tried to locate the politics of Objectivism in local and specific circumstances; it seems to me the only way they make sense.

The Trotsky letters are held in the Houghton Library, Harvard University, and are printed here for the first time by kind permission of the Houghton Library. Philip Rahv's letters to Trotsky, which are also held at the Houghton Library, are printed here for the first time by kind permission of Mrs B. T. Rahv and the Houghton Library. James Brewster's letter to Upton Sinclair appears by kind permission of the Lilly Library, Indiana University. I am grateful to David Sinclair and Penguin Books for permission to quote from Upton Sinclair's *The Jungle*.

1 Jack London

Jacob Riis noted in *How the Other Half Lives* (1890) that Hamilton Street in New York contained no picturesque dives, only a sailor's mission, saloons and tenements. 'Suppose we look into one?', he asked. Riis's book issued a serious invitation to look at urban life in America. 'Be a little careful, please! The hall is dark . . . Here where the hall turns and dives into utter darkness is a step, and another, another. A flight of stairs. You can feel your way, if you cannot see it. Close? Yes! . . . That was a woman filling her pail by the hydrant you just bumped against . . .'[1] To visit the 'sweaters' of 'Jewtown', one must take the Second Avenue El:

> Every open window of the big tenements, that stand like a continuous brick wall on both sides of the way, gives you a glimpse of one of these shops as the train speeds by. Men and women bending over their machines, or ironing clothes at the window, half-naked. Proprieties do not count on the East Side; nothing counts that cannot be converted into hard cash. The road is like a big gangway through an endless work-room where vast multitudes are forever laboring.[2]

Riis brought his prejudices along with him to 'Jewtown'. When Basil March travels downtown on the Third Avenue El in William Dean Howells's *A Hazard of New Fortunes* (1890) he indulges in one of his 'public-spirited reveries' over the future of 'our heterogeneous commonwealth'

> It must be owned that he did not take much trouble about this; what these poor people were thinking, hoping, fearing, enjoying, suffering; just where and how they lived; who and what they individually were – these were the matters of his waking dreams as he stared hard at them, while the train raced further into the gay ugliness – the shapeless, graceless, reckless, picturesqueness of the Bowery.[3]

By temperament March chose not to look too closely at the 'vast hive of population' swarming throughout lower Manhattan. He found the variety greater on the East Side than on the West, and travels on the El with the curious, bland demeanour of the flâneur. Riis was a police reporter working out of Mulberry Street, and knew enough about life in the slums for its 'gay ugliness' to hold little charm for him. The 'sweaters' are observed working 'half-naked'. It is obviously high summer in New York, but it is also 1890 and convention and the public proprieties assume a standard of behaviour which makes no concession to the weather, nor to the kind of work done in the tenements of 'Jewtown': pants-pressing, the operating of sewing machines, in close, poorly-lit buildings. The men in shirt sleeves or undershirts, and the women workers in what one imagines to be sleeveless blouses, draw forth Riis's further reflection that, on the East Side, nothing 'counts' that does not have cash value. 'Money is their God', he wrote of Jews in the preceding chapter.[4] 'Life itself is of little value compared with even the leanest bank account.' Travelling on the El allowed one to see 'the endless panorama of the tenements', now revealed to be an 'endless work-room', a hellish cathedral to Jewish materialism. For Riis the Jews are a people threateningly alien to the civil values of his culture. Buried within the East Side scene was a portent, a racist nightmare of Western culture just beginning to form on the horizons: the immigrant, the oriental, the foreigner. Behind Riis's invitation to visit the tenement is a dread, the anxiety of a civilization losing its codes and distinctions, being swamped by values which previously were under control (materialism), and which now seem to threaten the fragile structures of society. Enough people went along, at least in imagination, with Riis into 'darkest' New York, as they followed Booth, Sims, Mayhew, Stead and the Social Settlement workers into the slums of England, and then the United States, to make the invitation significant. The 'alien presence climbing higher and higher', as Henry James put it in *The American Scene* (1907), was a source of anxiety to most Americans. To enter that threatening world, a helpful guide was needed. One of the very best was Abraham Cahan. His extended walks through the ghetto with writers like Lincoln Steffens and Hutchins Hapgood helped outsiders to see ghetto life without Riis's sentimentality, as in this description of the old houses of the poor:

Of the handsome cornice barely a trace is left. Dirt and desolation reign in the wide hallway, and danger lurks on the stairs. Rough pine boards fence off the roomy fire-places . . . The arched gateway leads no longer to a shady bower on the banks of the rushing stream, inviting to day-dreams with its gentle repose, but to a dark and nameless alley, shut in by high brick walls, cheerless as the lives of those they shelter.[5]

Only the oldest residents of Manhattan could recall 'shady bower' or 'rushing stream': such things had long disappeared, and the immigrants were hardly to be held responsible. The invocation of arcadia in this context had more to do with the emotions Riis wishes to convey than with the historical reality of Manhattan in the 1890s. And those emotions are powerfully coloured by regret at the passing of a world of the 'handsome cornice' and 'roomy fire-place'. Cahan reserved his sentimentality for the religious piety of Jews in the old world: like Riis's 'roomy fire-place', their lives in the new world were covered over by modern materialism; but Cahan seems to have felt there was no return to the ancient pieties. (Before the immigrant Jew lay the whole of Modern American life.)

Riis's solution to the tenement problem seems utterly non-political. He called at the end of *How the Other Half Lives* for a recognition that the gap between classes was widening day by day: 'No tardy enactment of law, no political expedient, can close it . . . I know of but one bridge that will carry us over safe, a bridge founded upon justice and built of human hearts.'[6] While socialists would disagree with Riis's scepticism before politics and the law (and some, notably the direct actionists on the left of the Socialist Party after the turn of the century, would have agreed with this much of Riis's analysis), they, too, believed in the main in the need to change people's hearts.[7] Those who were unaware of the problem, or indifferent to its true human cost, had to be appealed to, invited, as Riis proposed, to enter the world of the tenement and the sweated labourer. Socialists and social investigators shared the belief that social improvement must come through organizing and manipulating sympathy, with a consequence that socialists could easily fall into the approach of progressives to social problems, and vice versa. There was a fluidity and ease of movement between ideologies which is a striking characteristic of the age.

Half-ironically, Jack London feared that *The People of the Abyss* (1903) might in time become 'a sort of sentimental-radical-reformer's classic'.[8] He, too, appealed strongly to instincts of common decency and justice; he anticipated the need for a change of heart among the public (and other unspecified changes in society); and issued, not unlike Jacob Riis, an invitation to the 'dear, soft people' to follow him through the squalor of the East End of London.

At several points in *The People of the Abyss* London seems angrily puzzled by the problem of how his readers could be made to understand the lives of tramps and of the homeless of London. It is a problem which everyone who writes on poverty and low life must confront, and since there are still so many indications of a general public ignorance and hostility on this question, answers had better be provisional: none seem to have worked particularly well.[9] Upton Sinclair in *The Jungle* asks: 'How . . . could anyone expect to excite sympathy among lovers of good literature by telling how a family found their home alive with vermin, and of all the suffering and inconvenience and humiliation they were put to, and the hard-earned money they spent, in efforts to get rid of them?'[10] Sinclair's thoughtful approach is to transform an abstract into a specific account of Jurgis and how his family attempt to cope with vermin: their story makes the general point accessible. But there are other dimensions to the vermin problem, dimensions which are ignored or misunderstood by the kind of story which Sinclair tells, and which are discussed in detail in the second chapter; there were efforts to improve hygiene through legislation, municipal ordinances, and educational propaganda conducted through public schools and in the Social Settlements. But such efforts were generally reduced to that remote category of middle-class do-gooding which were either comic or ineffectual in stories about the poor. The kind of story told isolates Jurgis and Ona, and accentuates their helplessness.

In the same way Jurgis and Ona are as cut off from the 'lovers of literature' as the Jews and Chinese in *How the Other Half Lives*. Sinclair understood the need to humanize their plight, thus enabling the reader to participate in their struggle. But the language of Darwinian naturalism used to describe the poor and their environment is profoundly dehumanizing. It is a contradiction which Sinclair escapes only when he extricated Jurgis from Packingtown. Jack London was at ease with such a language, and its consequent tendency to dehumanize, while at the same time writing: 'But, O dear, soft people, full of meat and blood, with white beds and airy rooms waiting you each night, how can I make you know what it is to suffer as you would suffer if you spent a weary night on London's streets.'[11] Like Sinclair's 'lovers of good literature', London's 'dear, soft people' constitute an imputed audience who have a role to play within the story. Their cultural values are repeatedly invoked: it is assumed such values form a bond between author and reader, and give them both an agreed basis for judging the poor and the slums. London's implied reader plays an important part in the rhetoric of *The People of the Abyss*. London's references to the 'sacredness of motherhood' and condemnation of the 'ugly and repulsive philosophy' of the man who lived for nothing but drunken excess, are wholly free from irony or defensiveness. He assumes that such moralizing value-judgements are shared by the readers and by the society at large. (Riis's bland racism falls exactly into the same category.) There was felt to be a larger community of moral and ethical values which transcended class division, and which might be appealed to above and beyond any political or ideological position. The point is self-evident, but worth emphasizing; socialists did not necessarily remove themselves from the common discourse of their culture when they addressed social problems. Their works may be thereby tainted by bourgeois, sexist and racist assumptions which later generations of scientific thinkers will vigorously seek to eliminate. But socialists of Sinclair's and London's generation were probably more successful at reaching that audience of middle-class and middle-ground opinion, which remained impervious to the rhetoric of radicalism after the First World War.

What separated London from Riis and Sinclair was his decision to go and live among the slums. Sinclair travelled to Chicago as a muck-raking journalist, an investigative journalist on a story, while Riis was a mundane police reporter. London in 1903 was twenty-six, a year younger than Sinclair when he went to Chicago; he was keen to extricate himself from a failed marriage. The original plan was to travel to South Africa to write about the aftermath of the Boer War, stopping off in London on the way. Before leaving New York he discussed with George P. Brett, President of the Macmillan Publishing Company an idea he had about writing an account of the slums of the East End of London.

There were dozens of Englishmen who had written about the poor and about the slums in the preceding two or three decades, but a book by an American on the London slums would be a novelty, especially by a writer with such a remarkable background. London had roughed it, knew life on the tramp, and his adventures at sea and in the Klondike had given him a legendary claim to know the 'real' world of men on the frontiers of civil society. He had since become a successful writer, and would be even more successful in the years to follow. It is perhaps correct to wonder whether the process of bourgeoisification had gone so far that London saw the tramps as an alien species, meanwhile attempting to distance himself from them by becoming 'an investigator, a social student'.

The book begins with London's decision – not explained – to go into the East End. Despite the incomprehension of friends, he buys an appropriate outfit, rents a 'port of refuge', a little *pied-à-terre*, where he can store his notes, clean up, and work on his book. From this convenient base he sallies forth to study the East End. Once he leaves the apartment, the transformation from middle-class man of letters into rough proletarian (a theme he later used in *The Sea-Wolf* and other works) is effected without difficulty. London notices that he no longer receives the automatic deference of servants and working people, and is regarded with suspicion by the well-to-do. The workers he meets treat him with casual acceptance and in a spirit of rough equality. It is a form of play-acting which London as a foreigner can only push so far. An American accent, no less than an Etonian drawl like Orwell's, stands out too much for the impersonation to be seriously attempted. A plausible justification, that he is an American sailor temporarily down on his luck, is all he really needs.

The People of the Abyss is loosely constructed of brief sketches of things seen, and of the people and places of the East End: from Frying-Pan Alley to the Whitechapel casual ward or 'Spike' to the Salvation Army 'Peg' where a free meal could be had at the cost of several long hours of sermons, hymns and prayers. No less vivid are the series of brief portraits of people he meets: the sailor who lives only for his drunken excess at the end of every voyage; Thomas Mugridge and his wife, who in their old age embodied 'that vast incomprehensible patience' of utter poverty; and the carter and carpenter, who 'shut up like clams' when they realize that London is a slumming visitor in the East End. The connecting link between the sketches and stories is London himself. Joan London observed that her father's experiences in the East End 'produced no radical change in him'. The episodic structure of the book does not contain a defined moral itinerary on the part of the author. He is able to dip in and out of the life of tramps and the slums at will. After his struggle to get out of the Salvation Army hostel after a meal, London says that he 'disconnected' himself from his 'poor' self and boarded a bus. After explaining the dire prospects of the hop-pickers, who, having earned sixpence, had no place to stay or any more money expected for two days, he wrote: 'What was to be done? We [London and his travelling companion] looked at each other in despair – Not a bit of it. We joyfully thanked God that we were not as other men, especially hoppers, and went down the road to Maidstone, jingling in our pockets the half-crowns and florins we had brought from London.' There is an uncomfortable delight in this. The ability of London to produce a gold sovereign which he had sewn into the armpit of his stoker's singlet, after going through the 'acts of a contortionist' to get at it, is mentioned with at least a mild twinge of guilt:

> After a shave and a bath, with my clothes all off, I got in between clean white sheets and went to sleep . . . And as I lay there drowsily, my mind went back to the seven hundred unfortunates I had left waiting [at the Salvation Army hostel] for services. No bath, no shave for them, no clean white sheets and all clothes off, and fifteen hours' straight sleep. Services over, it was the weary streets again, the problem of a crust of bread ere night, and the long sleepless night in the streets, and the pondering of the problem of how to obtain a crust at dawn.[12]

A bourgeois might feel greater guilt than London, whose familiarity with poverty was considerable. No American writer since Melville had lived so various a life, with such strong contrasts of prosperity and poverty. His experiences, particularly in the scene when he walked out of the Salvation Army jingling the money in his pocket, seem to have left London able to shed his middle-class inhibitions and self-consciousness when necessary.

It is the book of an angry young rebel, and its most distinct impression upon readers is as an emotional cry of outrage. Earle Labor is right to talk about London's compassion in *The People of the Abyss*.[13] Equally characteristic of his tone is a bitter anger at the sheer *unnecessariness* of the conditions in the East End. He sees how the law operates in an irrational fashion, locking up the parks at night, for example, while requiring the police to keep tramps from sleeping in the streets. The same parks were allowed to be opened at 4.30 a.m., when the tramps entered and slept undisturbed by the police. Petty irrationalities and unkindness run throughout English society as the poor experience it. He wonders why the recipients of charity were treated with cruel and needless harshness. Professing Christians share in the 'general heartlessness' towards the poor. The manager of the fruit brokers where Dan Cullen worked for thirty years rejects an appeal for help: 'Oh . . . you see, we make it a rule never to help casuals, and we can do nothing.' Coachloads of 'beanfeasters' 'cheered and jeered and shouted insulting things' after London and his friend as they walk towards the Kent hopfields. It is an old English theme. It is striking that London assumes a greater sympathy and concern on the part of his American readers than he finds about him in the East End, with its widespread but unpredictable cruelty and indifference to the poor:

> Where sights and sounds abounds which neither you nor I would care to have our children see and hear is a place where no man's children should live, and see, and hear. Where you and I would not care to have our wives pass their lives is a place where no other man's wife should have to pass her life.[14]

There is a world of difference between Riis's comment about the 'half-naked' Jews in the tenements and Jack London's direct and manly appeal to equal standards of decency. He wants to break through the hard shell of callous indifference which allows such treatment for some, while others enjoy privilege and leisure.

At one point in *The People of the Abyss* he quotes a brief newpaper account of a coroner's inquest upon a death which took place in Devonshire Place.[15] An elderly woman has been found dead in her room. The description of the scene surpasses anything in *The Jungle* in ugly detail: a doctor who examined the corpse testifies at the coroner's hearing that

> she had one garment and her stockings on. The body was quite alive with vermin, and all the clothes in the room were absolutely grey with insects. Deceased was very badly nourished and was very emaciated. She had extensive sores on

her legs, and her stockings were adherent to those sores . . . Her hair, which was matted with filth, was simply a nest of vermin. Over her bony chest leaped and rolled hundreds, thousands, myriads of vermin.

London's comment – any comment was superfluous – repeats the appeal he made elsewhere for equal standards of decency. It was useless simply to rail against the world in which such a death occurred. London rather asks his readers, as Riis had, to consider such things as if they affected themselves: 'If it is not good for your mother and my mother so to die, then it is not good for this woman, whosoever's mother she might be, so to die.' Whatever social meanings which might be read into the newspaper account, one of many cited by London, the author refrains here from piling on to the bare facts of the coroner's citation a political interpretation.

London's stance of dignified restraint is not maintained throughout *The People of the Abyss*. His own feelings are often very clear, and powerfully expressed. But he knew, or perhaps the middle-class writer in him knew, that he would be accused of overdoing his description of the slums. A recent biographer of London writes that his conclusions about the East End were 'prejudged': 'To cooler observers, the place seemed to be a group of working urban villages with a strong sense of tradition and community . . . His prose and point of view were overwrought, more propaganda than philosophy, more passion than description.'[16] London anticipated this sort of response:

> Is the picture overdrawn? It all depends. For one who sees and thinks life in terms of shares and coupons, it is certainly overdrawn. But for one who sees and thinks life in terms of manhood and womanhood, it cannot be overdrawn.[17]

In the second half of *The People of the Abyss*, where London devotes himself to the presentation of documentation and contemporary opinion, he pauses to consider the same problem:

> Sometimes I become afraid of my own generalizations upon the massed misery of this Ghetto life, and feel that my impressions are exaggerated, that I am too close to the picture and lack perspective. At such moments I find it well to turn to the

testimony of other men to prove to myself that I am not becoming overwrought . . .[18]

Like Upton Sinclair confronted with the slaughterhouses in Chicago, London's reaction is immediate and highly emotional. The facts and figures are marshalled to give his readers a sober justification for sharing London's outrage. Perhaps even more revealing are the passages where London tries to imagine himself permanently stuck in a room such as Dan Cullen's in the 'Municipal Dwellings': 'If I looked into a dreary future and saw that I would have to live in such a room until I died, I should immediately go down, plump into the Thames, and cut the tenancy short.' And at the end of the book, when he considers the uselessness of high cultural ideals in the slums, the speculation irresistibly returns:

> Did Destiny today bind me down to the life of an East End slave for the rest of my years, and did Destiny grant me but one wish, I should ask that I might forget all about the Beautiful and True and Good; that I might forget all I had learned from the open books and forget the people I had known, the things I had heard, and the lands I had seen. And if Destiny didn't grant it, I am pretty confident that I should get drunk and forget it as often as possible.[19]

London feared such a 'dreary future', and the tone of those passages in his book when he is able to 'disconnect' himself from the fate of the homeless and poor betrays an uneasiness which might be more precisely described as anxiety. No less than the middle-class readers who were assumed to know little about the slums and to fear its denizens, Jack London dreads the entrapment which the abyss meant for so many of its inhabitants.

He wrote *The People of the Abyss* during seven weeks in August and September 1902, while he was living in the East End. It was serialized in *Wilshire's Magazine* beginning in March 1903. Even before serialization was completed, Macmillan brought it out in volume form. Among the various projects which London undertook upon completing the manuscript was an essay for *The Comrade* in the series 'How I Became a Socialist.' It appeared in the same month that serialization of *The People of the Abyss* began in *Wilshire's*: this was the real beginning of London's public recognition within the American socialist movement. Within three years his opinions were prominently reported in the bourgeois press, and his books attentively reviewed in the main journal of the European socialist movement, Kautsky's *Die Neue Zeit*.[20] London's essay 'How I Became a Socialist' is a classic account of conversion.[21] As a young man London exulted in hard work, and relished the chance to demonstrate his physical strength. His view of the world was optimistic, and was rooted in a cult of masculinity: 'To adventure like a man, and fight like a man, and to do a man's work (even for a boy's pay) – these were things that reached right in and gripped hold of me as no other thing could.' Describing himself in those days as 'a rampant individualist', London's self-image was a compound of aggression and physical strength: 'I could see myself only raging through life without end like one of Nietzsche's *blond beasts*, lustfully roving and conquering by sheer superiority and strength.'

Early in 1894 London explained that he 'took it into my head to go tramping'. What followed was a months-long journey across America. He joined 'Kelly's Army' of unemployed Californians who intended to join the march on Washington led by Coxey. But London abandoned his fellow marchers in Missouri. His further adventures took him to Buffalo where he was gaoled for thirty days for vagrancy. What left the strongest impression were the human wrecks he met on the road, men 'all wrenched and distorted and twisted out of shape by toil and hardship and accident'. Listening to their stories along the march, and while in prison, he had a glimpse of 'the shambles at the bottom of the Social Pit'. The dread which he expressed in *The People of the Abyss* about being trapped in the slums of the East End reappears in his essay in *The Comrade*: 'I saw the picture of the Social Pit as vividly as though it were a concrete thing, and at the bottom of the Pit I saw them, myself above them, not far, and hanging on the slippery wall by main strength and sweat.' His travels throughout America 'pretty effectively hammered "rampant individualism" out of me'. Without quite knowing why, he had become a socialist. 'I had been reborn, but not renamed . . .' London returned to California, enrolled in high school and vowed to pursue his education with energy. London's conversion to socialism was a matter of emotion and psychology, not logic or science:

I have opened many books, but no economic argument, no

lucid demonstration of the logic and inevitableness of Socialism affects me as profoundly and convincingly as I was affected on the day when I first saw the walls of the Social Pit rise around me and felt myself slipping down, down, into the shambles at the bottom.

The argument that London converted to socialism because it afforded him a vehicle for upward social mobility is not quite satisfactory.[22] In the 1890s the socialist movement and its 'intellectuals' were hardly visible in middle-class American life, to say nothing about the upper class. Nor were there very many intellectuals in the movement, and the motive for self-improvement was as likely to be accompanied by anarchist, Single Tax or Nietzschean individualistic political attitudes. The socialists held no privileged place in education. In any event, such a view gives little credence to London's own account of his conversion, which emphasizes that his conversion took place before London sought out either education or contact with socialists in Oakland. An even more crucial point: as Martin Eden soon learned, the one sure way to block upward social mobility in America was to be branded a socialist.

London wrote *The Sea-Wolf* in 1903. It was the most important of his various writings immediately following *The People of the Abyss*. It might be argued that in significant ways *The Sea-Wolf* owes as much to London's experiences in the East End as it does to his adventures as a sailor. When faced with the prospect of a lifetime to be spent in Dan Cullen's room, London thought of suicide; and he felt all of his cultural aspirations would be meaningless if he were to be reduced to the level of a slave to poverty. A bold, physically daring Jack London quailed at the thought of being trapped in the Social Pit. In *The Sea-Wolf* he asks what would have happened to a believer in 'the Beautiful and True and Good', one of Upton Sinclair's 'lovers of good literature', if he or she suddenly found themselves plunged into the violence and degradation of arbitrary and tyrannic rule on board a ship. The story had to be removed from land, from the reach of the law and civil authority, to save it from the excesses of Gothic melodrama. In all other respects, Wolf Larsen's ship is the Social Pit. Not the least of the surprises in the novel is London's insistence that the narrator, a 'man of letters', has important things to learn – about himself, his values and human nature – from the rough life aboard the *Ghost*.

Humphrey Van Weyden's distinction as a critic, slight though it is, rests upon a study of Poe's place in American literature. A decent, well-meaning, harmless person, Van Weyden is the sort of 'scholar and dilettante' who sees life through books. While crossing San Francisco Bay one evening, his ferry is involved in a collision and sinks amidst a chaos of fog, whistles, shouts and despairing cries. He is luckily hauled on board the *Ghost*, bound on a seal-hunting cruise in the Pacific. Van Weyden's education begins at once: he notices that the sailors hands are rough, and how the dry clothes they offer him stink of fish: 'on the instant my flesh was creeping and crawling from the harsh contact'. The sailors' oaths leave Van Weyden with 'a wilting sensation, a sinking at the heart, and, I might just as well say, a giddiness'. When questioned by the captain as to what he did for a living, Van Weyden uncertainly replies 'I – I am a gentleman.' The unmanly traits of the man of letters are summed up in Larsen's comment about Van Weyden's hands: 'Dead men's hands have kept it soft. Good for little else than dish-washing and scullion work.' There is a sexual undercurrent to the relationship between the two men which is seen elsewhere in London's work. The captain's superior strength and will-power is unchallengeable. Van Weyden rapidly passes into 'a state of involuntary servitude' to Wolf Larsen. The contrasts between the two men are carefully arranged: the strength of Larsen is 'primitive' while Van Weyden embodies the higher, cerebral and cultural ideals of civilization. Van Weyden believes in the reality of ethical values while Larsen is a materialist and a believer in the philosophy of might; altruism pitted against selfishness. It is as though London took himself before his conversion to socialism, in his period of rampant individualism, and opposed to that the sum of the values which he held to represent civilization. It is true that no one in the crew opposes Larsen on political grounds; there are no socialists on board the *Ghost*.

Van Weyden is able to adapt, survive and eventually triumph over Larsen not because his values are superior to the captain's, but because he has shown superior ability to learn and accommodate himself to varying conditions. *The Sea-Wolf* is a study in the triumph of civilization over primitive force and individualism. By the time London wrote *The Iron Heel* and *Martin*

Eden, its optimism and romantic conclusion will seem out of place, its lack of politics a flaw.

Van Weyden's initial conclusion is that life at sea is 'cheap and tawdry, a beastly and inarticulate thing, a soulless stirring of the ooze and slime'. The 'general heartlessness' of life in the East End of London is evident in the 'total lack of sympathy' on board the *Ghost*. Larsen embodies the Emersonian doctrine of self-reliance, now transformed by Darwin and naturalism into a cold and aggressive materialism. He challenges Van Weyden precisely at the core of the latter's unexamined humanism: 'The sacredness of life I had accepted as axiomatic. That it was intrinsically valuable was a truism I had never questioned. But when he challenged the truism I was speechless.' Larsen dismisses altruism as 'slush and sentiment', and as the cruise continues Larsen's rage grows more violent at the attempts by Van Weyden and others like him to attribute transcendent meaning to life. In turn, these bitter arguments bring out a new, snarling aggressiveness in Van Weyden. Sustained exposure to life on board the *Ghost* gradually brings Van Weyden to share their values. He faces down Mugridge after hours spent mutually whetting knives before the galley. The very idea that he might have a knife fight seems incredible to him: 'I had not been called "Sissy" Van Weyden all my days without reason, and that "Sissy" Van Weyden should be capable of doing this thing was a revelation to Humphrey Van Weyden, who knew not whether to be exultant or ashamed.' He begins to observe other kinds of changes in himself. His muscles toughen up, and his general physical condition is greatly improved. He now argues, after Larsen, that individuals make or break themselves. His early life had left him 'innocent of the realities of life'. Now Van Weyden seems to find 'a more adequate explanation of life' in Larsen's individualism than he found in his own altruism. He has learned to stand on his own two feet, and secretly prides himself that his adaptation to his new way of life has been so successful.

At this point in the voyage, when Van Weyden could say

. . . I knew these men and their mental processes, was one of them myself, living the seal-hunting life, eating the seal-hunting fare, thinking, largely, the seal-hunting thoughts. There was for me no strangeness to it, to the rough clothes, the coarse faces, the wild laughter, and lurching cabin walls and swaying sea-lamps . . .[23]

the transformation of the 'scholar and dilettante' has been completed. He now wears a thick beard, his hands are rough and dirty, the sleeve of his jacket ripped, and there is a knife in a sheath on his hip. He has at last become one of the crew. The appearance on board the *Ghost* of Maud Brewster, a young and beautiful poet, instantaneously transforms Van Weyden back to what he was, a gentleman. A look of sympathy from Maud, coming after a sneering insult from Larsen, softens Van Weyden: '. . . I became then, and gladly, her willing slave.' His process of accommodation to the *Ghost* had began with the recognition that he was in a 'state of involuntary servitude' to Wolf Larsen's strength. What Larsen hoped the 'scholar and dilettante' would learn has, seemingly, been lost. In his discussions with Maud as the voyage continues Van Weyden argues with diminishing conviction the materialistic philosophy of Wolf Larsen. But the virtuous example of Maud (and a slight hint of sexual ambiguity: she wears a boy's cap) gradually loosens the harsh veneer of his materialism. At first he loves her remotely, idealistically and without passion, but jealousy stings Van Weyden into an understanding of what he pompously refers to as 'the physical characteristics of love'. But the return of civilizing influences does not deprive Van Weyden of his cunning or his strength. When he and Maud are shipwrecked in an escape attempt, he fixes the windlass and the masts. Larsen had brought him to the world of practicality. Maud returns him to ideals and principles.

Maud herself is changed by her experiences. When the blinded but still powerful Larsen seizes Van Weyden by the throat, as if to throttle all those values which Van Weyden had refound, Maud proves that she too is capable of adapting herself to new challenges. She hits Larsen with a seal-club. 'Truly', Van Weyden concludes, 'she was my woman, my mate-woman, fighting with me and for me as the mate of a caveman would have fought, all the primitive in her aroused, forgetful of her culture, hard under the softening civilization of the only life she had ever known.'[24]

It is an interesting notion that it was possible, as Van Weyden suggests, to be 'forgetful' of one's own culture. Part of what Van Weyden learns is that the culture of idealism and the genteel world of *belles lettres* can be put aside. He becomes a different man physically, and in sexual terms is transformed from an effete writer into London's conception of true masculinity. Though he is able to enter the world of the *Ghost*, he does not find solidarity or enlarged social horizons among the crew. London's affirmation of the possibility of self-transformation in such a context of extreme conflict touches upon a central dimension of socialist hopefulness in the period after the formation of the Socialist Party in 1901. One speaks of 'socialist hopefulness' because in the process of self-transformation, in the capacity to 'forget' one's culture and class-bound view of the world, is found the promise of releasing society, eventually, from what looked like fixed and inescapable class and ideological conflicts. While it is true that the man of letters and the Nietzschean sea captain cannot be reconciled, the Van Weydens of this world can still be shown in a hopeful light: change and growth are still possible. The politics of *The Sea-Wolf* are to be found more in the development of Van Weyden than in the Nietzschean Wolf Larsen, and the politics are those of the constructive socialists on the right of the party. When he wrote *The People of the Abyss* and *The Sea-Wolf*, London was not the revolutionary firebrand that he became later in the decade. Ironically, as he became more revolutionary he became increasingly pessimistic.

The Iron Heel (1907) is in effect two distinct books. The structural break which divides it has a political and ideological dimension. It reveals the deepening of London's socialism, while at the same time it indicates his sceptical rejection of the tendency of the Socialist Party from the middle of the decade. What can be described as the first book (Chapters 1–12) tells the story of the transformation of Avis Cunningham, her father (a professor at the University of California), and Bishop Morehouse. Through the speeches and personal influence of a young proletarian socialist militant, Ernest Everhard, all three are brought over to the side of the revolution, and suffer unexpected penalties for their political courage. Theirs is a socialist conversion story of a pessimistic sort, quite out of key with the 'How I Became a Socialist' series in *The Comrade*, to which London contributed. The glimpses of the new age which Everhard helps them achieve serve to isolate them from the values of conventional society, and eventually destroy them. London understood that it was dangerous to become a socialist in America. Many socialist novels conclude, as with the renewal of Jurgis in *The Jungle*, with a hopeful intimation of the forthcoming victory of the cause. The socialist revolution in *The Iron Heel* is placed in the remote future, and indeed is so inexplicable in terms of the movement of the plot that it serves as a Sorelian myth which binds socialists together.

The political climate in 1905 and 1906 was undoubtedly worse, from a socialist point of view, than a few years earlier. The initial promise of the Russian Revolution of 1905 ended with defeat, suppression of the soviets, and imprisonment or exile for the leading figures. (Trotsky spent part of his time in exile editing a Russian-language socialist periodical in New York.[25]) The leadership of the Socialist Party insisted that party activities be directed towards elections, to the point where it seemed that the party mainly existed to elect socialists to office. Attempts to bring the American Federation of Labor over to socialism were abandoned. The leadership of the party were seeking respectability and discouraged the use of confrontational or revolutionary language; like good social democrats they rejected the industrial use of direct action for political purposes. Jack London viewed the signs of reformism in the Socialist Party with growing impatience. He played a major role, along with Upton Sinclair, in launching the Inter-Collegiate Socialist Society in 1905, and was an indefatigable speaker on campuses across America. (His lecture on 'Revolution' was given, with minor revisions, to Ernest Everhard for delivery in *The Iron Heel*.)

The second half of the book tells a different story: the political instability produced by strikes and growing socialist activity is answered by a *coup d'état* in which socialists are killed or imprisoned, and the unions repressed or bought off by the Iron Heel, a conspiratorial league of big capitalists (the Oligarchs) and their armed forces (the Mercenaries). The surviving socialists are forced to go underground where they prepare a terrorist reply to the terrorism of the Iron Heel. A plan for insurrections in American cities is uncovered by agents of the Oligarchs, but there is no time to call off the rising in Chicago. The resulting mutual slaughter of the 'Chicago Commune' leaves the underground weakened and dispersed, though it still survives as a revolutionary organization. Avis Cunningham's 'manuscript' breaks off in 1932, on the eve of yet another failed uprising. The editor indicates that after hundreds of years of repression the Iron Heel is eventually overthrown in a successful socialist revolution. This is the story which has been repeatedly praised for its prophetic insight into

European politics of the interwar years. In an introduction to a 1932 translation of *The Iron Heel* (as *Talon de fer*), Paul Vaillant-Couturier, member of the Central Committee of the French Communist Party and from 1934 editor of *l'Humanité*, saw in

> ... le chomage, l'échec de la grève générale, l'avènement du Talon de fer avec la complicité – assurée par la corruption – de l'aristocratie ouvrière et des syndicats réformistes, l'écrasement du soulèvement des *farmers*, l'horrible vie du 'people de l'abîme,' les provocateurs, les enlèvements à la manière des *gangsters*, la terreur, la bombe de Washington, l'emprisonnement des leaders parlementaires, leur déliverance, le cynicism intelligent des oligarques, la Commune de Chicago et sa répression, tout cela constitue un tableau parfois prophétique ou l'on découvre déjà le fascisme européen ... [26]

Trotsky's letter to Joan London of 16 October 1937, perhaps a more familiar source, praised 'the audacity and independence' of London's 'historical foresight':

> One can say with assurance that in 1907 not one of the revolutionary Marxists, not excluding Lenin and Rosa Luxemburg, imagined so fully the ominous perspective of the alliance between finance capital and labour aristocracy ... Over the mass of the deprived rise the castes of labour aristocracy, of praetorian army, of an all-penetrating police, with the financial oligarchy at the top. In reading it one does not believe his own eyes: it is precisely the picture of fascism, of its economy, of its governmental technique, its political psychology. [27]

Within the socialist movement, London's activities were criticized (some comrades deplored his racism, for others he was politically too extreme). The viewpoint of the constructive socialists is suggested by John Spargo's review of *The Iron Heel* in the *International Socialist Review* in April 1908:

> The picture he gives is well calculated ... to repel many whose addition to our forces is sorely needed; it gives a new impetus to the old and generally discarded cataclysmic theory; it tends to

weaken the political Socialist movement by discrediting the ballot and to encourage the chimerical and reactionary notion of physical force, so alluring to a certain type of mind. As a statement of the cataclysmic theory and an argument against political action, it is worthy the careful study of every Socialist and every student of Socialism.

While on the centre and right of the Socialist Party *The Iron Heel* was regarded as 'an unfortunate book' (Spargo), on the left it was praised as its most effective piece of propaganda.[28]

The Iron Heel can be seen to offer a conclusive answer to the utopian fictions of Bellamy (and by implication William Morris), and to the established views of the constructive socialists, who expected the advent of socialism by peaceful consensus, persuasion and finally through an electoral victory. London anticipated a capitalism ruthless in defence of its own interests, capable both of manipulating and suppressing its opponents. London understood American capitalism better, at least in certain crucial aspects, than his critics among the constructive socialists. His prophetic insight into what would later be described as the coopting of the labour aristocracy was much admired, but even London in his pessimism did not foresee the virtual disappearance of the class struggle a half-century after his death. An American working class without class consciousness would have confirmed his criticism of the tactics of the Socialist Party leadership, and heightened his scepticism about the likely prospects of the revolution.

The first two chapters of *The Iron Heel* are wordily disputatious. Professor Cunningham, anticipating an interesting evening's discussion, has invited a group of local worthies to meet Ernest Everhard, and to hear from him the socialist case. Everhard is aggressive; his listeners are inevitably provoked and outraged; certain ideas are introduced. Everhard abuses the clergymen (in terms which echo Wolf Larsen's criticism of Van Weyden) as fat parasites: 'Your hands are soft with the work others have performed for you . . . And your minds are filled with doctrines that are buttresses of the established order . . . [you] guard, with your preaching, the interests of your employers . . .' A subsequent conversation with Professor Cunningham, Bishop Morehouse and Everhard brings out the essential difference between them. Like a good materialist, Everhard argues that the conflict between capital and labour is inevitable and irreconcilable. The bishop, on the other hand, blames the wrongs of industrial society upon the ignorance of the capitalist class. If only men of good will honestly sought to remedy the social ill, serious conflict could be avoided. The opposition of their views, between meliorative and deterministic social philosophies, is starkly set forth, and cannot be reconciled. Everhard challenges the bishop, the professor and his daughter, to test their social philosophies against the way the world actually works. He tells them about Jackson, a workman at the Sierra Mills who lost an arm in an industrial accident, and challenges them to look into the case to see if his model of class relations, or theirs, is more appropriate. The cool logic of his argument is quickly replaced by a stomach-wrenching appeal to emotion which assaults Everhard's listeners (and the book's readers) with equal ferocity:

> . . . the gown you wear is stained with blood. The food you eat is a bloody stew. The blood of little children and strong men is dripping from your very roof-beams. I can close my eyes, now, and hear it drip, drop, drip, drop, all about me.[29]

London once remarked (in his 'Revolution' lecture) that socialist propaganda was basically intellectual, and that 'the movement is based upon economic necessity and is in line with social evolution'.[30] A significant part of his imagination needed that drip of blood, and remained unsatisfied by the scientific and intellectualized propaganda which he, and the Socialist Party, offered to the American public.

Investigating Jackson's case, Professor Cunningham's daughter Avis learns a great deal about the powerlessness of the poor, and the overweening arrogance of the big companies. Her research, she writes, helped to tear away 'the sham from the face of society, and gave me glimpses of reality that were as unpleasant as they were undeniably true'. She is led step by step through a conversion experience. The world now looks differently to Avis, and the superficial pleasures of her class have become repellent. Everhard's conclusion has become her own: 'Our boasted civilisation is based upon blood, soaked in blood, and neither you nor any of us can escape the scarlet stain.'

The investigation into Jackson's case has consequences for them all. Avis at first notices a 'certain aloofness' in her friends. The opinion gains ground, especially among the wives of prominent members of the faculty of the University of California, that Avis has become 'a too-forward and self-asserting young woman'. Professor Cunningham is reprimanded by the President of the University for entertaining socialists and radicals: such behaviour is likely to bring the institution into disrepute. As the investigation proceeds, pressure on Professor Cunningham asserts itself unmasked. He is asked to resign from the university, and his book, *Economics and Education*, is abused and misrepresented by the press. The bishop experiences a similar fate.[31] After being taken by Everhard through the slums of San Francisco, the bishop vows to dedicate himself to the ancient spirit of the church. But his sermons scandalize the wealthy, are suppressed by the press, and the poor bishop is committed to a sanatorium, from where he manages to disappear into the slums: 'he was seeing life in the raw, and it was a different life from what he had known within the printed books of his library'. Professor Cunningham's shares in the Sierra Mills are stolen from the bank where they were kept, and a fake mortgage robs him of his home. He moved south of Market Street – in San Franciscan terms a terrifying plunge into the Social Pit. 'Now we shall become real proletarians', he remarks to his daughter Avis. (The far-fetched lengths to which London has to go to pitch the professor and his daughter into the slums does him no credit as a writer; the most interesting point is that London clearly felt that an abstract or distant sympathy or comprehension was not enough. The exposure must be complete and irrevocable, unlike his own experiences in the slums of London.) Both the bishop and the professor accept their fates without resentment. '"... I have learned a great lesson," the Bishop remarked to Avis and Everhard: "The soul cannot be ministered to till the stomach is appeased. His lambs must be fed with bread and butter and potatoes and meat; after that, and only after that, are their spirits ready for more refined nourishment."' When they last see him the bishop is dressed in rough workman's overalls. In London's opinion, the Social Gospel was merely so much hot air unless it issued out in such a transformation. The story of the conversions of the professor, his daughter and the bishop is finished by the twelfth chapter. In the harsher, more pessimistic political climate of *The Iron Heel* there was no happy ending awaiting the convert to socialism, only ridicule, hardship and persecution.

The second half of the novel allows Avis Cunningham to step to centre stage. The commentators on London's novel are just beginning to find this worthy of attention. Everhard is absent for long stretches of the narrative, and Avis's 'manuscript' (that moth-eaten literary pretext) is mainly concerned with the early development of the underground socialist resistance. As a convert to the cause, and as someone overwhelmingly in love with Everhard, there are some curious aspects to her story. The larger framework recounts the New Order imposed upon America by the Iron Heel. Within that narrative is Avis's story of her transformation. She is held in prison for six months after the coup and then released. In order to shake off the spies who follow her, she must adopt a disguise. She cannot pass herself off as a proletarian. Unlike Maud in *The Sea-Wolf*, who shows a capacity to 'forget' her culture at a moment of dire necessity, Avis passes herself off as the pampered wife of a lesser Oligarch. Later, at the underground base at Glen Ellen (north of San Francisco, where London lived), she works at perfecting her disguise. Everhard insists that the change was needed in order to save her life:

> You must cease to be. You must become another woman – and not merely in the clothes you wear, but inside your skin under the clothes. You must make yourself over again so that even I would not know you – your voice, your gestures, your mannerisms, your carriage, your walk, everything.[32]

Avis, it must be remembered, is a bourgeois convert to the revolutionary cause. Everhard is telling her that she must once again become part of the bourgeois world, a further twist of the spiral which leaves Avis uncertain what she actually was:

> . . . it seemed impossible either that I had ever lived a placid, peaceful life in a college town, or else that I had become a revolutionist inured to scenes of violence and death. One or the other could not be. One was real, the other was a dream, but which was which?[33]

In order to reemerge into the world again, Avis must transform herself, or at least her appearance and outward behaviour, into yet another self. She proves happily adept at deception and disguise, to the point where Everhard does not recognize her true identity when he returns to Glen Ellen after escaping from prison.

The shifting and uncertain identities of Avis have an unexpected political dimension, for the socialist Fighting Groups have to disguise themselves in their struggle against the Iron Heel. Through the use of spies and double-agents the underground penetrates to the core of the Oligarchy. Communications between prisoners are established, including an elaborate underground railway; safe houses are set up to assist revolutionary fugitives. The process works the other way round. The Fighting Groups are themselves penetrated by spies and *agents provocateurs*. So extensive is the mutual penetration that Ernest and Avis decide, without serious misgiving, to emerge from the underground as Iron Heel double agents. They now enter a morally indeterminate world where ideology and identity have become desperately confused. Avis describes their emergence:

> It was not until January, 1917, that we left the refuge. All had been arranged. We took our place at once as agents-provocateurs in the scheme of the Iron Heel. I was supposed to be Ernest's sister. By oligarchs and comrades on the inside who were high in authority, place had been made for us, we were in possession of all necessary documents, and our pasts were accounted for. With help on the inside, this was not difficult, for in that shadow-world of secret service identity was nebulous.[34]

In the beginning of *The Iron Heel* the socialist movement, embodied in the stern rectitude of Ernest Everhard, bristled with dedication and integrity. It was the capitalists who were morally bankrupt. But under the rule of the Oligarchs there has been a remarkable transformation of the ethics and character of the ruling class. They are no longer to be symbolized by the conspicuous consumption of the idle rich, as described by Veblen in *The Theory of the Leisure Class* (1899); as Avis's narrative makes clear, the plutocrats have evolved into a genuine aristocracy, moved by the highest ideals:

> They served as leaders of troops and as lieutenants and captains

of industry. They found careers in applied science, and many of them became great engineers . . . They were, I may say, apprenticed to education, to art, to the church, to science, to literature; and in those fields they served the important function of moulding the thought-processes of the nation in the direction of the perpetuity of the Oligarchy.[35]

The 'manuscript' ends with an even more remarkable description of the Iron Heel, 'impassive and deliberate . . . punishing without mercy and without malice, suffering in silence all retaliations that were made upon it and filling the gaps in its fighting line as fast as they appeared'.[36] The Oligarchs now combine the discipline of an army with the zeal and conviction of missionaries. It is as though in the confusing atmosphere following the *coup d'état*, the strength and integrity of the socialists has been transferred to the Oligarchy. The moment in *The Jungle* when Sinclair reversed the meaning of hog and butcher carried with it an interrogatory purpose. The reader's emotions were challenged (i.e. manipulated) in the cause of humane values. *The Iron Heel* lacks that design upon its readers, though the judgements which the 'manuscript' makes are explicitly those of Avis; it is worth recalling that the sympathetic judgements upon the Oligarchy emerge directly out of Avis's experiences in the Chicago Commune.

By becoming an agent for the Oligarchy, she is able to travel across America in some style. Dressing well turns out to have been the best disguise. Avis goes to Chicago, aware that the Oligarchy are preparing a provocation, but is unable to do anything before the mob explodes in suicidal violence. When Avis and a fellow double-agent are spotted by the rioters they are in immediate danger: 'We were well dressed, and that was enough.' They are in the end rescued by soldiers of the Mercenaries who were going through the piles of corpses and shooting the wounded or those merely feigning injury. Avis and her friend talk to the soldiers during the killing, and are then released. Avis recalls that she fixed up her hair and pinned together her torn skirt. 'Sometimes the revolver shots drowned the voices of Garthwaite and the officer, and they were compelled to repeat what they had been saying.' Later that day Avis comes face to face with a wounded rebel:

Once he looked straight across at me, and in his face was all the dumb pathos of the wounded and hunted animal. He saw me, but there was no kinship between us, and with him, at least, no sympathy of understanding; for he cowered perceptibly and dragged himself on.[37]

He at least knows what Avis is, or rather, what she had become. The scene invites an interpretation which runs against the grain, but is worth following: Avis, in the ambiguous atmosphere following the *coup*, has found her identity, her former identity, and is now truly an enemy of the revolution.[38] The process of transformation which made her a socialist is unstable. The ambivalent role of Avis during the Chicago Commune is understood by the 'fiendish' mob. Dressed like the women of the Oligarchy, she is treated by the mob as an enemy. They seem to intuit the inner changes in Avis, though having only her dress, an objective sign of class, to go by. Avis, one concludes, has gone over emotionally to the side of the Oligarchs. She has become an intense admirer of their dedication and morale, observing that 'The aristocratic idea was woven into the making of them until it became bone of them and flesh of them.' Despite the many changes in Avis, her respect for aristocracy remains unchanged. She first saw in Everhard 'a natural aristocrat . . . in spite of the fact that he was in the camp of the non-aristocrats'.

The changes in Avis, both those forced upon her and those which emerged out of her situation, seem to have been ignored by most readers. As a result, the ambiguity of London's novel has not been correctly understood. Ernest Everhard reverts to the background. It is Avis who betrays the movement. The mutual penetration of revolutionaries and Oligarchs, the changes of physical identity and political loyalties, and the reversal of roles between opponents, do much to cloud the moral atmosphere so clearly drawn in the first half of the book. It is as though London strayed by accident into the landscape of *Under Western Eyes* – but Conrad's novel was published four years after *The Iron Heel*.

London wrote a letter to the socialist intellectual William English Walling on 30 November 1909 which clearly revealed the full extent of his pessimism, and which, more than any other comment by London on the novel, provides a key for the interpretation of its strange ending.

Depend upon me for one thing. I am a hopelessly non-compromising revolutionist, and I shall stand always for keeping the socialist party rigidly revolutionary. Any compromise such as affiliation with the American Federation of Labor would be at this time suicidal . . . If the socialist movement in the United States goes in for opportunism, then it's Hurray for the Oligarchy and the Iron Heel . . .[39]

Avis's inner evolution and betrayal of the revolution carries within itself in an inverted form London's dismay at the betrayal of the Socialist Party, and its inner evolution towards revisionism. *The Iron Heel*, so widely regarded as an example of left-wing socialist propaganda, is more a monument to his despair at the opportunism of American socialism.

London had begun to think about a 'Novel on Literary Struggles' as early as 1902 or 1903.[40] Various manuscript notes and drafts suggest that he returned to the project intermittently over the next five or six years. The 'struggling writer idea' was heavily autobiographical, but from the start he envisaged a tragic conclusion to the conflict between idealism and crass materialism. In July or August 1907 he began *Martin Eden*, completing the novel on Tahiti in February 1908. Published a year later, it was praised for its considerable power and intensity, though it was felt to lack the full dimensions of tragedy. It is better described as a melodrama of social mobility, summing up concerns running through the whole of London's work. The theme of the 'empty success', as London described the book in an early note, invites an ironic narrative perspective. It is a very American preoccupation: the hero experiences a 'success' tainted by symbolic personal failure and frustration, as well as ethical disintegration. But London's book is almost wholly without the ironic distance. The story was too closely modelled upon London's own career and temperament, and the emotions it aroused were too painfully subjective, to acquire that high finish of ironic perspective. Written at the height of Jack London's power as a novelist, *Martin Eden* is a book of 'quivering sensibilities'.

Martin Eden's story describes his attempt at self-transformation and its consequences. Culture is his fatal Lorelei. Proletarian origins and a lack of formal education set him at a distance from the high bourgeois culture of California. He enters the Morse home as a crude, alien being, precisely reversing the dilemma facing Humphrey Van Weyden in *The Sea-Wolf*. But where Van Weyden's transformation ended in growth and successful adaptation to new circumstances, Eden is destroyed by his attempt to rise out of the working class.

Culture and romance are united for Eden in Ruth Morse and her home. 'Here was intellectual life', he thought, 'and here was beauty, warm and wonderful . . . She lent wings to his imagination . . .' Everything else about his life is narrow and oppressive: when at the theatre working-class girls stare at him, 'he felt the fingers of his own class clutching at him to hold him down'. The real meaning of his origins is expressed in such imagery:

> He was appalled at the problem confronting him, weighted down by the incubus of his working-class station. Everything reached out to hold him down – his sister's house and family, Jim the apprentice, everybody he knew, every tie of life. Existence did not taste good in his mouth.[41]

When he thought of a life spent with working-class girls, exchanging 'the stupidities of stupid minds', a dream rose before him of towering bookshelves 'filled with the wisdom of the ages'. Even books, however, could be ominously threatening: 'From every side the books seemed to press upon him and crush him. He had never dreamed that the fund of human knowledge bulked so big.' His desire for self-transformation takes on spatial as well as symbolic dimensions: 'Down below where he lived was the ignoble, and he wanted to purge himself of the ignoble that had soiled all his days, and to rise to that sublimated realm where dwelt the upper classes.'[42] Culture and romance have an unspoken economic and social dimension in Martin Eden's fantasies, though his idealism makes him unable to accept that there are other considerations at work:

> On the screen of his imagination he saw himself and this sweet and beautiful girl, facing each other and conversing in good English, in a room of books and paintings, and tone and culture, and all illuminated by a bright light of steadfast brilliance . . .[43]

The first hint of disturbance in Martin's idealistic fantasy comes when he notices that cherries have stained Ruth's lips. Eden had never even thought of Ruth in that way; she was a 'being apart', 'an emanation', whose body was to him 'a pure and gracious crystallization of her divine essence'. The tell-tale cherry stain on her lips teaches Eden that she 'was subject to the laws of the universe just as inexorably as he was. She had to eat to live, and when she got her feet wet she caught cold.' Martin discovers the writings of Herbert Spencer, and through the ideas of evolution glimpses a universe obeying the laws of science and not random chance or divine will. The scientific world-view fascinates Martin, showing him an inner kinship between 'love, poetry, earthquake, fire, rattlesnakes, rainbows, precious gems, monstrosities, sunsets, the roaring of lions, illuminating gas, cannibalism, beauty, murder, levers and fulcrums, and tobacco'. Love alone seems outside the claims of the scientific world-view; it is transcendent, non-rational, utterly removed from ordinary life. He willingly submits himself to be moulded by Ruth. Her ideals, her values, are accepted by Martin as his own: 'He was clay in her hands immediately, as passionately desirous of being moulded by her as she was desirous of shaping him into the image of her ideal man.' Ruth's values are exemplified by her father, and by Andrew Carnegie, men who preached the necessity of austerity, sacrifice, patience, industry and high endeavour. Martin seeks to follow their advice, but a job working in a resort laundry rapidly disillusions him. Martin's fellow work-mates have no such high ideals; they are all people of 'small mental calibre'. Any thought of self-improvement after a day working in the laundry is unrealistic: his work leaves him too exhausted to read. He becomes little more than a beast through such work. The simple pieties of Ruth gradually lose their hold upon him before the actual nature of hard physical labour.

The gap between his experiences and Ruth's values widens in other ways. The desire to be a writer had come out of his basic love of reality. He had hoped to write about the things he knew, a rough and low world of adventure and hard work. His sister Gertrude, however, after listening to several of Martin's stories, points out that on the whole she preferred happy endings. 'There is [*sic*] too many sad things in the world anyway. It makes me happy to think about happy things.' Eden's brother-in-law thinks that Martin's poems are obscene. (The 'magazine taste' so contemptuously attacked by Mrs Atherton and Upton Sinclair, and which is discussed in the second chapter, was not simply invented by an overly-protective band of editors.) Ruth, his great mentor in all cultural matters, finds Martin's stories crude and amateurish. His subjects disgust her. 'Oh, it is degrading! It is not nice! It is nasty!' Both Gertrude and Ruth reflect the taste prevalent among the editors of magazines: his manuscripts, with their rough realism, are unpublishable. 'He was puzzled by countless short stories', wrote London,

> written lightly and cleverly . . . but without vitality or reality. Life was so strange and wonderful, filled with immensity of problems, of dreams, and of heroic toils, and yet these stories dealt only with the commonplaces of life. He felt the stress and strain of life, its fevers and sweats and wild insurgencies – surely this was the stuff to write about! He wanted to glorify the leaders of forlorn hopes, the mad lovers, the giants that fought under stress and strain, amid terror and tragedy, making life crackle with the strength of their endeavour. And yet the magazine short stories seemed intent on glorifying the Mr. Butlers, the sordid dollar-chasers, and the commonplace little love-affairs of commonplace little men and women. Was it because the editors of the magazines were commonplace? he demanded. Or were they afraid of life – these writers and editors and readers?[44]

(Both Upton Sinclair and London were attempting to support themselves by writing for the market which they despised, and which rejected or tried to tone down their dealings with the 'fevers and sweats and wild insurgencies' of life.) Ruth feels that his 'Love Cycle' of sonnets is impractical, and does nothing to make their marriage possible. Eden's attempts at hack-work for the magazines, abandon Ruth ('that pale, shriveled, female thing'), sides with incomprehension. Ruth least of all understood his literary aspirations. She points out that the rough talk of his characters offended readers and would inevitably result in his stories being rejected by editors. Eden defends his stories with the classic realist argument: '"Because the real Wiki-Wiki would have talked that way." "But it is not good taste." "It is life," he replied bluntly, "It is real. It is true. And I must write life as I see it."'

Martin is forced to oppose his own standards to those of society. He is being inexorably driven into a lonely, proud isolation, which is only disturbed when he meets Russ Brissenden, a *fin de siècle* consumptive and aesthete who advises Eden to forget the magazines, abandon Ruth ('that pale, shriveled, female thing'), and leave the corrupting cities of the bourgeoisie. Martin, he argues, should return to the sea, and 'pick out some great wanton flame of a woman, who laughs at life, and jeers at death, and loves one while she may'. In an attempt to wean him from bourgeois influences, Brissenden takes Eden to the working-class district of San Francisco, south of Market Street. There he meets rebels, men of independent minds, who bristle with opinions and recondite learning. Brissenden is a socialist and hopes to see Eden converted to the cause. At one point he brings Eden to a party meeting in Oakland, but Eden views the speaker, 'a clever Jew', in uncompromisingly Darwinian terms:

> To Martin this withered wisp of a creature was a symbol. He was the figure that stood forth representative of the whole miserable mass of weaklings and inefficients who perished according to biological law on the ragged confines of life. They were the unfit. In spite of their cunning philosophy and of their ant-like proclivities for cooperation, Nature rejected them for the exceptional man. Out of the plentiful spawn of life she flung from her prolific hand, she selected only the best.[45]

During a conversation with Ruth's parents and a local judge, Eden proclaims himself an opponent of socialism: 'I look to the State for nothing. I look only to the strong man, the man on horseback, to save the State from its own rotten futility.'[46]Like Wolf Larsen, he is as critical of 'mongrel Democracy' as of socialism and its 'slave-morality': 'The world belongs to the true noblemen, to the great blonde beasts, to the non-comprisers, to the "yes-sayers."' Ironically, Eden's speech at the socialist meeting is deliberately misreported by the press, where he is presented as a dangerous radical. This serves to deepen the wedge between Eden and Ruth Morse.

The suicide of Brissenden and Martin Eden's exhaustion from overwork bring him near to breaking point. He bitterly regrets abandoning his old working-class friends, and attends a plumbers' picnic in a local park where he meets an old girlfriend. For a moment the 'old days' have returned, but the zest of combat soon dies down. He is far too self-analytical to sink back into his earlier way of life. 'The old days of licence and easy living were gone.' He is saddened by the distance which now separates him from his old friends. 'Too many thousands of opened books yawned between them and him. He had exiled himself.' The books which once threatened to crush him have been opened and mastered; but the hoped-for liberation is purchased at a high cost, a new kind of self-imprisonment, a closing of certain human possibilities.

Eden retreats into a bitter nihilism. He cannot believe in Ruth's world, for its culture has revealed its true basis in the cash nexus. Ruth herself in the end prefers bourgeois standards to the higher idealisms of Martin Eden. When she comes to him in his belated success, there is nothing left, no feelings or even an emotional response to the woman who once embodied his shining ideal of love. He tells her: '. . . you would have destroyed me out of your well-meaning . . .':

> Realism is imperative to my nature, and the bourgeois spirit hates realism. The bourgeois is cowardly. It is afraid of life. And all your effort was to make me afraid of life. You would have formalized me . . . you wanted to formalize me, to make me over into one of your own class, with your class-ideals, class-values, and class-prejudices.[47]

Even on board the ship carrying him to the South Pacific, Eden's isolation is brought home. He cannot go back to 'his own class' and he detests the first-class passengers around him. He concludes that there is nowhere for someone like himself to go but through the porthole and into the sea.[48]

Martin Eden is a study of the failure of self-transformation. He has come unstuck in the class system; more significantly, his naive idealism has been undermined. The shrines where he worshipped – Ruth and culture – have been emptied of their meaning. Eden has nothing to put in their place: hence his suicide. His fate was implicit in his individualism. In 1910 London placed the meaning of the book squarely upon the failure of Martin Eden's individualism: 'Being an Individualist, being unaware of the needs of others, of the whole human collective need, Martin Eden lived only for himself, fought only for himself, and, if you please, died for himself.'[49] Eden's fate seemed to justify London's politics: 'I am not an individualist', he wrote to Professor Philo M. Buck, Jr in 1912. '*Sea-Wolf, Martin Eden, Burning Daylight*, were written as indictments of individualism. Martin Eden died because he was an individualist. Individualism failed him . . .'[50] What is omitted in this view of his fate is the connection between Martin Eden's development as an artist and his idealization of Ruth. He aggressively proclaimed his individualism in two scenes (at the Morse home and at the Socialist Party meeting), to the detriment of the book, perhaps. It enabled London to flatten the ideological burden of the book, to reduce it to Eden's proclaimed ideas. But Eden was also an artist, and had to learn the hard way that there was no alternative to fighting for his own values. The alternative in such a society was 'the needs of others'. In his case, that meant the needs (and literary taste) of his sister Marian, who liked happy endings; and his sister Gertrude's husband, who thought the sonnet cycle of love poems was obscene. It also included the editors of magazines, who wanted optimistic, light fiction that would be inoffensive to their readers. Ruth Morse, too, was one of the 'others' whose opinions and taste were exceedingly conservative. In each case Eden's individualism, his resistance, was the proof of his integrity as a writer.

There is an alternative in the book, introduced by Brissenden: socialism, at least in notional form, is the body of values which Martin Eden rejects at once and out of hand. He takes years to see through capitalism, but the 'slave-morality' of socialism requires no such careful examination before being rejected. The reason why is not hard to divine. There are no socialist conversion stories with happy endings in London's work. He was frankly too pessimistic about the prospects of the movement after 1905 to write otherwise. The belief, so deeply rooted in constructive socialism, in the power of persuasion and the inevitability of conversion, did not fire his imagination. Martin Eden's diatribes against socialism are uncomfortably eloquent – no less eloquent, it must be said, than London's protestations of socialist fidelity. He felt by 1916 that he was too much a socialist to remain in the Socialist Party:

> Trained in the class struggle, as taught and practised by the Socialist Labor Party, my own highest judgment concurring, I believed that the working class, by fighting, by never fusing, by never making terms with the enemy, could emancipate itself. Since the whole trend of socialism in the United States of recent years has been of peaceableness and compromise, I find that my

mind refuses further sanction of my remaining a party member.[51]

And so he resigned.

Martin Eden's conversion to socialism, amidst the self-educated intellectuals of Oakland and San Francisco south of Market Street, would have lacked credibility. To have accepted Brissenden's socialism involved the abandonment of Ruth, and the high bourgeois culture which she represented. A happy proletarian marriage, after his relationship with Ruth, would have been pure pastoral. Besides, American society as he had hitherto experienced it had no other values than the materialistic ones Eden sensed everywhere around him. Had there been a real alternative, a genuine socialist culture, the book might conceivably have had a different ending instead of the one it has, with its loneliness, bitterness, nihilism and emotional unresponsiveness. While others hopefully celebrated 'How I Became a Socialist', in *Martin Eden* London presented a society in which socialism was a remote and unattractive doctrine. The inner ambiguity of *Martin Eden*, and of Jack London as a writer, lies in the fact that the individualism which kept Martin Eden remote from socialism was also the integrity which made him a writer.

2   Upton Sinclair

'American literature today', wrote Gertrude Atherton in 1904, 'is the most timid, the most anaemic, the most lacking in individualities, the most bourgeois that any country has ever known.'[1] A modestly successful and highly industrious lady scribbler, with over fifty books under her belt in a career which continued for a half-century from 1892, Mrs Atherton waved the banner of a high and serious art. She advised her contemporaries to abandon the snug and the conventional; writers must learn to 'fight unceasingly' for literature, and face the prospect of having 'to stand absolutely alone'. Cynics, as is their wont, quickly pointed out how much easier it was for Mrs Atherton at forty-seven, the widow of a wealthy and socially prominent San Francisco landowner, to preach such austere integrity than it was for young writers like Upton Sinclair and Jack London, who had to support themselves by their writing. But Mrs Atherton had a splendid case to make, and her analysis of American culture at the turn of the century (echoed by Martin Eden: 'The bourgeois is cowardly') anticipates the attitudes of figures such as Van Wyck Brooks, Lewis Mumford and Matthew Josephson in the 1920s. She answered her question, 'Why Is American Literature Bourgeois?', through a scathing analysis of the domination of 'magazine taste' in America. In her opinion, the magazines of the day rejected originality in the subject-matter of the stories they printed, and wanted only acceptable subjects treated in conventional ways. They allowed only a censored view of human nature which, among other things, excluded adult sexuality.[2] Editors preferred works which lacked either vitality or audacity; their magazines were contemptuous of the intellect. Their ideal story was one which would not disturb those with delicate nerves. The American bourgeoisie was basically responsible for this situation: 'magazine taste' was, Mrs Atherton felt, 'the expression of that bourgeoisie which is afraid of doing the wrong thing, not of the indifferent aristocrat; of that element which dares not use

34

slang, shrinks from audacity, rarely utters a bold sentiment and as rarely feels one'. The appearance of Kate Douglas Wiggins's *Rebecca of Sunnybrook Farm* and Gene Stratton-Porter's *Freckles* on the bestseller lists in 1903–4 would have been greeted by Mrs Atherton with a disdainful nod. These were the sorts of books the editors wanted. But the appearance of *The Call of the Wild*, *The Pit*, *The Sea-Wolf* and *The Jungle* on American bestseller lists for 1903–6 suggests she was making a partial case.[3] She seems to have been unaware of the challenge which realistic and naturalistic novels were offering to contemporary taste.

Among the flurry of replies to Mrs Atherton's article, easily the most passionate was by Upton Sinclair in *Collier's Weekly* of 8 October 1904. Sinclair was then twenty-six, and had published four undistinguished novels. His contempt for the bourgeoisie was no less real than Mrs Atherton's, but it lacked her haughty and aristocratic disdain. The bourgeois, he wrote,

is well fed himself, his wife is stout, and his children are fine and vigorous. He lives in a big house, and wears the latest thing in clothes; his civilization furnishes these to everyone – at least to everyone who amounts to anything; and beyond that he understands nothing – save only the desire to be entertained. It is for entertainment that he buys books, and as entertainment that he regards them; and hence another characteristic of the bourgeois literature is its lack of seriousness. The bourgeois writer has a certain kind of seriousness, of course – the seriousness of a hungry man seeking his dinner; but the seriousness of the artist he does not know. He will roar you as gently as any suckling dove, he will also wring tears from your eyes or thrill you with terror, according as the fashion of the hour suggests; but he knows exactly why he does these things, and he can do them between chats at his club. If you expected him to act like his heroes, he would think that you were mad.[4]

Sinclair's argument in 'Our Bourgeois Literature: The Reason and the Remedy' attributed bourgeois timidity to the knowledge of the possibility of revolution. A 'mighty revolution' was coming in America from the 'under-world of the poor', but was not yet grasped by Americans, because socialism, as they observed it, had not yet impinged upon culture. In Europe there was a substantial socialist literature (though the figures mentioned by Sinclair were in most cases not socialists at all: Bjørnsen, Maeterlinck, Sudermann, Hauptmann, Ibsen, Tolstoy, Zola and Gorky are paraded as examples), but writers in America who were socialists were generally forced to send their socialistic writings to 'some obscure Socialist paper that you never heard of' because the editors of bourgeois magazines were hostile to their message. The writers he mentions (Bliss Carman, Richard LeGallienne and Jack London) were, with the exception of London, established men of letters, hardly likely to threaten the social order, and London's most important socialist writings had not yet appeared. Where Mrs Atherton blamed bourgeois timidity, Sinclair argued that Americans have a capitalist culture, obedient to the interests of capital. The very idea that great art, or a high civilization, could be nourished by an unjust and exploitative society, brings forth from him a moral cry of indignation. Sinclair was an idealist in matters of culture. The arts belonged to a higher and purer realm of human endeavour than money-grubbing capitalism; but a corrupt society dragged down its highest impulses and cultural ideals:

> there can be among us neither political virtue, nor social refinement, nor true religion, nor vital art, so long as men, women, and little children are chained up to toil for us in mines and factories and sweatshops, are penned in filthy slums, and fed upon offal, and doomed to rot and perish in soul-sickening and horror.

In 1904 Sinclair was a recent convert to socialism, and showed all the convert's passionate conviction. There was little in his background to suggest the likelihood of such a conversion: he grew up in Virginia and New York, where he was a student at City College in the 1890s.[5] Sinclair's father was a wholesale whisky salesman, and appeared to his wife and son mainly as a troublesome drunk. Sinclair describes his mother as a long-suffering, puritanical woman who scrupulously avoided artificial stimulants like coffee, tea or alcohol. Brewers and saloon-keepers were the source of unmitigated evil to the young Sinclair, but while at City College he was exposed to other kinds of corruption:

> I can remember speculating at the age of sixteen whether it could be true that women did actually sell their bodies. I

decided in the negative and held to that idea until I summoned the courage to question one of my classmates in college.

The truth, finally made clear, shocked me deeply, and played a great part in the making of my political revolt. Between the ages of sixteen and twenty I explored the situation in New York, and made discoveries that for me were epoch-making. The saloonkeeper, who had been the villain of my childhood melodrama, was merely a tool and victim of the big liquor interests and politicians and police. The twin bases of the political power of Tammany Hall were saloon graft and the sale of women. So it was that, in my young soul, love for my father and love for my mother were transmuted into political rage, and I sallied forth at the age of twenty, a young reformer armed for battle.[6]

By 1902 Sinclair had written a vast quantity of popular ephemeral literature (stories, articles, serials, thousands of jokes, etc.), and three novels, two of which had been published. He described himself as being 'in revolt against Mammon'. '. . . I was intellectually a perfect little snob and Tory. I despised modern books without having read them, and I expected social evils to be remedied by cultured and well-mannered gentlemen who had been to college and acquired noble ideals.'[7] In the autumn of 1902, while calling upon the offices of the *Literary Digest*, Sinclair met 'a tall, soft-voiced, and gentle-souled youth' by the name of Leonard D. Abbott. He was soon impressed by the sincerity of Abbott's socialist beliefs, and took away several pamphlets and magazines to read. Abbott brought Sinclair along to meet John Spargo, editor of the *International Socialist Review*, and the young writer was soon drawn into the party. The effect of meeting socialists seems to have been electrifying: their doctrine, he discovered, was very congenial to his own; socialists also gave Sinclair the possibility of becoming part of a community, a brethren of fellow-believers:

It was like the falling down of prison walls about my mind; the amazing discovery, after all those years, that I did not have to carry the whole burden of humanity's future upon my two frail shoulders! There were actually others who understood; who saw what had gradually become clear to me, that the heart and centre of evil lay in leaving the social treasure, which nature had created and which every man has to have in order to live, to become the object of a scramble in the market place, a delirium of speculation. The principal fact the socialists had to teach me was that they themselves existed.[8]

One of the tracts which Abbott gave Sinclair was by George D. Herron, the Indiana congregational minister and socialist writer whose sensational divorce and remarriage to Carrie Rand in 1901 had ended his career in the ministry.[9] Herron was a leading proponent of Christian Socialism, and his criticism of the damaging effects of money upon organized Christianity, in his famous sermon 'The Message of Jesus to Men of Wealth', delivered in Minneapolis in 1890, was likely to receive a sympathetic hearing from Sinclair, still strongly influenced by his mother's Episcopalian piety. 'In no nation on the earth is there such abject submission to mere money in both church and state as there is in America': which might just as easily have come from Sinclair in 1904 as it did from Herron a decade earlier.[10] Herron's new wife had money, and he was able to help Sinclair throughout 1903, when he was writing *Manassas*, a heavily-researched novel about the Civil War. Herron made Sinclair a cash gift of several hundred dollars, and a small sum each month until the project was completed. It enabled Sinclair to keep afloat as a writer, and relieved him of the hack work by which he had supported himself in the past. *Manassas* did not reflect Sinclair's conversion to socialism, but his next book, *The Jungle*, became the most famous and influential novel written by a socialist in America.

The idea for a study of wage slavery came from the editor of a right-wing socialist weekly, *The Appeal to Reason*. The paper would stake Sinclair for $500 in return for serial rights to the book. Sinclair would be free to make his own arrangements for book publication, translation and foreign rights. He set out for Chicago in October 1904, where he spent seven weeks talking to workers, walking around the plants where butchery had been developed into an industrial technique. The simple act of carrying a lunchpail seemed to grant him unrestricted access to the stockyards. One of the first people he spoke to was Algie M. Simons, who knew Chicago in great detail and who had written about conditions in the canning factories.[11] The stockyards had been for two decades the scene of intense labour struggles, but Sinclair seems to have known nothing of the background of the situation in 1904. There had been two general strikes. One, in 1886, was led by the Knights of Labor and resulted in the complete destruction of the union movement in the stockyards and packing houses. For fifteen years union members were hounded and eliminated from the industry. The second major strike, in 1894, was spontaneous and unorganized. The unions began to return to the stockyards by the turn of the century, and in 1904 the skilled butchers went on strike on behalf of the unskilled labourers, specifically over a claim for a combined scale of pay for all departments and classes of labour. This was a remarkable show of class consciousness and solidarity, particularly since the skilled workers were mainly immigrants from Ireland, Germany and Bohemia, whereas the unskilled were Lithuanians, Slovaks, Poles and Blacks. The strike lasted from May to September 1904, under the leadership of the Amalgamated Meat Cutters and Butcher Workmens' union. It was finally defeated when men were brought in from the five major packers' other factories, and when Greeks and Blacks were brought in for the unskilled jobs.[12] When Sinclair arrived in Chicago the strike was fresh enough to have suggested that a 'strike novel' could have been quickly put together. In 1914 Sinclair travelled to Colorado with a similar purpose, which is discussed in Chapter 3. But Sinclair seems to have preferred to take a long-term view of the stockyards, and particularly of the substitution of ethnic groups which had led, by the turn of the century, to the arrival of great numbers of Lithuanians in Chicago to work in the stockyards. It was from the most recent immigrants that Sinclair chose his characters, and their experiences in Chicago constitute his story. All that survives in *The Jungle* of the 1904 strike is told through Jurgis's eyes at a time when he was a strike-breaker and *agent provocateur*; neither the specific issues nor the history of the struggle of the workers appear in his novel. Sinclair was, however, highly impressed by racist accounts of the behaviour of black strike-breakers, and described 'black bucks' going wild.

The most complete account of his activities in Chicago appeared in an interview he gave to Frederick Boyd Stevenson in *Wilshire's Magazine* in August 1906. 'I went to Chicago and spent seven weeks studying the stockyards and the conditions there', he explained:

I really had no need to study the lives of the people, for the poverty of the characters in the book are the experiences of my own life, only metamorphosed. Three times I went through the packinghouses. The first time I went through with ordinary visitors and saw just what the proprietors cared to show us. On the next occasion I went through with the correspondent of the London *Lancet* [Adolph Smith], who is an expert sanitarian, and has been through the abattoirs of all the important cities of the world. He told me that never in all his life had he seen such abominations as he had witnessed in the Chicago slaughter houses. He said he would not believe that such horrible atrocities had existed since the Dark Ages. He afterwards wrote in the *Lancet* that these conditions in Packingtown were 'a menace to the health of the civilized world' . . . The people whom I talked with there were settlement workers, doctors, policemen, saloon keepers, workingmen and packers' representatives. But the key that opened the most doors to me was Socialism.

Representatives of the packing houses, and their interests, immediately attempted to discredit Sinclair's account of the insanitary conditions. In reply, Sinclair prepared affidavits, eye-witness accounts, legal records and other circumstantial material. He defended *The Jungle* in terms of verifiable truth. In the *Wilshire's* interview Sinclair explained how he heard of some of the more gruesome details:

One night I sat in the kitchen of a Hungarian cattle-butcher whose hands were so slashed with deep knife-cuts that he could not use his thumbs, and he gave to me all the details of a man's daily life on the killing beds. And the next night I sat in the back room of a saloon and listened to the story of a man who had worked in the fertilizer mill where, in the month of November, out of 126 men, only six had been able to continued.

The claims he made for the book were unequivocal. *The Jungle* does not assert a 'poetic' or artistic truth, but a literal one: 'Every statement of importance in the book is based on some actual occurrence, either something I myself saw or something that was told to me by eye-witnesses.' Akin to the work of reforming journalists like Riis, Steffens and Tarbell, the 'literary' dimension of *The Jungle* was at the service of its documentary purpose. For many years Sinclair's novel was a model of what literature ought to be in the eyes of radicals. In the interview in *Wilshire's* he denied that there was anything imaginary or invented about the characters. He had seen them all at a Lithuanian wedding party in Chicago: 'Now that is the story of *The Jungle*, and that is the way I created the people of *The Jungle* – in fact I did not create them at all, for they are real people.'

When Sinclair began work on his novel on Christmas day, 1904, the conditions in the stockyards were about to become an international concern. While in Chicago Sinclair met the 'Special Sanitary Correspondent' of the *Lancet*. This man, identified by Sinclair as Adolph Smith, was engaged in a similar exercise in investigative reporting. His reports in the *Lancet* for two years, beginning with the issue of 24 December 1904, were of such detail and seriousness that the United States government issued a formal reply (which Smith rebutted in the issues of 14 July and 29 December 1906). The *Lancet* could not be silenced or discredited in the fashion the meatpacking industry sought to do with Sinclair, and Smith's reports were believed to have resulted in legislation banning meat and especially pork imports from Chicago: they constitute a parallel effort, justifying Sinclair, but belonging to a higher level of 'public health' seriousness. Sinclair had the *Lancet* reports available to him while writing *The Jungle*, and in follow-up articles on 9 June and 29 December 1906, the *Lancet* referred to Sinclair's role as reinforcing their own, prior indictment. Smith's reports constitute an important and hitherto unnoticed 'source' for the novel.

But the *Lancet* was not the first to bring to public notice the conditions in the stockyards. Nor were Smith's reports, especially those published in January 1905, the only source available to Sinclair. In 1899 Algie M. Simons, who had been assigned the stockyard district by the Bureau of Charities in Chicago, published a propaganda tract, *Packingtown*, which may have suggested some aspects of Sinclair's approach. Simons discussed the stockyards as a visitor might experience them, and tried to explain the industrial process which they represented. (Simons defended *The Jungle* in the *International Socialist Review* in June 1906). Ernest Poole published a sketch of the experiences of a Lithuanian immigrant who settled in Chicago and worked in the stockyards (*Independent*, 4 August 1904). Sinclair, in fact, turns out not to have been the discoverer of the problem so much as a successful dramatizer of the issues. It would be unkind to suggest that he exploited the conditions in the stockyards, because the problems were of such magnitude that any definition of the public interest would accept the legitimacy of his interest.

The American public was selective and intermittent in its attention to the complaints of reformers and muckrakers. There was a major scandal during the Spanish–American War over the quality of tinned beef shipped to the army in Cuba. Shrewd bribery and effective public relations, though on a less scientific basis and on a smaller scale than that conducted on behalf of the Rockefeller interests (described in Chapter 3), kept the public profile of the meatpacking industry generally below the horizon of concern. Henry Demarest Lloyd did much to publicize the operation of the Beef Trust in his book *Wealth Against Commonwealth* (1894). The Trust was undoubtedly a mighty force in Chicago life, and, when Lloyd was writing, was becoming an increasingly potent factor in national politics. The industry was a comparatively new one, made possible by the invention of the refrigerator car in the 1870s. The ability to transport cut and trimmed or 'dressed' sides of meat across the country enabled butchery for the whole nation to be centralized in Chicago. The major packing houses arranged a cartel to push down the prices paid for the best grade of beef cattle. At the same time the Trust undermined competitors who continued to butcher their own cattle by undercutting prices, threatening to open rival businesses, and by the usual forms of intimidation employed by cartels. They negotiated preferential terms with the railroads which were denied to shippers of live cattle.[13] The Trusts were a power in the land; by taking them on so boldly and so devastatingly, Sinclair came close to the real sources of power in the United States. But the idea that the packing houses were blankly hostile to inspection would seem to be incorrect. They saw the inspection of meat as a desirable protection against foreign competition, especially from Argentina; it was also to the advantage of the Beef Trust as against their smaller competitors within America. But inspection would cost money, and they were concerned that some of the cost was picked up by the government.[14] The campaign to discredit *The Jungle* was an aspect of the attempt by the Beef Trust to sustain and extend its dominance in the industry. It would be too flattering to Sinclair to suggest that the novel was either responsible for the moves to reform the industry or to improve conditions. As with the elimination of flogging in the United States navy and the powerful anti-flogging case made by Herman Melville in *White-Jacket* (1850), the cause-and-effect relationship is elusive and probably unprovable. Which is not to deny that for many people Sinclair's novel had an overwhelming impact, and that the sentiment for President Roosevelt's reform legislation owed a great deal to the climate in part created by the novel.

At the heart of *The Jungle*, permeating the human reality of Packingtown, is the idea that sudden transformations of life were always possible. For the characters in the novel there are two major transformations. The first changes Jurgis and Ona from healthy, optimistic young immigrants into degraded 'beasts' destroyed by their work. The second phase begins after the death of Ona. Jurgis's picaresque career takes him from the life of an ex-convict and fertilizer worker to his later experiences as a smart thief, political operator and labour scab. He is saved from this corrupting life by the discovery of socialism. For Sinclair, socialism was embodied in the liberation and transformation of human nature. Solidarity was the goal of socialism, not its prerequisite. (Like Jurgis, Sinclair found community with the discovery of socialism.) The structure of the book, so often brutally criticized, becomes more comprehensible in view of Sinclair's vision of the possibilities of transforming human nature. The first part of the book is naturalistic, the second picaresque: an uneasy conjunction. But within the conditions of work in the slaughterhouses, how could the decline of Jurgis be reversed? How in those conditions could his health recover? How could he be made to gain a broader grasp of the way the system works, and thus be led to socialism? As Sinclair saw the matter, it was hardly possible for the slaughterhouses to reform themselves. He was sufficiently sceptical of Progressivism and reformism generally to doubt whether that sort of change was at all plausible in American conditions. But the book was locked into a Naturalism which seemed to point relentlessly towards Jurgis's defeat and death. Yet belief in the capacity for change, so much a central feature of the socialist imagination in America, kept Sinclair by main force from a Zolaesque conclusion. If Sinclair's belief that work and housing conditions could not, under capitalism, be meaningfully altered, then Jurgis's subsequent career makes a little more sense. The structural problem of the novel was solved by ideology and temperament: Sinclair was a deeply hopeful person. Jurgis's sudden conversion to socialism has often left critics dissatisfied, and in some respects did not please Sinclair himself. We live in a political climate more sceptical of such conversions, more cynical of their likely endurance; and for this reason find it harder to share fully the optimism of a novelist in 1905 about socialism and American politics, and about socialism as such. It is impossible to foresee a time when the gap between our own wizened realism and Sinclair's blazing hopefulness will ever be reduced.[15]

Analysis of *The Jungle* should begin with the long passage describing the butchery of hogs, the way they were hoisted by chains upon an iron wheel:

At the same instant the ear was assailed by a most terrifying shriek; the visitors started in alarm, the women turned pale and shrank back. The shriek was followed by another, louder and yet more agonizing – for once started upon that journey, the hog never came back; at the top of the wheel he was shunted off upon a trolley, and went sailing down the room. And meantime another was swung up, and then another, and another, until there was a double line of them, each dangling by a foot and kicking in frenzy – and squealing. The uproar was appalling, perilous to the eardrums; one feared there was too much sound for the room to hold – that the walls must give way or the ceiling crack. There were high squeals and low squeals, grunts, and wails of agony; there would come a momentary lull, and then a fresh outburst, louder than ever, surging up to a deafening climax. It was too much for some of the visitors – the men would look at each other, laughing nervously, and the women would stand with hands clenched, and the blood rushing to their faces, and the tears starting in their eyes.

Meantime, heedless of all these things, the men upon the floor were going about their work. Neither squeals of hogs nor tears of visitors made any difference to them; one by one they hooked up the hogs, and one by one with a swift stroke they slit their throats. There was a long line of hogs, with squeals and life-blood ebbing away together, until at last each started again and vanished with a splash into a huge vat of boiling water.

It was all so very businesslike that one watched it fascinated. It was pork-making by machinery, pork-making by applied mathematics. And yet somehow the most matter-of-fact person could not help thinking of the hogs; they were so innocent, they came so very trustingly; and they were so human in their protests – and so perfectly within their rights! They had done nothing to deserve it, and it was adding insult to injury, as the thing was done here, swinging them up in this cold-blooded, impersonal way, without a pretence at apology, without the homage of a tear. Now and then a visitor wept, to be sure; but this slaughtering machine ran on, visitors or no visitors. It was like some horrible crime committed in a dungeon, all unseen and unheeded, buried out of sight and of memory.

One could not stand and watch very long without becoming philosophical, without beginning to deal in symbols and similes, and to hear the hog-squeal of the universe. Was it permitted to believe that there was nowhere upon the earth, or above the earth, a heaven for hogs, where they were requited for all this suffering? Each one of these hogs was a separate creature. Some were white hogs, some were black; some were brown, some were spotted; some were old, some were young; some were long and lean, some were monstrous. And each of them had an individuality of his own, a will of his own, a hope and a heart's desire; each was full of self-confidence, of self-importance, and a sense of dignity. And trusting and strong in faith he had gone about his business, the while a black shadow hung over him and a horrid Fate waited in his pathway. Now suddenly it had swooped upon him, and had seized him by the leg. Relentless, remorseless, it was; all his protests, his screams, were nothing to it – it did its cruel will with him, as if his wishes, his feelings, had simply no existence at all; it cut his throat and watched him gasp out his life. And now was one to believe that there was nowhere a god of hogs, to whom this hog-personality was precious to whom these hog-squeals and agonies had a meaning? Who would take this hog into his arms and comfort him, reward him for his work well done, and show him the meaning of his sacrifice? Perhaps some glimpse of all this was in the thoughts of our humble-minded Jurgis, as he turned to go on with the rest of the party, and muttered: '*Dieve* – but I'm glad I'm not a hog!' (Chap. 3)

Herman Melville had not yet been rediscovered when Sinclair wrote this passage early in 1905. The description in *Moby-Dick* of the cutting up and rendering of whales might have taught Sinclair how to make this description more economical, and also more serious. Sinclair's sincerity is obvious; his intense concern to make his readers participate in the pig-holocaust leads him into sentimentality, repetition and naïveté.

The slaughterhouses transform living animals into meat products (and into profits for the packing houses). During the slaughtering the animals are endowed with human reactions ('they were so very human in their protests') while the men in the slaughterhouse are like remorseless machines, 'a horrid Fate', indifferent to the tragedy of the hogs. Human beings have lost their humanity. It is the hogs who have the sensitivity and imagination not customarily associated with animals. The 'signified' attributes of animal and man have become, in the process of industrializing the slaughterhouse, detached from their customary 'sign' and reattached to its opposite. This passage tells us something important about Sinclair's humanism. He retains the knowledge that there is another arrangement available to mankind, in which human nature was not alienated from the human subject. (Though what form of butchery would provide a similar service to the hogs is unclear; more to the point, the humane answer to this passage is the end of butchery in any form, a complete vegetarianism.) In current social and economic conditions, as Sinclair viewed them, the dream of integral wholeness is denied, and only with the transformation of human nature made possible by socialism is it possible to think once again of the reintegration of the human subject.

The novel begins with a traditional Lithuanian wedding. Justly praised as one of the best scenes in the whole of Sinclair's fiction, the wedding scene has a cultural specificity and symbolic resonance which is destroyed by the economic reality of life in Packingtown. At the core of the wedding is the *veselija*, the symbolic compact which binds Ona and Jurgis to each other and to the community. But already the elders, Teta Elzbieta and Dede Antanas, fear that the force of the ties was weakening. Some guests at the wedding have given less money to the young couple than they should have done; others sneak out without giving anything, or spend their time at the bar, ignoring everyone else. The 'subtle poison' in the air, which seemed especially to affect the young men, comes from America itself. Traditions like the *veselija*, which the immigrants brought with them from the old world, seem somehow starved for oxygen in the new. Such rituals could not put

down roots in the American soil. The communal sanctions seem to
the elders less secure or final. The failure of the *veselija* is the first in
a series of disappointments and cruel twists which turn Ona into a
'hunted animal' and Jurgis into a 'dumb beast of burden'.

There is no need to retrace here the precise sequence of events.
They are related with considerable effectiveness and pessimism
by Sinclair. The young couple seem caught 'like rats in a trap'.
They are victims, guilty only of being poor and foreign: and they
are seen as 'victims of a relentless fate, cornered, trapped, in the
grip of destruction'. Jurgis is 'the victim of ravenous vultures that
had torn into his vitals and devoured him'. Sinclair gives a very
plausible account of the mechanisms of fraud, from the tricksters
to deceitful manufacturers; sheer ill-fortune is seen to play an
important role in transforming Ona and Jurgis into victims. A
close student of the petty commercial deceptions which consumed
the resources of the poor, Sinclair emphasizes the destructive and
degrading work conditions which left the workers exhausted,
demoralized and unable to think for themselves, or even to defend
their interests. The decline of Jurgis's strength, and the corruption
of his moral character, are painfully recited. The animal imagery,
for victim and victimizers, was by 1905 part of the intellectual
luggage of Sinclair's and London's generation. They thought
in Darwinian terms, as did almost the entire American
intelligentsia.

Precisely at the middle point in the novel, when he has been
imprisoned for attacking Connor, the boss who tricked Ona into a
whorehouse, Jurgis feels himself flung aside 'like a bit of trash'.
He goes over, almost without being fully aware of what was
happening, to the cause of rebellion, outlawry and unbelief.
Jurgis's home is repossessed while he is in prison, and his wife dies
in childbirth. Their son drowns, and Jurgis finds that he has been
blacklisted in Packingtown. The iron determinism of his plight, in
which his physical decline is closely related to the impossible
pressure of economic circumstance, has been swept away. Jurgis
is thus enabled to enter a more fluid environment in which rapid
changes of fortune become possible. Jurgis's health is restored by
weeks on the tramp, but on his return to the city in the autumn
Jurgis sinks down to drunkenness and begging. Befriended by a
rich young drunk who gives him $100, Jurgis is easily tricked out
of the money. A further spell in prison brings him to crime, graft
and political corruption. He is set up in a political career and helps

fix the defeat of a 'sheeny' Democrat. He next appears as a scab worker in the slaughterhouses, but this turn of fortune is cut short when he again assaults Ona's former boss. He is advised to jump bail, and returns to life on the tramp. The suddenness of changes in his life, the variety of incident and scene, suggest the picaresque. The shift from one literary mode to another, from the naturalistic novel to the picaresque adventure story, is effected with little difficulty, although at the expense of the traditional novelistic qualities of coherence and consistency.

On impulse Jurgis attends a political meeting. Exhausted and hungry, he soon falls asleep. A prosperously-dressed woman addresses him as 'comrade' and gently suggests that Jurgis might be interested in the speeches if he stayed awake. He struggles to pay attention, all the while observing the reactions of the young lady to the speech:

> There was a look of excitement upon her face, of tense effort, as of one struggling mightily, or witnessing a struggle. There was a faint quivering of her nostrils; and now and then she would moisten her lips with feverish haste. Her bosom rose and fell as she breathed, and her excitement seemed to mount higher, and then to sink away again. (ch. 28)

The speech raises the young lady to a higher spiritual and emotional plane. She has quite literally been transformed by what she has heard. The speaker is described as tall, gaunt and haggard, with a thin black beard and a rapid manner of speech. 'His voice was deep, like an organ.' Sinclair claimed in a letter in 1958 that the orator was based on Algie M. Simons, who had been a charity worker in the stockyards (and from whose 1899 pamphlet, *Packingtown*, Sinclair had borrowed a number of details on stockyard conditions for *The Jungle*).[16] Sinclair also said that the speech was one that he himself had made shortly before leaving Chicago. It seems possible that the speaker included certain qualities of Sinclair's patron, George D. Herron. Certainly there is very little political content in the speech, and a great deal of sermonizing rhetoric. The speaker's tactic is to implore his listeners to open their eyes, and thus to 'shake the most sluggish soul to action!' 'I am here to plead with you, to know if want and misery have yet done their work with you, if injustice and oppression have yet opened your eyes!' The word 'socialism' is not mentioned in this message of salvation. The appeal is specifically aimed at those for whom religious salvation was a familiar phenomenon:

> I feel sure that in the crowd that has come to me tonight, no matter how many may be dull and heedless, no matter how many may have come out of idle curiosity, or in order to ridicule – there will be some one man whom pain and suffering have made desperate, whom some chance vision of wrong and horror has startled and shocked into attention. And to him my words will come like a sudden flash of lightning to one who travels in darkness – revealing the way before him, the perils and the obstacles – solving all problems, making all difficulties clear! The scales will fall from his eyes, the shackles will be torn from his limbs – he will leap up with a cry of thankfulness, he will stride forth a free man at last! (ch. 28)

Listeners to this lay sermon are repeatedly urged to 'realize once in your lives this world in which you dwell'. The effect on Jurgis is to leave him 'smitten with wonder'. He listens motionlessly, completely seized by the spiritual meaning of the speech:

> It was his presence, it was his voice . . . that gripped the listener like a mighty hand about his body, that shook him and startled him with sudden fright, with a sense of things not of earth, of mysteries never spoken before, of presences of awe and terror.

There are wild shouts of joy, and a spontaneous singing of the 'Marseillaise' at the end of the meeting. Jurgis remains, to have a word with the speaker:

> 'You want to know more about Socialism?' he asked. Jurgis started. 'I – I –' he stammered. 'Is it Socialism? I didn't know. I want to know about what you spoke of – I want to help. I have been through all that.'

Sinclair soon rectified the absence of politics with a simplified exposition of socialist teaching about capitalism, class conflict and the coming revolution:

> It was a slow and weary process, but it would go on – it was like

the movement of a glacier, once it was started it could never be stopped. Every Socialist did his share, and lived upon the vision of the 'good time coming' – when the working class should go to the polls and seize the powers of government and put an end to private property in the means of production.

The novel ends with a dramatic rise in the socialist vote in Chicago, and a vision of ultimate electoral victory. Jurgis has a steady job as a porter in a hotel owned by a prominent local socialist.

What separated Sinclair, on the right of the Socialist Party, from those, like Jack London on the left wing, was this faith that socialism would and could come from municipal election victories. Having once won Chicago, there was still Illinois, with its rural and conservative majority. Beyond that lay Washington, the constitution and the Supreme Court: 'a slow and weary process' indeed. A socialist victory in Chicago would constitute a heady tonic to the movement, but from the point of view of socialist militants 'municipal socialism' had such serious drawbacks, and local politics were notoriously so corrupt, that the left wing of the Socialist Party were highly critical of the ultimate prospects of a purely electoral stategy.

It is remarkable that the crucial moment in Jurgis's conversion to socialism should have so little political content. As with so many conversion experiences studied by psychologists at the turn of the century, doctrinal theology was less required than a deep and urgent desire on the part of the subject to rid him- or herself of the 'incompleteness' which rendered life meaningless. The socialist preacher concentrated almost exclusively upon the wrongness of the present, thus confirming William James's belief that it was the intense specificity of 'sin', rather than the imaginary ideal of salvation and grace in the future, which was central to the process of conversion.[17]

The Jungle appeared throughout 1905 in *The Appeal to Reason*. Commercial publishers, as Sinclair soon discovered, were unwilling to publish the manuscript as it stood. Macmillan, who had given Sinclair a substantial advance, withdrew from the contract as serialization progressed: they asked Sinclair to delete 'objectionable' passages, but the novelist refused to do so. He announced in the *Chicago Socialist* on 25 November that he would publish *The Jungle* himself, in an edition selling for $1.50, and invited advance orders. Sinclair feared that the Beef Trust would throttle the book, and prevent it from reaching a large reading public. But before his own publication plans were complete, Doubleday, Page agreed to print the manuscript without alteration. Copies were sent to President Roosevelt when it was published early in 1906.

Within the socialist movement the book created an immediate sensation. Jack London, supporting Sinclair's plan for self-publication, advised Chicago socialists to

> . . . take notice and remember, comrades, this book is straight proletarian. And straight proletarian it must be throughout. It is written by an intellectual proletarian. It is written for the proletariat. It is published by a proletarian publishing house. It is to be read by the proletariat. And depend upon it, if it is not circulated by the proletariat it will not be circulated at all. In short, it must be a supreme proletarian effort.[18]

Debs was no less enthusiastic than Jack London:

> The first really great and distinctively proletarian novel has been written. Upton Sinclair's masterpiece, *The Jungle*, is entitled to that distinction. Here we have the tragic story of *Les Misérables* hot from the brain and soul of a living genius. In *The Jungle* we have a startling, shocking, world-arousing revelation. The pictures of Sinclair are as real as the palpitant flesh that inspires them. It is an awful panorama that is here unfolded, and all its colorings are so mercilessly true to life that they fairly quiver with its misery and groan with its despair. The minutest details, like the boldest outlines, are traced with the consummate skill of a master. All the passion that sweeps the soul of this inspired young author is aglow in these pages. It is a marvelous work. No possible review can do it justice. Every man, woman and child, rich and poor, should read it. The tragic fate of the children of poverty and ignorance is so thrillingly presented, and with such subtle power, that even the most gruesome pictures have potent charm and irresistible fascination.
>
> The pulse of the proletarian revolution throbs in these pages. It is a novel of the impending crisis, and will prove a powerful factor in precipitating it.

The Jungle, as a masterful literary achievement, will mark a luminous epoch in the social revolution.

A million copies should be in demand the first year, and every Socialist and every sympathizer, and every other human being with a heart in working order, should join in giving it world circulation.[19]

A. M. Simons described *The Jungle* as 'the great novel of capitalism'.[20]

The novel contained material of such a sensational nature that its publication was planned with care. Isaac Marcosson, who handled the publicity for Thomas Dixon's *The Clansman*, planned a similar campaign for Doubleday, Page. Advance page proofs were sent to hundreds of leading American newspapers, with an invitation to quote freely. The release date, 15 January 1906, saw Sinclair suddenly transformed into a famous writer. Across the country front pages were filled with the more sensational passages from *The Jungle*. Marcosson was peppered with demands for photographs of Sinclair; theatrical managers wanted rights to adapt it for the stage; famous writers were lavish with praise; and when Marcosson received a wire from Jack London ('*The Jungle* is the *Uncle Tom's Cabin* of wage slavery') the publicity campaign had its perfect slogan. Marcosson was quick to suggest a similar novel on steel, and a third on coal-mining or the railroads, but he found Sinclair increasingly distracted by socialism, and by 'a weird experiment in sociology' in New Jersey which made the author a figure of ridicule. That *The Jungle* was so successfully marketed by a publisher and publicity agent is by no means the least of the ironies which surrounded it.[21] As expected, it gave President Roosevelt useful impetus in a campaign to require federal inspection of meat. But Sinclair found the President resolute in his opposition to socialism:

. . . while I agree with you that energetic, and, as I believe, in the long run radical, action must be taken to do away with the effects of arrogant and selfish greed on the part of the capitalist, yet I am more than ever convinced that the real factor in the elevation of any man or any mass of men must be the development within his or their hearts and heads of the qualities which alone can make either the individual, the class or the nation permanently useful to themselves and to others.[22]

The royalties enabled Sinclair to keep the issue before the public, but as an exercise in propaganda *The Jungle* was somewhat less successful than Sinclair hoped, and had its chief influence in ways he did not anticipate. The specific measures of hygiene and meat inspection which resulted from an aroused public opinion, and Roosevelt's legislation, although desirable in their own right, were humanitarian rather than socialist, and more characteristic of the objectives of progressives and reformers than socialists.[23] The long-suffering workers in Packingtown did not appreciate Sinclair's efforts, or at least not as much as he would have expected. One of the first reforms compelled them to get rid of their old, dirty work clothes and to purchase a new outfit. With wages at $5.00 per week, Sinclair and his meddling was bitterly resented.[24] The Socialist Party, which might have been expecting a boost from *The Jungle*, by 1906 had lost some of its earlier momentum and popular appeal. And in Chicago, where the novel might have been expected to have its greatest impact, the socialist vote collapsed in the 1907 mayoral election. Socialist voters abandoned their own candidate to support a reform Democrat named Dunne, who, like Tom Johnson in Cleveland, advocated the municipal ownership of the traction companies which ran civic trolley lines. The regular Democratic Party machine, fixed by the political clubs of 'Hinky Dink', 'Bathhouse John' and others (the political bosses who used Jurgis as scab and *agent provocateur*), swung over behind the Republican candidate Busse. It was a nice example of Chicago democracy at work. The radical vote was split and discredited, and the new mayor, as reported in the *International Socialist Review*, was 'frankly and openly the candidate of plutocracy'.[25]

Sinclair revisited Chicago in 1909. He gave a lecture in which he described the President's reaction to *The Jungle*, the subsequent investigations, and the resulting legislation. The novelist's disillusionment was transparent:

> You have perhaps heard my remark, concerning *The Jungle*, that I aimed at the public heart and by accident hit it in the stomach. You see, a great deal of fuss was made about the book, but there was never the least thing done in behalf of the poor laboring man who has to support a wife and children on $5.00 a week. I am told that they have whitewashed the walls of the packing houses, and that manicure parlors have been established for the

use of the girls who handle the meats; but they have done nothing for the workingman. They have done nothing to protect his wife from the brutal foreman, and they have done nothing for the children who work in the cellars and should be at school.

And even the so-called reforms in the packing of meat have amounted to nothing.[26]

Sinclair attempted to dramatize *The Jungle*, but the New York production was a flop which cost him several thousand dollars.[27] A silent film version of the novel was made by the All-Star Feature Corporation in 1914. Directed by Augustus Thomas in five reels, the film featured George Nash as Jurgis and Gail Kane as Ona (Sinclair himself played the socialist orator), but the company went bankrupt not long after completing the film and it was never released commercially. Sinclair purchased the negative, and showed it to socialist audiences across the country. The film was banned in Chicago. In 1920 the Labor Film Service proposed to re-edit the now rather old-fashioned film and reissue it with additional scenes. The picture is lost, but something of its original conception may be gathered from Sinclair's correspondence with Joseph D. Cannon, Field Director of the Labor Film Service. Cannon wrote to Sinclair in September 1920:

> The picture does not measure up to the story; it seems that economy in its production was carried too far . . . We can improve this by having some large strike meetings made which would fill it out . . . the picture . . . The last reel needs almost entire remodeling . . . Instead of the Socialist Party meeting, Jurgis should stroll into a big union meeting. It might be a celebration of the winning of their strike by the workers in the packing-house industry a few years ago; or what would be better still a meeting preceding the winning of the strike and the appeal should be for solidarity and unity of purpose, to hold intact, to join together, to stick together . . . the picture ending with the audience spontaneously coming to its feet, cheering enthusiastically and tumultuously, and when this is quieting down and a few leave their seats going to the exits, there suddenly is heard a song, and they halt and listen as a voice of a child, in the far-off corner of the great hall is heard singing the opening words of the Marseillaise . . .
>
> You see I do not wish to change the philosophy of *The Jungle*,

but I want to make it the more inspiring, more gripping, and I want the people to leave the theatres whistling or singing the Marseillaise, to go out with a spirit of revolt awakened in their heart.[28]

These changes, best described as radical *schlock*, seemed acceptable to Sinclair. In a letter to Cannon on 27 September 1920 he repeated a proposal he had first made in 1914 for the ending of the film:

Let me suggest that you look up in the Rand School library and the public library a collection of some twenty or thirty drawings on Socialist themes by Walter Crane. One of these shows a pageant, a May Day festival of labor, a number of symbolic figures, men, women and children marching with a chariot symbolizing peace and plenty. It seems to me that this particular vision could be an admirable way of conveying a very happy ending of *The Jungle* – that is to say, happy ending for all the workers and not merely for Jurgis and a new wife working on a glorified tenant farm.[29]

Sinclair's socialism, with its roots in the great urban centres of New York and Chicago, has an unexpected dimension. The iconography of Walter Crane, so much a part of the Arts and Crafts approach to socialism, and so closely associated with William Morris and his American heirs writing in *The Comrade*, a socialist monthly published in New York 1901–4, seemed an adequate vehicle for Sinclair's 'vision of a redeemed society'. The details of the revised ending, including Jurgis's new wife and their life on 'a glorified tenant farm', confirm the impression that the redemption cannot seriously be envisaged as taking place *within* Packingtown. It will occur, if at all, in the form of an escape from the slaughterhouses, and the closed world of industrial capitalism they symbolize. This conclusion seems to have emerged from Sinclair's activities in the year following publication of *The Jungle*. His meetings with President Roosevelt, the numerous public lectures, interviews with the press, and the notoriety of his book, seem to have left Sinclair (normally a self-advancing and publicity-conscious person) hungry to withdraw from society.

Part of the money he received from *The Jungle* was spent in 1906 on a nine-acre plot of land near Englewood, New Jersey, where he proposed to found an 'experiment in co-operative distribution'. Called Helicon Hall Home Colony, the project lasted from July 1906 to March 1907 when the hall was burned down.[30] Helicon Hall was not designed along ascetic lines: it consisted of the grounds and buildings of a former school, complete with a bowling alley, theatre, organ and tropical plants. The hope was that the Colony would be run 'as one big happy family'. Radicals from all over the country came to visit the experiment, including John Dewey and Emma Goldman. Sinclair Lewis lived in the colony for a month before escaping to write an article for the New York *Sun* about 'Two Yale Men in Utopia'.[31] The American press portrayed the experiment with innuendo and vilification, but at the time of the fire in 1907 there was a substantial waiting list to enter. The colony represented something of a throwback to the socialist politics of the end of the nineteenth century when utopian socialists, anarchists, Single Taxers and prohibitionists, argued against the exclusively electoral strategy of the 'political actionists'. The Socialist Party itself emerged out of this argument, when the Milwaukee socialist leader, Victor Berger, led political actionists out of the Social Democracy of America into the Social Democratic Party, which in 1901, after further mergers, formed the Socialist Party.[32]

By placing Jurgis in a 'glorified tenant farm', with the socialist symbolism of Walter Crane, Sinclair tacitly acknowledged the impossibility, in contemporary American social conditions, of extending the process which made Jurgis a socialist to the whole workforce. In this he was well attuned to the revisionist tendency within the Socialist Party. Leading figures such as Morris Hillquit and John Spargo had, by 1907, essentially agreed that the revolutionary perspective of orthodox Marxism did not seem to fit American conditions. In lectures delivered at the Cooper Union in the winter of 1907–8, and published as *The Spiritual Significance of Modern Socialism* (New York, 1908), Spargo abandoned class conflict, the dictatorship of the proletariat, and the whole economic and historical dimension of socialism in favour of a 'spiritual interpretation' of the movement which rooted it in dreams of universal peace and the brotherhood of man. Spargo believed that socialism would come to America only gradually, one step at a time. The platform of the Socialist Party convention in 1908 was wholly preoccupied with issues of municipal reform. Plans for a Karl Marx memorial celebration were dropped. The bible of the Socialist Party was the second edition of W. D. P. Bliss's *The New Encyclopedia of Social Reform* (1909) which carried detailed accounts of every aspect of 'municipalism' throughout the world. Hopes for the sudden, violent transformation of the political order seemed irrelevant to American socialists. The issue now was how socialism could be adapted to the modern world of industrialism and democracy. Spargo wrote that 'no Socialist whose works have any influence in the movement believes that there will be a sudden, violent change from capitalism to Socialism'.[33] Sinclair felt that the old hope that 'the co-operative commonwealth could be established at once upon a small scale' carried little weight in the party. It proved difficult, however, to transform a millennial rhetoric into a meliorative one, as Sinclair shows: 'The modern "Scientific Socialist" believes that the end of the competitive wage system will come by a revolutionary change affecting the whole of society at once, and coming as the end of a long process of industrial evolution.'[34] Two audiences were being appeased here, and neither with much conviction. Sinclair's social thought is as muddled as that of the party itself, which wanted to be respectable and revolutionary – sometimes in the same sentence. Having declared that the cooperative spirit was now dead, he devoted his considerable energies, and the royalties from *The Jungle*, to found a cooperative community called Helicon Hall.

Sinclair shared the perspective of the right-wing leadership of the Socialist Party in believing that the future of the movement lay in patient electoral work, party propaganda, and not rubbing Samuel Gompers the wrong way. Writing about a bitter industrial dispute in *King Coal* (1917), which is analyzed in Chapter 3, he clearly sided with the wise heads of the union and not with the syndicalists who advocated direct industrial action for social change. The transformation of Jurgis, an immigrant workman in a Chicago slaughterhouse, was a model of the coming of socialism as anticipated by the right wing of the party. It was a conversion based on oppression and victimization on a personal level. Jurgis's political consciousness was untouched by organized industrial conflict, and in this Sinclair was undoubtedly false to the experience of the socialist movement in Chicago. Sinclair shows how effectively the industrial system pitted workers against each other, and how these divisions were exacerbated by racial and ethnic conflicts within the workforce. But he does not show how *some* workers did, in fact, learn solidarity through industrial conflict. Jurgis had to be extracted from the packing-houses, and from the industrial system, before the socialist message could reach him. The effects of the socialist speech were instantaneous and permanent. At the end of the book Jurgis shares the urgent, impatient certainties of the new convert. In a brief but acute observation, John Chamberlain noted that while Sinclair's critics have pointed out that the conversion 'solves' nothing, the portrayal of Packingtown was the real substance of the book, its true call to action.[35] In trying to reconnect the harsh naturalism of the description of the slaughterhouses with the remarkable transformation with which the book ends, one senses the limitations of the socialist perspective it conveys. It is a problem which Sinclair could not solve in the novel, any more than the Socialist Party could, in political terms, find a way to link its detailed criticism of American capitalism with its belief in the advent of socialism by persuasion and propaganda.

3 Greenwich Village Intellectuals and the Ludlow Massacre, 1914

The Colorado coal-miners' strike of 1913–15 was on a scale and of a ferocity which outstripped even the IWW-led strikes at Lawrence and Paterson in 1912 and 1913.[1] Because it occurred near Manhattan, the Paterson strike made a particular impact upon the editors of *The Masses*, Max Eastman and Floyd Dell, and upon the circle of poets, bohemians, artists, anarchists and hostesses in Greenwich Village in which they moved. The celebrated strike pageant held in Madison Square Garden in support of the Paterson strike was conceived and organized by left-wing Villagers, and made a highly original contribution to the lexicon of American protest politics.[2] But when the pageant left a deficit of several thousand dollars, instead of an anticipated surplus, the morale of the strikers collapsed and the strike was lost. The position of the Wobblies on the East Coast was fatally weakened by the defeat at Paterson, and by the subsequent recriminations. The Villager's intervention in Paterson was symptomatic of the many uncertainties facing left-wing intellectuals who were drawn to industrial conflicts. The Socialist Party was engaged in an acrimonious disagreement about the place of middle-class intellectuals in the party.[3] Some forms of social concern had to create new institutions, such as the Social Settlements, through which they could be expressed.[4] For Villagers with rebellious attitudes towards social and ethical conventions, and especially for those with elite educations and middle-class backgrounds, there was a problem in simply grasping the ethnic diversity and social aspirations of the American worker. When he visited a meeting of strikers and their families at Paterson, Max Eastman recalled that it seemed to him less a political rally than a Sunday School picnic.[5] Expecting militant fervour, he found the strikers relaxed and hopeful. In *Venture*, a novel published in 1927, Eastman portrayed the visit to Paterson of a Greenwich Village intellectual, Jo Hancock, who was closely modelled on John Reed. When asked to give a talk to the strikers, Hancock can think of nothing to do but to lead them in college football songs with new words composed on the spot.[6] The cause was desperately important, but the role of intellectuals as intellectuals was not yet fully serious. Eastman heard speeches at Paterson by Elizabeth Gurley Flynn, Carlo Tresca and Bill Haywood, vivid personalities all, but he was most strongly impressed by the ordinary people he met. 'I felt at home, and knew that I would always feel at home, not with the proletariat, but with simple men and women anywhere.'[7] In Colorado, Eastman found these same simple folk, only now in isolated feudal company towns, confronted by viciously armed camp guards, Baldwin-Felts 'detectives' who specialized in labour intimidation and strikebreaking, and behind them a trigger-happy state militia. College songs had no place in the Colorado mining camps. Where there had been pockets of sympathy and support for the striking silk weavers in Paterson, friendly municipalities nearby where they could hold rallies and plan their course of action, and a reservoir of potential support across the Hudson River in New York, in Colorado the miners lived in closed mining camps, far from the major centres of population. They were isolated and threatened by overweening and aggressive employers. The conflict was so violent that something near civil war existed in Colorado in the spring of 1914. It seemed to many radicals a foretaste of the coming class warfare in industrial America. The trains west were soon crowded with radical journalists and intellectuals making their way to Ludlow and Trinidad in search of the revolution.

In 1902 the socialist writer W. J. Ghent held up the Colorado Fuel and Iron Company (CFI) as an outstanding example of the new 'benevolent feudalism'.[8] He noted that the company, which by the turn of the century had become the largest coal and steel producer west of the Mississippi, had a 'sociological department' which maintained free kindergartens, night school and libraries, and which provided free band concerts and organized Fourth of July picnics.[9] The CFI published a weekly magazine, *Camp and Plant*;

Ghent noted that the CFI hospital at Pueblo was one of the best equipped in the west. John Osgood, who organized the CFI in 1889, donated 500 volumes to form the nucleus of a camp library. Funds were provided to purchase a circulating art collection for local schools. The CFI was altogether an unusual demonstration of capitalist paternalism. But after a secretive and complex negotiation, Osgood sold the controlling interest to John D. Rockefeller in 1902. Osgood and the leading managers remained in place, but a newer, less obliging managerial style was soon noted. When Osgood eventually departed to assume control over a rival company, *Camp and Plant* was discontinued, the sociological department reined in and confined to a subordinate role within the company's medical department. Altogether a different spirit prevailed.

Colorado had for a generation been notorious for the violence and lawlessness of its conduct of industrial disputes. The militia were ordered out to quell labour disturbances no less than ten times between 1880 and 1904[10] Strikes at Cripple Creek in 1894 and Telluride in 1901, and an unsuccessful attempt to win an eight-hour day in 1902, culminated in a massive series of strikes in 1903–4. John Graham Brooks, sent by President Roosevelt to investigate the conflict, described it as 'a strike in which the lawlessness of labor was matched and outmatched by the lawlessness of capital'.[11] Ray Stannard Baker, in an influential article in *McClure's* in 1904, powerfully indicted both sides in the dispute for their contempt for the rule of law.[12] In *Violence and the Labor Movement* (1914) Robert Hunter condemned the 'terrorism of powerful and influential anarchists' no less than the violence of the strikers.[13] (This was precisely the even-handedness which Theodore Roosevelt insisted upon in a powerful letter to Edward Costigan, Progressive Party candidate for Governor of Colorado in 1914: 'The impression left upon my mind by the testimony accessible to me is that both the employers on the one side and the employees on the other have much responsibility and much blame.'[14]) Even-handedness in response to the situation which prevailed in Colorado was a 'practical' response. Liberal-minded observers like Brooks, Baker, Hunter and others hoped that the very excesses of violence in Colorado would serve as warnings to the general public that labour unrest was not solely due to trouble-making or immigrant lawlessness. It was a problem which could not simply be repressed by draconian law-and-order policies. By so arguing they supported the cause of labour, with careful reservations and qualifications, and always from a perspective clearly distinguished from the antagonists. Baker magisterially condemned lawlessness, but in doing so did not attempt to apportion blame. The stance of impartiality was a crucial one in preserving the writer's integrity before an audience which was generally suspicious of unions. The high ground of public rectitude and even-handedness upon which such writers stood involved a complex rhetorical act of balancing and judging. But in the light of events as they unfolded in 1903–4, it is easy to see how the limitations of balance and practicality could be undermined by powerful emotional responses. In almost uncanny anticipation of the events of 1914, the mine-owners forced the governor to call out the militia to defend property. Strikers were arrested or simply held in large numbers without bail. A Citizens' Alliance of small businessmen directed attacks on strikers and their families and supporters. Martial law was declared, *habeas corpus* suspended, and in certain counties of southern Colorado the press was subjected to rigorous military censorship. Baker described how the military authorities openly defied the civil courts. The strike was broken by the mass deportation of the strikers and by the importation of foreign scab labour. When confronted by such events, a younger and perhaps more radical generation were no less angry than Baker (whose article was passionately written), but were less constrained by scruples about objectivity and the rhetoric of fairness. The expressive freedoms so much admired in modern painting, the new literature, dance (Isadore Duncan was a cultural goddess to the radicals of *The Masses* [see Appendix II]), and photography, reflect a similar pressure and restlessness. The distinguishing feature of the Villagers' response to the events in Colorado in 1914 was the purity of their outrage.

In September 1913 those same strike-breakers who had come to Colorado as scabs staged a massive walkout under the leadership of the United Mine Workers of America (UMWA). The immediate issue was union recognition, but there were economic demands as well. The UMWA housed strikers and their families, summarily evicted from their company-owned homes, in a string of tent colonies. The largest camp was just outside Ludlow, a small town near the border with New Mexico. The CFI management remained intransigent in its refusal to negotiate on the miners' demands, despite the fact that many of these were supposed to be guaranteed by Colorado statute. An aggressive open-shop policy was well established with Rockefeller companies, and was presented to the public as a way to protect the rights of the individual workman. As John D. Rockefeller Jr wrote to President Wilson on 27 April 1914:

> if the employees of the Colorado Fuel & Iron Company had any grievances, we felt sure that the officers of the Company would be willing now, as they have always been, to make every effort to adjust them satisfactorily, but that the question of the open shop, namely the right of every American citizen to work on terms satisfactory to himself without securing the consent of the union, we regarded as a question of principle which could not be arbitrated.[15]

Testifying before a congressional committee, the younger Rockefeller heroically defied ruination in defence of the open shop:

> We would rather that the unfortunate conditions should continue, and that we should lose all the millions invested, than that American workmen should be deprived of their right, under the Constitution, to work for whom they please. That is the great principle at stake. It is a national issue.[16]

Behind this cloud of humbug, there was a long history of 'yellow-dog' contracts, blacklistings, beatings, spies and violent company guards at the CFI.

The company's tactic was to starve out the strikers and, as in 1903–4, to intimidate the workforce. Gunmen were imported from all over the west by the Baldwin-Felts Detective Agency. An automobile was equipped with steel panels and fitted with two machine guns. It was called the 'Death Special' and designed to intimidate the tent families. Powerful searchlights were prepared, and stocks of rifles and ammunition were rushed to the mine camps. Provocations in such a situation were inevitable, and attempts to decide which side fired first are a legalistic nicety scarcely relevant to the fundamental fact which confronts students of the strike: the mine-owners were intransigent and were spoiling for a fight. Throughout the events of 1913–15, it was the owners who had the initiative and could determine the pace of events. Violence on both sides escalated until Governor Elias Ammons was forced to call out the militia. Funds to pay their salaries were borrowed from banks controlled by the mine-owners, and guards from the mines and Baldwin-Felts gunmen were enlisted into the militia. Some guards and detectives were appointed as deputy sheriffs. As the crisis deepened in Colorado, the conflict no longer was between capital and labour: the distinction between state and mine-owners blurred and virtually disappeared, as the strikers were forced to take up arms against the state.

The militia, which at first had been instructed to preserve the peace and to remain neutral in the strike itself, was, after a sudden, unexplained reversal of policy by the governor, set on a more aggressive course against the strikers. Tension in the tent camps grew steadily, until, on 20 April 1914, the camp on the outskirts of Ludlow was attacked and burnt out by militiamen. Two women and eleven children died in what was immediately called the Ludlow Massacre. A military tribunal was quickly summoned and promptly exonerated serving members of the Colorado National Guard from any responsibility for the massacre. A Grand Jury in Las Animas returned indictments against 124 of the striking miners. The massacre was to be firmly blamed on the victims. In such a supercharged atmosphere no miner in the state believed that justice would be done, and, in the event, none of the officers in charge of the attack was blamed. The miners did not wait for sham trials, but went on a rampage in response to the massacre. Mines were attacked, company buildings blown up or set ablaze. Union leaders, and their sympathizers in Colorado, set about the task of arousing public opinion in defence of the miners. It was far from clear whether the massacre was an isolated incident, or the prelude to a general attack on all of the miners' camps. Telegrams were sent to President Wilson, demanding the use of federal troops. An appeal brought George Creel back to Denver from New York.[17] Formerly a newspaperman and reforming police commissioner in Denver, Creel was a good man to launch a counterattack on the mine-owners. He called a mass meeting on the statehouse lawn in Denver on Sunday, 26 April, which was attended by a crowd variously estimated at between 5000 and 10 000 people. Of all the speeches given that afternoon, Creel's denunciation of the spineless Governor Ammons was the most bitter. Representatives of the UMWA, and delegations composed of striking miners and their families, travelled east to meet union members, and to speak to journalists. Public meetings were arranged, many impassioned speeches delivered. A committee of prominent figures was formed to win support for the strike, which included such progressive stalwarts as Judge Ben Lindsey of Denver, Upton Sinclair, and journalists like John Reed.

Max Eastman, editor of *The Masses*, arrived in Colorado on 21 April, having travelled west with Frank Bohn, an economic historian at Columbia University, left-wing socialist and associate editor of the *International Socialist Review*.[18] John Reed, who had just returned from his adventures with Pancho Villa in Mexico, was sent to cover the massacre and its aftermath by the *Metropolitan Magazine*, and arrived not long after Eastman and Bohn: the three men travelled together to Ludlow. The experience of revolutionary Barcelona in 1937 caused George Orwell to write to Cyril Connolly: 'I have seen wonderful things & at last really believe in Socialism, which I never did before.'[19] Colorado came close to becoming that kind of transforming experience for Eastman and Reed. 'I never came nearer to a sense of identity with the working class than I did there in Colorado', Eastman wrote in his autobiography.[20] Of Reed's various biographers, it was Granville Hicks who sensed the full significance of Reed's response:

> Emotionally aroused, he realized that Ludlow was a clear and terrifying example of what the I.W.W. meant by the class struggle. This was what he must show, beyond any possibility of misunderstanding, in his article. If, for the sake of their profits, employers would put into motion machinery that ruthlessly extinguished the lives of whole families, there was but one conceivable conclusion: justice could be won for the workers only if they would fight back, using the deadly weapons that the employers did not hesitate to use against them.[21]

The articles on Colorado by Eastman and Reed are marked in the highest degree by intense feeling and personal commitment.

The tent colony at Ludlow was still smoking when Eastman arrived. He tried to explain the nature of the conflict and to apportion responsibility for the massacre in 'Class War in Colorado', which appeared in the June 1914 issue of *The Masses*. The miners were on strike, he argued, for reasonable and moderate demands: 'there is nothing we are accustomed to call "revolutionary" in the local aspect of this strike. One sees here only an uprising of gentle and sweet-mannered people in favor of the laws they live under.' There was no middle ground of opinion in Colorado to which the miners could have turned. On the one side there were the 'money interests', determined to crush the strike, and on the other the 'gentle' people who were being driven to take up arms:

> For once in this country middle ground was abolished. Philanthropy burned in rage. Charity could wipe up the blood. Mediation, Legislation, Social-Consciousness expired like memories of a foolish age . . .
> I think the palest lover of 'peace' after viewing the flattened ruins of that colony of homes, the open death-hole, the shattered bedsteads, the stoves, the household trinkets broken and black – and the larks still singing over them in the sun – the most bloodless would find joy in going up the valleys to feed his eyesight upon tangles of gigantic machinery and ashes that had been the operating capital of the mines. It is no retribution, it is no remedy, but it proves that the power and the courage of action is here.

Public opinion, manipulated by a conservative press and news agencies, blamed labour violence on the strikers and their unions. Eastman's 'Class War in Colorado' was written against the background of a publicity campaign on behalf of the mine-owners which was funded by John D. Rockefeller Jr. The public was not allowed to forget the bombing of a trainload of non-union miners in Independence, Colorado, in 1903, which was blamed on the Western Federation of Miners; nor the bombing of the Los Angeles *Times* building in 1910, for which two union officials, the McNamara brothers, were convicted. Eastman was clearly writing with that hostility in mind: his miners are too patient and gentle to resemble real miners, in Colorado or anywhere else. He says less about their intimidation than objectivity would seem to demand. On the other hand, the inner working of the plan to break the strike was not known at that time. Eastman attributed greater importance to the role of prejudice (anti-union and anti-foreign) than to calculation and planning within the top management of CFI, conducted with the full support of John D. Rockefeller Jr, and attempted to infer a coordinated strategy for which he had no evidence. It is a nice irony that the inference was not far off. Much of what he implied was no more than the truth of what actually happened and was revealed in the hearings on the Colorado strike held by the Commission on Industrial Relations in 1915. Eastman's article is very powerful journalism, but it was forced to rely upon emotional appeals to make up for what it lacked in documentation.

A month later he published a further article in *The Masses* on 'The Nice People of Trinidad' and a briefer piece on 'Class Lines in Colorado' in the independent Marxist journal, *The New Review*. In the former he attempted to present the strike as seen by the more prosperous class of people in Colorado. Adopting the role of a social scientist seeking to test the thesis that attitudes were generated by the holder's place in the class structure, Eastman described how a tea party was arranged in Trinidad for him to meet 'a dozen of the most representative ladies of the elegance of the town'. What he heard from them was 'a debauch of murder-wishing class-hatred'. The wives of a Presbyterian minister, a coal company lawyer, and the sister of Governor Ammons – the 'quality' – furnished Eastman with abundant proof of the thesis in question. The bitterness and aggression of the ladies seems to have shocked Eastman, and he quotes the most extreme sentiments with grim relish: 'they're nothing but cattle, and the only way is to kill them off.' The nice people in Trinidad turn out to be not 'nice' at all. Their intransigence helped Eastman understand the emotions behind the massacre itself: 'I want to record my opinion, and that of my companions in the investigation, that this battle was from the first a deliberate effort of soldiers to assault the tent-colony, with purpose to burn, pillage and kill . . .' Testimony then follows: that of Mrs Toner, who crawled into a pit beneath her tent when it was fired on by the militia, and who heard Mrs Snyder's cry when her son was hit in the head by bullets; of Mrs Low, the wife of a railroad worker, who was shot at by militiamen despite waving a white handkerchief in an attempt to rescue her child; and of Mrs Petrucci, whose babies died in the pit of a burnt-out tent. 'If there is more fineness or more tenderness in the world than dwells in those now pitifully vague and wandering eyes, I have lived without finding it.' Eastman wrote in his autobiography that he emerged from his experiences in Colorado 'in search you might almost say, of a battle. I truly wanted to fight for Mrs. Toner and her babies against the bosses, and if necessary against all bourgeois society. And to the extent that I could do so in *The Masses* I did.'[22] What began as pseudo-scientific investigation, and was couched in an objective language, ended with a frank confession of the essentially emotional and sympathetic roots of Eastman's radicalism.

It is puzzling that Eastman chose to present himself, while writing for *The Masses*, as an 'impartial investigator'. After all, the readership of the magazine, bohemian and socialist, hardly needed persuading that the oppressed proletariat were stoically virtuous, and that the strike-breakers, police and militia were the ones who provoked the violence. There was no *need* to persuade, or at least not in this way. He later recalled that during one afternoon while in Colorado he felt himself to be like a spectator at classical Greek drama, 'where inexorable conflict is the theme, and the fatality with which each side acts out its will and opinion is the only truth'. He felt he had entered a world in which there was no common ground, in which wildly conflicting versions of events competed for public sympathy. Climbing to a butte outside Trinidad, Eastman drifted off into revery. 'I thought not only about Greek drama, but about my poems.'[23] Colorado, that afternoon, seemed a place where there could be no meeting between the sides of his own personality.

This division within Eastman was often noted by his critics, and sometimes with sincere regret. 'This man who could think on politics with the clean beauty of a running athlete', wrote Mike Gold,

had the flabbiest, most reactionary notions of poetry. It was something that had no connection with the struggle of human beings, with their epic movements, with their dramatic aspirations and day by day labors. Poetry was a mere langourous sensual melancholy, in Eastman's eyes; why he believed so I could not understand, and I was one of those who esteemed his intellect this side of idolatory . . .[24]

Eastman's poems seemed frankly anachronistic to Gold, himself no enthusiast for modern poetry. In a revealing preface to *Colors of Life* (1918), Eastman explained that though he had often partaken of the world's struggle for liberty, he had never invested his whole 'undivided being' in such public struggles. 'I have found that rather in individual experience and in those moments of energetic idleness when the life of universal nature seemed to come to its bloom of realization in my consciousness.'[25] He regarded poetry as something concerned with the enhancement of experience for its own sake, which had nothing to do with ideologies. In a review of *Colors of Life*, Floyd Dell reflected on that side of the poet which showed such delight in a 'singularly childlike wholeheartedness of surrender' to his emotions:

I read this book with a curious feeling which I had more than once about myself during our recent adventures in the federal courts. I sometimes wondered then, in the midst of some legal argument, suddenly: What am I doing here? Why am I not at home writing a story? The scene became, in such moments, utterly unreal. The fact was that I was an artist – not a politician. How in the world did I come to be mixed up in the political *cause célèbre?* And now I have the same surprise, as I read this book and think of you back there in that musty court-room . . . For you are revealed by these pages as so pre-eminently a lover of beauty and so delicately sure-handed a creator of it, that your participation even in the most vital politics seems incongruous. For I am not ashamed to say that *to me art is more important than the destinies of nations*, and the artist a more exalted figure than the prophet . . .[26]

Dell's review appeared in *The Liberator* in December 1918. One month later the same journal published Lenin's 'A Letter to American Workingmen'. This was where Eastman's essay in praise of 'Lenin – A Statesman of the New Order' appeared, and where Eastman's poem, 'To Nikolai Lenin', was published (October and November 1918). *The Liberator* was the most widely-read defender of Leninism on the American left. But Dell's review reminds us that its cultural policy was virtually untouched by socialist or Marxist thought. Both Dell and Eastman opposed attempts to politicize art when they edited *The Masses*, and Dell's dislike for 'sociological' novels caused no little vexation.[27] Both writers maintained a distinction between art and politics which the younger staff writers on *The Liberator*, people like Mike Gold and Joseph Freeman, were beginning to reject.[28]

Poetry for Eastman was something precious, delicate and organic. It is hard to quote him with a straight face, however, so little was he gifted as a poet. 'I have sung lightly or languidly all of the songs of love', he wrote, determined to be 'poetic'. He celebrated 'quiet space' and 'tranquil pools' of love. Time in his poems goes upon its 'immortal quest'. Lips are 'crimson', limbs are 'hot' or 'slim'. Girls are 'naked footed' and 'lovely'. Eastman's unfailing instinct for the clichéd epithet, the leaden extended simile, the 'poetic' sexual euphemism, revealed a conception of creativity and a notion of the poetic subject and language which was at once untouched by the revolutionary artistic ideas of the European avant garde, and closed to the social ideas and concerns which were elsewhere preoccupying the poet.[29] On that afternoon in Colorado, the divisions in Eastman's sensibility drew him away from the miners and their struggles. However intensely felt, the articles on the strike were in an inward sense detached from Eastman's truest nature. There were limits to the battles Eastman was prepared to fight on behalf of Mrs Toner, limits not always visible behind the impassioned facade of his rhetoric.

John Reed returned to New York to write his article, 'The Colorado War', for the *Metropolitan Magazine*.[30] In it, Reed told the story of how an ethnically divided workforce found a common purpose and mutual respect in their struggle against 'profits'. Within this parable was an inner tale of conflict growing fitfully but inevitably into violence. The dominating moment of Reed's narrative occurred on 20 April, when the militia attacked the camp near Ludlow. During that terrible massacre one moment seemed to Reed to capture the essential character of the struggle. Louis Tikas, a leader of the Greek strikers, was arrested by militiamen while trying to save the Petrucci family from the fire. He was brought before Lt. Karl Linderfelt, a bravo who had been overheard urging his men during the attack to 'Shoot every son-of-a-bitchin' thing you see moving!'[31] Taken before soldiers in such a frame of mind, and with such leaders, Tikas's fate was sealed:

He tried to explain his errand; but they were drunk with blood lust and would not listen to him. Lieutenant Linderfelt broke the stock of his rifle over the Greek's head, laying it open to the bone. Fifty men got a rope and threw it over a telegraph wire to hang him. But Linderfelt cynically handed him over to two militiamen, and told them they were responsible for his life. Five minutes later Louis Tikas fell dead with three bullets in his back; and out of Mrs Petrucci's cellar were afterward taken the charred bodies of thirteen women and children.

Militiamen explained Tikas's death by arguing that he was killed in crossfire while attempting to escape. McGovern and Guttridge dismiss this as superficial, and point to the evidence produced at the inquest in which Tikas was shown to have been shot in the back by three bullets, two of which were from the standard issue Springfields which the militia carried. The third was a soft-nose bullet from a gun not of official issue.[32]

Reed brilliantly captures the frantic alteration of mood within the strikers' camp. After small but heartening victories, he describes the joyous relief which swept the camps. The turning back of an armoured train in late October 1913 was such a moment. The strikers poured back to Ludlow, where they held a gigantic banquet and dance,

. . . at which all the visitors were entertained, and the warriors told their stories over with much boasting and adulation. But in the midst of the festivities word came that the guards were loading a machine gun into a wagon and were coming down the canyon. The dance broke up in a panic, and all night no one slept.

Another such dramatic alteration of mood occurred in mid-April 1914, when the Greek strikers and their families celebrated Easter with a baseball game, festive dances in national costume, and then a lunch:

There was beer for the men and coffee for the women; and whenever a Greek drank he rose and sang a Greek song instead of a toast. Everybody was very happy, because this was the first real day of spring they had had. At night there was a ball; and then about ten o'clock a man came in and whispered to the

other men that the militia were riding silently through the
colony and listening at the walls of the tents.

The dance broke up . . .

The miners' victory in late October in effect prevented the
owners from bringing up reinforcements for the guards and
detectives guarding the mines. As a result, the owners forced the
governor to call up the militia. An initial ban, forbidding the
troops to break the strike, was reversed at the demand of the
owners. The local victories of October and November were soon
forgotten. By the new year the militia were conducting aggressive
armed searches of the camps. A parade in Trinidad was broken up
by mounted troops. In the face of repeated provocations, the
miners began to understand that they were fighting the state itself.
The buoyant mood of the Greek miners in April was partially due
to the recall of units of the militia on 23 March, when money to
pay their salaries ran out. Welcomed at first by the strikers, their
attitude soon changed when the militia failed to protect the
camps, and when the troopers insulted the strikers and stole from
their tents. Reed writes that the militiamen 'openly began a
campaign of tyranny and intimidation'. On the morning after the
Greeks' baseball game, the remaining companies of the militia,
composed almost exclusively of enrolled company detectives and
mine guards (who remained on the owners' payroll), attacked and
burnt out the camp near Ludlow. Reed shows the elation of the
strikers turning twice into panic and then despair. More than any
other writer on the strike, he conveys an intense, sympathetic
grasp of the rhythm of events, the way excitement and hope
turned into gnawing anxiety, anger and bursts of frantic activity.
For someone who only made a brief visit to Colorado, and who
was deeply preoccupied with events elsewhere, Reed's 'The
Colorado War' was an impressive achievement.

Upton Sinclair attended a meeting at Carnegie Hall in New
York on 27 April 1914, where he heard eye-witness accounts of the
massacre at Ludlow.[33] Finding that the New York press ignored
the meeting, he decided to break the news blackout himself. He
attempted to interview John D. Rockefeller Jr, but was refused.
(Judge Ben Lindsey, who had travelled from Denver for a similar
purpose, was also refused an interview with Rockefeller.) Sinclair
organized a silent picket of people dressed in black (the 'mourning
picket') outside Rockefeller's office on lower Broadway. Other

public demonstrations were held. The Reverend Bouck White staged a demonstration in Calvary Church, where the Rockefellers attended worship, for which he was sentenced to six months in prison.[34] Sinclair was arrested, and the press coverage of his protest did much, he felt, to break the wall of silence around the issue. After his release from the Tombs, Sinclair went to Denver on 12 May to investigate conditions for himself, and, inevitably, to collect material for a novel on the strike. He spoke at a mass meeting on behalf of the strikers, and was present in the capital when the Colorado legislature debated the issue. The Associated Press report of the legislature's actions contained what Sinclair believed to be a deliberate distortion. In reply to President Wilson's repeated appeals for conciliation, the news agency reported that a committee of the legislature was attempting to resolve the dispute. With the relevant piece of legislation before him, Sinclair knew that no such effort was being made. Governor Ammons's letter to President Wilson of 16 May contained the deception ('. . . a committee on mediation on the present strike has been provided for and appointed'),[35] and the story was widely circulated by the AP. When Sinclair claimed that the measure referred only to 'investigation' and not to 'mediation', and was prepared to support his claim with documentary proof, the news agency still refused to see the story his way, or to print his version of events. Sinclair and other radicals had long believed that the AP was suppressing news of the strike in Colorado, and that it customarily presented industrial disputes in ways prejudicial to labour. *The Masses* had been conducting a determined campaign against the AP over the news service's coverage of the strikes in West Virginia in 1913. The classic Art Young cartoon in the July 1913 issue, in which the AP was caught in the act of furtively poisoning the reservoir of news with a vial of lies, resulted in criminal libel proceedings against Eastman and Young. The case was subsequently dropped, which provided Young with further opportunities to ridicule the agency.[36]

Sinclair carried the attack on Rockefeller to the latter's country estate at Pocantico Hills, near Tarrytown, New York. Denied permission to speak in the town, Sinclair defended his constitutional rights of free speech. He also brought a lawsuit against a New York newspaper which criticized his actions in Tarrytown. The case was eventually settled out of court, with Sinclair receiving $2500 in damages. No small amount of publicity was generated by Sinclair's campaigns against Rockefeller and the AP, but his real work did not begin until he settled down to write a novel about the strike.

By the time *King Coal* was published in 1917, the American public had lost interest in the Ludlow massacre and its aftermath. Events in Europe dominated the nation's newspapers. Radicals like Eastman and Reed were far more obsessed with the revolutionary situation in Petrograd than with the fate of the miners in Las Animas and Huerfano Counties in Colorado. The strike was lost; but changes of a sort were certainly taking place. A fraudulently-elected sheriff of Huerfano County was thrown out of office by the state Supreme Court. The Mackenzie King 'Colorado Plan' was gradually introduced in the CFI mines, and a new generation of managers brought forward. Rather than telling the story of a failed strike, Sinclair chose to set his novel in the period between the strikes of 1903–4 and the events of 1913–15, when the owners' feudal regime was at its peak. According to Philip S. Foner, 'not a single change took place to improve the conditions of the miners' during this period. Never one to shirk his homework, Sinclair prepared a detailed and comprehensive account of the oppression of the miners: themselves ethnically divided, constantly spied on, cheated in the company shops, robbed of full payment for the coal they mined, they were virtually defenceless: '. . . I am doing the Colorado strike at present', he wrote to Jack London in November 1915.[37]

The 'education' of Hal Warner, a high-spirited college student who posed as a miner to investigate industrial conditions, gave Sinclair sufficient pretext for his muckraking exposition. Warner is at first sceptical of the wilder claims of oppression and wage slavery, but when he assumes the lead of a campaign for a check-weighman he is threatened with violence, falsely arrested and blackmailed. The sheriff offers him the choice of being imprisoned on a false charge, or destroying his reputation with the men by admitting that he had accepted a bribe. In *The Jungle* Jurgis was trapped by a pessimistic naturalism, only to be freed by the deaths of his wife and child to begin his picaresque wanderings. In *King Coal* Sinclair's naturalism yields to a similar adventure fantasy: Hal lets the sheriff know his real identity as someone who cannot be so easily trapped, for he is the son of a mining magnate. He thus leaps out of the sheriff's clutches, as the novel dissolves into chases and escapes, secret conferences and earnest appeals for justice. The son of the mine-owner, a college chum of Hal's, is by chance travelling nearby with a party of friends in a private rail carriage. Among them is Hal's fiancée, Jessie Arthur. In a desperate appeal Hal tries to interest them in the fate of the miners. A decade earlier socialist writers would have hoped that a 'cry for justice' would succeed.[38] But Hal cannot touch their consciences. Even Jessie Arthur remains indifferent. In his frantic words echo the many socialist writers who tried to arouse the concern of the public at injustice and oppression. It was greatly to Sinclair's credit, and perhaps also an indication of his realism, that Hal does not bring about a dramatic transformation of his friends' annoyed and puzzled indifference. At another point in the narrative, when the miners seem on the verge of going out on strike, Hal is persuaded by officials in the United Mine Workers that any such action is premature. The men must agree to wait until the union has completed the organizing of all the mining camps of the 'General Fuel Company'. Disguising himself as a widow, Hal secretly re-enters the North Valley camp where he explains to the men that they must not go on strike until the union is ready. The miners willingly accept his sensible advice, and enthusiastically bid good-bye to 'Joe Smith'.

Sinclair's novel closely reproduces the perspectives of the right wing of the Socialist Party. While sympathizing with the plight of the miners, Hal Warner's role is clearly to moderate their actions. Sinclair, in pursuit of moderation, dropped several of the strikers' demands of 1913–15, and toned down several others. Eastman and Reed saw the miners as gentle folk who were driven to take up arms; they wrote to help explain and to justify their actions. Sinclair, while no less graphic in his portrayal of the wrongs of the system, shared the right-wing Socialist Party condemnation of violence in labour disputes, and unease before the revolutionary rhetoric of the Wobblies and the left wing of the party. Sinclair preferred an image of the striking miners as humble victims, whose restraint and collective self-discipline would see them through in the end. Eastman and Reed ultimately praised the miners for fighting back; Sinclair praised them for refusing to act rashly. The differences of opinion within the Socialist Party are clearly present in their responses to the events in Colorado.

John Reed stopped off in Chicago on his way home from the strike, and talked to journalists about what was really going on in Colorado. He then travelled with Mabel Dodge to Provincetown, where he resumed work on the manuscript of his book about the Mexican Revolution. Reed was in Washington in June, interviewing Secretary of State Bryan and President Wilson about the situation in Mexico. A telegram reached him when war broke out in Europe, asking him to go to France as exclusive war correspondent for *Metropolitan*. The uproar caused by his article, 'The Colorado War' – a bookstore in Denver cancelled a standing order for fifty copies of the *Metropolitan* in protest at his account of the massacre [see Appendix I] – was no doubt satisfying, but events were moving too swiftly for Reed to return to the topic again. That summer Max Eastman went into psychoanalysis. His marriage with Ida Ruah was virtually over, and he settled down on 27 July, proposing to write 'a delineation in general outlines of my psycho-sexual character – my instinctive infantile selfishness, my neurotic pains, deficiencies, indolence, which are all doubtless in their root . . . an unconscious fixation of life-interest upon the early image of my mother'.[39] While Eastman was thus preoccupied, *The Masses*, and other socialist periodicals, were busy trying to keep America out of the war in Europe. Thoughts of Mrs Toner were far from his mind. When the war on the Western Front was stabilized, Eastman visited France for *The Masses*. Unable to get very close to the fighting, he returned home to publish an article on 'The Uninteresting War'. He attempted in a series of articles to apply Freudian psychology to the causes of war; as with Reed, the momentous events in Europe robbed domestic news of its urgency. He wrote nothing more about Colorado.

American progressives gave the impression that they had a clearer instinct than socialists for what, in the immediate context, could be done about the events in Colorado. The chairman of the President's Commission on Industrial Relations, Frank P. Walsh, invited George Creel to serve as special assistant to the commission during its investigation of the strike.[40] They set about the task of exposing industrial autocracy to an aroused public scrutiny: it was their most effective weapon. At the first hearing in January 1915, the younger Rockefeller denied responsibility for CFI managerial policies. Carefully coached by W. L. Mackenzie King, who had been invited by Rockefeller to study industrial problems in the Colorado mining camps, Rockefeller preferred to appear in public as someone not implacably hostile to unions.[41] He admitted that the violence and bitterness of the strike disturbed him. So remarkable were his protestations of ignorance that Walter Lippmann compared him to a 'weak despot':

> I should not believe that he personally hired thugs or wanted them hired; I should not believe that the inhumanity of Colorado is something he had conceived. It seems far more true to say that his impersonal and half-understood power has delegated itself into unsocial forms, that it has assumed a life of its own which he is almost powerless to control. If first impressions count for anything, I should describe Mr. Rockefeller as a weak despot governed by a private bureaucracy which he is unable to lead . . .[42]

Lippmann's thoughtful portrait of Rockefeller, and his evident willingness to take him at face value, was not widely shared in socialist circles. A correspondent in *The Masses* described Rockefeller as 'a master of evasion'.[43] Walsh, who shared some of the socialists' scepticism of Rockefeller's performance, subpoenaed the correspondence between Rockefeller and the CFI management for the period immediately before and during the strike. Walsh recalled Rockefeller to a second hearing (20–21 May 1915) at which Rockefeller once again claimed that he knew nothing of CFI policy and tactics. In his cross-examination, which made Walsh a hero overnight to the labour movement (and which strengthened labour's support for Walsh's boss, President Wilson, ironically at the expense of the Socialist Party), he devastatingly showed that Rockefeller's testimony consisted of deceptions and lies.[44] Walsh revealed that Rockefeller knew in detail his manager's opposition to unionization. In the words of the CFI chairman, L. M. Bowers, they would fight the unions 'until our bones were bleached as white as chalk in these Rocky Mountains'.[45] Walsh showed that Rockefeller had opposed every effort at industrial conciliation, including President Wilson's; and that he reassured the CFI management that their anti-union policy 'meets with our cordial approval, and we shall support them to the end'.[46]

The publicity which followed the massacre, and that which was generated by the Commission's hearings, produced a tidal wave of anti-Rockefeller sentiment. The effect of this was, in the words of Rockefeller's father's biographer, Allan Nevins, dramatic: 'a few weeks after Ludlow the younger Rockefeller was generously anxious to turn a new page in company history'.[47] Another report suggests that he had been brought to a 'new awareness of the iniquities and injustices of ignorant and outdated industrial practices'.[48] W. L. Mackenzie King's influence was soon felt. L. M. Bowers, who in Nevins's opinion 'belonged to a dying age in the relationship of capital and labor', was 'gently ousted' from his post as chairman of the board of CFI. On Mackenzie King's suggestion, Rockefeller visited Colorado in 1915, where he talked to miners and listened to their grievances. Mackenzie King succeeded in bringing Rockefeller together with union leaders. The legendary Mother Jones, who had helped organize the Colorado strikes of 1903–4, was said to have been captivated by Rockefeller's sincerity and good intentions.[49] Rockefeller published an article in the January 1916 *Atlantic Monthly* entitled 'Labor and Capital – Partners'. And later that year Rockefeller published the Mackenzie King proposals as *The Colorado Industrial Plan*. The only element omitted from this rehabilitation was a conversion to Christianity – unnecessary in the case of the Baptist Rockefellers; but it would have added the crowning touch.

The whole process nicely blended public relations and a sincere if measured change of heart. The CFI management, however, refused to have any dealings with the UMWA. Under Mackenzie King's plan, improvements were made in housing and schooling; some forms of consultation were envisaged. But the essential balance of power in this 'partnership' was identified by Walter Lippmann:

> in the face of it any talk of 'industrial representation' is a mockery. The company retains every essential of its old mastery, and the only difference is that it has been frightened into a willingness to listen to advice. No doubt Mr. Rockefeller means to use his absolute power in somewhat more enlightened fashion. But his power is supreme and unquestioned, and whatever is done will be an act of grace or of produce. The men remain helpless.[50]

Despite these reservations, it seemed that everyone who was drawn to the Colorado strike took away from it conclusions satisfactory to themselves. To Wilsonian liberals like Creel, Walsh and Judge Ben Lindsey, the active pressure of public opinion was necessary to act as a counterbalance to the concentration of unfettered industrial power.[51] For the *New Republic*, the Ludlow massacre provided decisive proof that different attitudes were needed in American industry, and that as things stood it was inevitable that the state would have to prepare itself to intervene to correct the balance between capital and labour.[52] John Reed saw the true face of brutal capitalism in Colorado, and learned that men in the face of oppression could rise in self-defence, even to the point of rebellion. Reed's 'The Colorado War' was a draft, a preliminary sketch, for the far greater canvas of *Ten Days That Shook the World*. Eastman seemed to draw similarly revolutionary conclusions from the massacre and the breakdown of a common ground in Colorado. Both had their socialism strengthened by their trip west, as did, in a different way, Upton Sinclair. As *King Coal* suggests, for Sinclair the gradualist strategy of the UMWA was the proper one for socialists to support. It was John D. Rockefeller Jr alone who seems to have been greatly changed by the strike and its consequent publicity. Was he, paradoxically, the moral victor, this man who was, in Lippmann's words, 'the supreme negation of all equality, and unquestionably a symbol of the most menacing fact in the life of the republic'?[53] By 1916 Rockefeller had become a voice of industrial conciliation, something of a prophet even of a new social order in which capitalism would be tempered by a sense of the social whole. He certainly was the winner in capturing the initiative in the public relations battle. The appointment of Mackenzie King closely followed the hiring of Ivy Lee, publicity expert of the Pennsylvania Railroad, who helped shape the public perception of the Rockefeller interests.[54] Standing behind Rockefeller were two men who symbolized the new approach of big business to the task of selling capitalism to the American public. Eastman, Reed and Sinclair, in their different ways, conveyed moral outrage as their response to the Ludlow massacre, not realizing that the real struggle for public opinion was passing from the hands of moralists to the smooth-faced shapers of image and manipulators of 'perceptions'.

4　John Reed

John Reed was twenty-two when he graduated from Harvard in 1910. After travelling extensively in Europe he settled in New York in 1911, where he turned to Lincoln Steffens for help and advice. Steffens, an old friend of Reed's father, did his best to launch Reed in New York journalism.[1] His view of Reed at that time, as he recalled in an obituary in 1920, was wholly remarkable: 'No ray of sunshine, no drop of foam, no young animal, bird or fish, and no star, was as happy as that boy was.'[2] Reed was every inch the poet, scouring the city over the next two or three years for material. Steffens did his best to keep Reed free from convictions, and for a while at least it seemed that such a hope might prevail. Reed's New York was seen through a 'poetic' language which was, from the point of view of American poetry in 1911, wrong from the start. One of Reed's earliest contributions to the *American Magazine*, on whose staff he had been guided by Steffens, was a sonnet in the October 1911 issue, 'The Foundations of a Skyscraper'. The pseudo-medievalism of his diction here, right down to candles, swords and even 'plumes of steam', is wonderfully risible. The site excavation seemed to Reed to be 'mouths of gloom, like dragon's lairs'. The final line ('A phantom of fair towers in the sky') reaffirms the deliberateness of the exercise, but does not explain why Reed thought it worth doing.[3] What was the nature of the 'poetic' that encouraged Reed, and many another poet in 1911, to approach such a subject in such a diction? The poem contains another kind of diction, or at least hints at another way of dealing with the contemporary, when Reed describes the 'Shouts and the dip of cranes, the stench of earth, – / Blinded with sweat . . .' But this intimation of realism did not, it would appear, look promising to Reed. Eight months later, 'June in the City' (again in the *American Magazine*), exchanged one set of clichés for another. He contrasted the 'warm sky', 'strolling lovers' and June's 'clean wind', with the dust and hardness of 'this iron city street!'

It is necessary to say of Reed that there was no 'modern' poetry in America in 1911 and 1912. Curiously, those hints and anticipations of the modern which we retrospectively understand show a dilemma not unlike Reed's. This is to say that he might have become such a poet. Consider the case of Ezra Pound, who was in America from June 1910 to February 1911. There are few echoes of this stay in Pound's verse, save the allusion to 'the flurry of Fifth Avenue' in the 'Und Drang' sequence in *Canzoni* (1911), a collection mostly notable for its calculatedly medieval poetic diction and use of elaborate and old-fashioned verse forms. 'Canzon: The Vision', which he published in the New York periodical *The Forum* in October 1910, is a good example of Pound's medievalism. Reed was in good company in 1911. Pound wrote in the *New Age* in September 1912, by which time he was back in London, about New York:

And New York is the most beautiful city in the world?
It is not far from it. No urban nights are like the nights there. I have looked across the city from high windows. It is then that the great buildings lose reality and take on their magical powers. They are immaterial; that is to say one sees but the lighted windows.
Squares after squares of flame, set and cut into the ether. Here is our poetry, for we have pulled down the stars to our will.[4]

In this sensitive, indeed beautiful, observation, a new kind of poetry of contemporary life is uncovered. The distance from this point in his career to the writing of the late *Cantos* is vast, but comprehensible. For Pound too the modern was intensely 'poetic', but the process of ridding himself of a second- and third-hand poetic diction was pursued with a seriousness and dedication which separates him from every American poet who was publishing in 1912, bar none. One of the first signs of a new direction in his work came in *Ripostes* (1912), which contained a poem entitled 'N.Y.', about the poet's vocation and the reality of New York. This was Reed's theme in 'The Foundations of a Skyscraper': what, after all, did the medievalism signify but Reed's yearning and unsatisfied imagination when confronted with an oppressive reality? Pound demands that the city listen to the poet: 'I will breathe into thee a soul.' Try as he might, the

contrary reality of New York refuses to be described as 'a maid
with no breasts' or a 'silver reed'. It bursts through such gestures
with appropriate contempt:

> *. . . here are a million people surly with traffic;*
> *This is no maid.*
> *Neither could I play upon any reed if I had one.*

Reed's poem and Pound's suggest a moment, one of many such, in
the evolution towards a modern poetry. Pound was never wholly
comfortable with the realism of his lines in italic, though he could
often manipulate it with considerable success. Reed perhaps
never understood its full meaning as a way out of the medieval and
'poetic'. The one poet who fully grasped the point was T. S. Eliot,
who had completed the first two of his 'Preludes' by October 1910.
The rest of the poem was written a year later, though it was not
published until it appeared in the second number of Wyndham
Lewis's *Blast* in 1915. The calculated use of sordid detail, no less
than Eliot's evocative symbolism, suggested what a fully adequate
poetry of the modern might have to encompass. Reed didn't begin
to understand what the issues were. It took Pound years before he
did.

During his extended stay in Portland, Oregon, during the
summer and autumn of 1912, Reed tried his hand at satirical
verse. Published as *The Day in Bohemia*, and dedicated to Steffens,
it contains numerous evocations of New York:

> Twixt Broadway and Sixth Avenue,
> And West perhaps a block or two, –
> From Third Street up, and Ninth Street down,
> Between Fifth Avenue and the town, –
> Policemen walk as free as air . . .[5]

Reed celebrated the joys of bohemian life in Greenwich Village,
where

> . . . nobody questions your morals,
> And nobody asks for the rent –
> There's no one to pry if we're tight, you and I,
> Or demand how our evenings are spent . . .

and gave a vivid picture of the villagers themselves:

> There spawn the overworked and underpaid
> Mute thousands; – packed in buildings badly made, –
> In stinking squalor penned, – and overflowing
> On sagging fire-escapes. Such to-and-froing
> From room to room we spied on! Such a thrill
> Cursing between brass earinged women, still
> Venomous Italian! Love-making and hate;
> Laughter, white rage, a passionate debate;
> A drunken workman beating up his wife;
> Mafia and Camorra, – yelling strife!
> The wail of children, – dull, monotonous,
> Unceasing, – and a liquid, tremulous
> High tenor, singing, somewhere out of sight
> 'Santa Lucia' in the troubled night.

The longest poem in *The Day in Bohemia*, 'Lines on the Dutch Treat', wittily commented on the circle of journalists and writers which Reed joined when he was elected to membership of the Dutch Treat Club. It was about as good as Clive James's poems, and rather shorter.

High-spirited work such as *The Day in Bohemia* was a diversion from a more serious confrontation with New York, and a struggle to become a poet. While still in Portland he wrote to Harriet Monroe, enclosing recent work for her new journal, *Poetry*. 'The pathetic, mawkishly religious middle class', he wrote,

> are our enemies. A labor-leader . . . read aloud to me John Neihardt's *Man Song* more naturally and beautifully than I have ever heard a verse read . . . Art must cease, I think, to be the aesthetic enjoyment of a few highly sensitive minds. It must go back to its original sources.[6]

(This was no small part of the teaching of William Morris, who wrote in 1877: 'I do not want art for a few, any more than education for a few, or freedom for a few.'[7]) Harriet Monroe was broadly sympathetic to Reed's argument:

> I agree with everything you say about present treatment of Poetry by the magazines, and also with your faith in the

essential appreciation of it and need of it by the people. If we can only reach them and convince them that they need it, we shall be doing a great work and gathering together our public.[8]

Reed's first appearance in *Poetry* was 'Sangar' in the issue of December 1912. The poem at once attracted enthusiastic praise. Alice Meynell, writing to Harriet Monroe, thought it 'very remarkably fine'.[9] Sara Teasdale, who met Reed in March 1913, wrote to him that 'Sangar' was 'truly glorious – such splendid, big, free music and such a wind of battle in it! I have read it over and over.'[10] Reed's poem received an honourable mention in the first annual *Poetry* prize award: proof, indeed, that Reed was a poet. The way people have reacted to this poem, he wrote to Percy MacKaye, 'opens up vast possibilities and stimulates my imagination to conceive when I shall be able to tell people a little part of the glorious things I see. Every day of my life I see more of them.'[11]

'Sangar' was written on a compelling contemporary theme, the efforts of Lincoln Steffens in Los Angeles the preceding year (1911) to save the McNamara brothers from a capital charge over the bombing of the Los Angeles *Times* building. The judge unexpectedly refused to accept the compromise Steffens had painstakingly effected, in which the brothers confessed responsibility for the bombing in return for reduced sentences. The judge gave them both heavy sentences, for which, at least on the left, Steffens was angrily blamed. 'Sangar' was dedicated to Steffens: the link was allegorical but hardly to be missed, despite the fact that the poem is a medieval ballad of warfare and parricide which takes place during an invasion by the Huns. (It is worth noting that Ezra Pound's 'Ballad of the Goodly Fere', written in energetic and manly rhythms against a 'certain cheap irreverence which was new to me' in 1909, attracted no less enthusiastic praise. It took Pound years to live down the reputation this poem gave him.)

The great chief Sangar was reluctantly drawn into the battle, and at a crucial moment turned to appeal to both sides:

> 'When will ye cast out hate?
> 　Brothers – my mad, mad brothers –
> Mercy, ere it be too late
> 　These are sons of your mothers . . .'

As Steffens learned in Los Angeles, where feeling ran particularly high against the McNamaras, there were no brotherly feelings on either side. Sangar's son, interpreted by Robert Rosenstone as an obvious symbolic representation of Reed's relationship to Steffens, denounces his father as a 'shameful old man – abhorr'd / First traitor of all our line!' and 'smote' him with his sword.[12] The poem ends with Sangar being joyously received into Heaven. Only there, by implication, can the conciliators be appreciated. Given what Reed was trying to do, like the 'Ballad of the Goodly Fere', it is strikingly well done. For all of its virtues, 'Sangar' did not help Reed find a way to write about contemporary life in the language of his day. He published a poem, 'A Hymn to Manhattan', in the February 1913 *American Magazine*, in which he tried to understand the 'world-wonder' of New York. Other great cities, from Babylon to Athens and Rome, were brought to the comparison but found to be inadequate:

> . . . the skyscrapers, dwarfing earthly things –
> Ah, that is how she sings!
> Wake to the vision shining in the sun;
> Earth's ancient, conquering races rolled into one,
> A World beginning – *and yet nothing done!*

It would be better, in response to this, to be perfectly frank: Reed had not the temperament, nor the discipline in language, to recognize a dud – as this poem unmistakably was. Oddly enough, when he was playing around with ideas for poems, just relaxing and allowing rhythms to work their way with him, he was far more a poet than when he was consciously trying to write 'poetry'. There is an unpublished undated draft of a poem entitled 'Eleventh Avenue Racket' among the Reed papers at Harvard. It was probably written in 1911 or 1912, and is contemporaneous with the other poems on New York which he wrote at that time.

ELEVENTH AVENUE RACKET

> There is something terrible
> about a hurdy-gurdy,
> a gipsy man and woman,
> and a monkey in red flannel
> all stopping in front of a bog house

with a sign 'For Rent' on the door
and the blinds hanging loose
and nobody home.
I never saw this.
I hope to god I never will.
    Whoop-de-doodle-de-doo.
    Hoodle-de-har-de-hum.
Nobody home? Everybody home.
    Whoop-de-doodle de-doo.
Mamie Riley married Jimmy Higgins last
    night: Eddie Jones died of whooping
    cough: George Hicks got a job on the
    police force: the Rosenheims bought
    a brass bed: Lena Hart giggled at a
    jackie: a pushcart man called *tomay-*
    toes, *tomay*toes.
Whoop-de-doodle-de-doo.
Hoodle-de-Har-de-hum.
    Nobody home? Everybody home.[13]

By a long way this is the most interesting of all of Reed's poems.
Being a poet meant a great deal to him in the early years in New
York, but by 1912 or 1913 he seems to have ceased writing poems.
The impulse, frustrated by the limitations of what he had been
able to achieve in verse, survived to encourage Reed to try to put
his experience of the city in the form of prose sketches or vignettes.

His preference for stories about prostitutes meant that they
were largely unpublishable in commercial magazines, such was
the magazine taste of the day; they were, almost by accident, to
play a crucial role in *The Masses*. The arrival of Max Eastman as
editor of Piet Vlag's cooperative journal, which had struggled
through four volumes without attracting much interest on the part
of anyone, was a no less significant moment for Reed. He
remained the star contributor to *The Masses* and then *The Liberator*
until his death, and the combination of Reed and Eastman was of
considerable importance for the direction of American radicalism
in this period. A story Reed wrote about a prostitute who travelled
to Europe and then South America before returning, out of
homesickness, to New York, was turned down by the *American
Magazine*. Having heard about Eastman's appointment, he spoke

to him on the phone and then brought the typescript to *The Masses* office. 'I was . . . not much impressed by John Reed when he arrived', Eastman recalled. 'He had a knobby and too filled-out face that reminded me, both in form and color, of a potato.'[14] Reed's sketch, 'Where the Heart Is', struck Eastman as being written with 'unlabored grace' and in a style which was both 'vivid and restrained'. 'The idea that *The Masses* might be *good*, that there really was a creative literature stifled by commercial journalism, took a firm grip on me after I read John Reed's story.' 'Where the Heart Is' appeared in the January 1913 *Masses*, and was followed by three further sketches later in the year. (Roughly from this period is Reed's draft sketch of life in a beer-hall nicknamed the 'Working-Girl's Home'.) He published two additional pieces in *The Masses* in 1916 about New York street life which were probably written in 1913.

The six published sketches were collected, along with other things, by Floyd Dell in his edition of Reed's prose, *Daughter of the Revolution and Other Stories* (1927), and are available in the City Lights volume, *Adventures of a Young Man* (1975). These sketches have occasionally been praised, but their role in Reed's development has not been appreciated. They are all very nicely written, as Eastman noted. The lucidity and directness which was lacking in Reed's poetry is clearly visible in his prose. There were many precedents and examples of prose vignettes of city life. Walter Benjamin's studies of Baudelaire and Paris during the Second Empire remind us that this kind of writing was popular at the middle of the last century. The vogue of 'O. Henry' was at its peak when Reed began to write his sketches, and it is hardly surprising that they show signs of having been influenced by the popular writer. Some eleven volumes of 'O. Henry' stories appeared between 1905 and his death in 1910. The thirteen volumes of his collected works reached a vast audience in America when they were published in 1913. Like 'O. Henry', Reed was both sentimental and ironic about New York. There are signs in Reed of the 'O. Henry' trademark of an ironic twist at the end of his stories. And Reed seems to have taken equal delight in the comic deformities of New Yorkese.

Like the scene of Eliot's 'Preludes', Reed's New York was a place of beer-halls and 'smoky days'. The skyscrapers, so potent a symbol of the dynamic energies of modern life for the Futurists in 1910, fascinated Reed. Even more, the curious romantic life of the city's people caught his imagination. 'New York was an enchanted city to me', Reed wrote in his posthumously published essay, 'Almost Thirty':

> Everything was to be found there – it satisfied me utterly. I wandered about the streets, from the soaring imperial towers of downtown, along the East River docks, smelling spices and the clipper ships of the past, through the swarming East Side – alien towns within towns – where the smoky flare of miles of clamorous pushcarts made a splendour of shabby streets . . . I knew Chinatown, and Little Italy, and the quarter of the Syrians; the marionette theatre, Sharkey's and McSorley's saloons, the Bowery lodging houses and the places where the tramps gathered in winter . . . The girls that walk the street were friends of mine, and the drunken sailors off ships newcome from the world's end, and the Spanish longshoremen down on West Street . . . I knew well the parks, and the streets of palaces, the theatres and hotels . . . Within a block of my house was all the adventure of the world; within a mile was every foreign country.[15]

Even in sketches of the poor and homeless, Reed detected something of the magical quality of New York: 'All the straight concrete walls are black onyx, jeweled in every unevenness with pools of steely rain-water.' In one interesting passage the flow of people was reduced to a blur of objects and sensations. 'The sidewalks ran like Spring ice going out', he wrote,

> grinding and hurried and packed close from bank to bank. Ferret-faced slim men, white-faced slim women, gleam of white shirtfronts, silk hats, nodding flowery broad hats, silver veils over dark hair, hard little somber hats with a dab of vermilion, satin slippers, petticoat-edges, patent-leathers, rouge and enamel and patches. Voluptuous exciting perfumes. Whiffs of cigarette smoke caught up to gold radiance, bluely. Cafe and restaurant music scarcely heard, rhythmical. Lights, sound, swift feverish pleasure . . . First the flood came slowly, then full tide – furs richer than in Russia, silks than in the Orient, jewels than in Paris, faces and bodies the desire of the world – then the rapid ebb, and the street-walkers.[16]

This kind of prose impressionism belonged more to the 1890s than to Woodrow Wilson's America.

In his vignettes Reed talked to a prostitute in a beer-hall, an old woman sitting on a park bench in the rain, a hungry bum in the street, a prostitute named Mae from Galveston, Texas, and to a street vendor of *Matrimonial News*. The range is curious and narrow, Reed's contact at best glancing and brief. These are people singled out from the crowd, people with whom Reed can talk; there is no fear in his approach, no apology or social anxiety, no self-consciousness. He is quite often surprised by the independence and wilfulness of others. The recipient of the narrator's charity in one sketch ('Another Case of Ingratitude') objects to being questioned and patronized: 'You t'ought just because you give me a hand-out, I'd do a sob-story all over you. Wot right have you got to ask me all them questions? I know you fellers. Just because you got money you t'ink you can buy me with a meal . . .'[17] In another ('The Capitalist') a broke young man, taking pity on a drunken and homeless old woman whom he sees sitting in a park, is accused of being a condescending toff, 'wid yer jinglin' money an' yer dainty manners!' Arrested by a policeman, the narrator in 'A Taste of Justice' finds an old friend sitting on the bench in the police court. He is promptly invited to join the judge on the bench, while the policeman receives a telling off. A young man named George in 'Seeing is Believing' cannot make up his mind whether or not to believe a girl of seventeen who tells him she has come to the city from Ohio, has no money, no place to stay, does not particularly want a job, and on the face of it has not become a street-walker. This is the best of Reed's New York sketches, a delightful *conte* of credulity and innocence. Floyd Dell, Louis Untermeyer, John Sloan – it seemed that all of the contributors to *The Masses* were fascinated by prostitutes, and perhaps also by the exciting freedom of being able to talk about them in print.

Reed's New York sketches show him reaching out beyond the medieval diction of his poetry. He has not really sought 'realism', at least not by the standards of Stephen Crane's *Maggie* and Dreiser's *Sister Carrie*; but his sketches constitute a step towards the real world. Mike Gold once wrote that 'Reality is more poetic and beautiful than romance.'[18] This certainly was the direction in which Reed was heading.

Meeting Bill Haywood, the larger-than-life leader of the

Wobblies, gave Reed a hefty push into the class war. He spoke to Haywood at one of Mabel Dodge's evenings, and, as we have seen in the third chapter, was invited to come across the river to Paterson to see what the strike at the silk mills was all about. By the end of April 1913, both sides in the dispute were deeply entrenched, and the struggle for public opinion was being waged in all seriousness. Reed talked back to a policeman, was arrested and sentenced to twenty days in the local prison. His telegram to Walter Lippmann ('Nothing to do for 20 days. Happy and Healthy. Jack.') caught an insouciant note, as did his article in the June 1913 *Masses*, 'War in Paterson'.[19] There is no doubt that Reed was galvanized by his contact with Haywood, Carlo Tresca, Elizabeth Gurley Flynn and other Wobblies. Impatient with the cautious hierarchy of the Socialist Party, who were reluctant to trespass on union affairs, and hostile towards the American Federation of Labor, he found in the militant workers of Paterson, and the Wobblies, a grit and determination which, from the vantage point of Greenwich Village, seemed lacking elsewhere in American industrial life. The physical repression of the strikers by the police, the activities of 'detectives' hired by the mill-owners, and the blatant bias of the courts, created the kind of situation which touched Reed in an immediate and visceral way. He was drawn to radical politics through his basic humanity.

There was certainly enough going on in the streets to justify the title of his *Masses* article. The only problem was that the article was based upon what appears to have been a ten-minute visit to the scene of the strike, and is devoted to a detailed and highly ironic description of his arrest, trial and brief stay in gaol. (He was bailed out after four days.) There may have been a 'war' in Paterson, but Reed concentrated upon the arbitrary and unfair nature of his arrest, and a criticism of the conditions of those held in Paterson gaols. The article was written in the midst of the series of vignettes about New York. His study of the Colorado strike, which is analysed in detail in Chapter 3, written a year later, was four times as long, and was based on a systematic effort on Reed's part to convey a complex sequence of events in a distant and unfamiliar setting.[20] The Paterson essay is cruder in its political analysis, and more aggressive in its partisanship. 'War in Paterson' is a testament, an explanation, of how Reed was won over to the side of the strikers ('. . . those gentle, alert, brave men, ennobled by something greater than themselves . . .'), and how *he* was ennobled by their example. In it, he proposes an elaborate balancing of values. On the one side Reed finds police acting arbitrarily and violently, a legal system heavily biased in favour of the mill-owners, organized religion opposing the strike, and gaol conditions badly overcrowded. The other side is characterized by patient solidarity, idealism and a fighting leadership provided by the Wobblies. Reed says nothing about the causes of the strike, the tactics of the leadership, or the attitude of the strikers themselves. The imprisoned strikers cheer and sing, applaud enthusiastically, boo the mayor and the chief of police, and console Reed in pidgin English for his misfortune in being gaoled:

'Too bad you get in jail . . .'

'We not take bail . . . We stay here. Fill up the damn jail. Pretty soon no more room. Pretty soon can't arrest no more pickets!'

The men show no signs of discouragement or uncertainty: 'As one little Italian said to me, with blazing eyes: "We all one big Union. I.W.W. . . ." ' And they are all organized by Reed in a one-dimensional enthusiasm and unity. A strikebreaker is ostracized and moans 'I've learned my lesson . . . I ain't never goin' to scab on workingmen no more!' Reed leaves prison a modest hero to those he left behind:

And as I passed out through the front room they crowded around me again, patting my sleeve and my hand, friendly, warm-hearted, trusting, eloquent . . .
'You go out,' they said softly. 'That's nice. Glad you go out. Pretty soon we go out. Then we go back on picket line.'

'War in Paterson' is basically the work of someone who was, in Paul Hollander's unflattering term, an 'ideological pilgrim'.[21] Reed was learning how to write about the real world in such a piece, but he was only slightly closer to the real thing than he had been in his vignettes about New York prostitutes. Reed's criticism of capitalism made him want to believe that the workers were capable of solidarity and militancy despite ethnic and religious divisions, the law, the police and the many cultural factors which made going along with the system easier in the short run than any other course. Lacking the scepticism of those more familiar with industrial disputes, and having little knowledge of the working class, there was no counterweight to his emotional response to the oppression of the working-class: 'Think of it!', he wrote. 'Twelve years they have been losing strikes – twelve solid years of disappointments and incalculable suffering. They must not lose again! They cannot lose!' He cannot explain why the American labour movement failed to support the Paterson silk-workers, except to suggest that 'a good share of the Socialist Party and the American Federation of Labor have forgotten all about the class struggle, and seem to be playing a little game with capitalistic rules, called "Button, button, who's got the vote!"' (In 'Almost Thirty' he wrote that 'Our Socialist Party seemed to me duller than religion, and almost as little in touch with labor.'[22] The 'our' in this case was a little hyperbolic: he did not join the Socialist Party until five years after the Paterson strike.) What an interesting contrast of temperament and politics is suggested, as we have seen, by the conclusion of Sinclair's *King Coal* (1917). The hard-bitten leaders of the United Mine Workers persuade Hal Warner that the strike in the North Valley pits is doomed to fail because the men are isolated and the strike premature. Hal accepts their judgement, and acknowledges that their perspective, the long-term view, is more realistic than his own, so totally concerned with righting immediate grievances. Reed was impervious to such cautious wisdom. The conciliator in 'Sangar' was turned-upon and slain by his hot-tempered son. Reed boldly declared his new allegiance by resigning from the staff of the *American Magazine* to work for the strikers. The pageant he helped organize at Madison Square Garden attracted considerable attention, but failed to raise the amount of money anticipated.[23] The strike collapsed in recrimination, but Reed was set upon his destiny: 'Here was drama, change, democracy on the march made visible – a war of the people.' He knew what side he was on.

Crossing the Rio Grande in late December 1913 was no less eventful for Reed than his journey earlier in the year across the Hudson River to visit Paterson. The Mexican Revolution was a major national story in late 1913, and powerful interests within the United States demanded military intervention. Reed's commission from *Metropolitan Magazine*, on Lincoln Steffens's suggestion, gave him a remarkable opportunity. Reed's articles on Mexico – he published no fewer than thirteen in 1914 – established him as a national figure, someone who was courted by editors, courteously received by the President and Secretary of State, and who was himself sought out by the press. Reed opposed American intervention, but the main contribution of *Insurgent Mexico*, which collected the best of his articles on the revolution, was to convey in vivid terms the feel of Mexico, the physical contexts and tones, seen first-hand, which so much of the American debate about the situation in Mexico lacked. Reed did not commit himself too unequivocally to one or the other cause in the confusing situation, though his sympathies with Pancho Villa and with the ordinary Mexicans influenced the way he saw events. He seems not to have known the powerful muckraking study by John Kenneth Turner, *Barbarous Mexico: An Indictment of a Cruel and Corrupt System* (1911), in which the 'contract slaves' of the Henequen ranches in the Yucatan, and those transported to Valle Nacional, were presented in writing which is magnificently disciplined in its outrage. The situation Turner described comes stunningly close to Solzhenitsyn's description of the Gulag archipelago. Beyond an attack on the Díaz dictatorship itself, Turner's targets were the American apologists for Díaz, the role which American capital played in Mexico, and the support which the American government gave to the dictator. Turner shows the Harriman interests dominating Mexican railways, the rubber industry controlled by the Continental Rubber Company, the American Sugar Trust largely dominating sugar production; smelting and mining were in the hands of the Guggenheims, copper output jointly controlled by Morgan and Guggenheim, petroleum production in the hands of Edward L. Doheny and Rockefeller's Standard Oil. This was the nightmare of the Iron Heel writ large. The trusts which in Colorado were constrained, at least to some degree, by public opinion, in Mexico exercised a free hand. There were American investments in Mexico of 900 million dollars in 1911. By 1914 the investment exceeded one billion dollars. Turner assumed that with such investment, American 'intervention' – of one kind or another – was inevitable: 'Wherever capital flows, capital controls the Government.'[24] In effect, the real intervention had already taken place, and a military follow-up was hardly surprising to protect such a vast investment. (Mexico was the largest area for foreign investment by American capital before 1914.) But Turner argued that the Mexicans were capable of democratic rule, under a restored constitution. 'Perhaps it will be said that in opposing the system of Díaz', he wrote,

> I am opposing the interests of the United States. If the interests of Wall Street are the interests of the United States, then I plead guilty. And if it is to the interests of the United States that a nation should be crucified as Mexico is being crucified, then I am opposed to the interests of the United States.[25]

Reed arrived in Mexico in the period following the army chief of staff Victoriano Huerta's *coup* against the legally-elected President, Francisco Madero. The new administration in Washington in 1913 refused to recognize the Huerta regime, and supported the governor of Coahuila, Venustiano Carranza, and the Constitutionalist forces he led in rebellion against Huerta. Under the leadership of Obregón, Villa and González, the Constitutionalist forces defeated the Federals in the northern provinces of Mexico by December 1913. John Reed joined the Constitutionalists as they turned south, towards Torreón, and the road to Mexico City. His narrative begins with his first sight of the defeated *Federales* on the other side of the Rio Grande. *Insurgent Mexico* ends before Villa took Torreón. Reed came back to New York early in April 1914, and was in Colorado when the US Marines landed at Vera Cruz, in President Wilson's words, to 'obtain from General Huerta and his adherents the fullest recognition of the rights and dignity of the United States'. (A party of American sailors was arrested at Tampico by Mexican forces. The apologies following their release were insufficiently abject.[26]) Reed was fortunate to have left before the intervention: even the Constitutionalists were hostile to the arrival of the Marines, and there were reprisals against American citizens. Early in 1914, however, he caught the crest of the Constitutionalist cause. A year later Villa's courageous Division of the North was largely destroyed in the civil war following the resignation of Huerta in July 1914.[27] In 1916 General John J. Pershing led a punitive column against the depredations of Villa, thus heightening the Mexican resentment of the American role. Early 1914 was the moment of the 'lyrical illusion', to borrow a phrase from Malraux, when the issues in Mexico could be presented in the clearest way imaginable: Reed pictures the revolution as the fight between the rich and the poor.

His first experience of the revolution came when he joined 'La Tropa' at Las Nieves. An irregular mounted force under the command of General Urbina, the 'lion of the Sierra', 'La Tropa' were dressed picturesquely in cowhide sandals and dusty uniforms. They wore immense sombreros, large spurs and serapes. They carried swords and German Mauser rifles. 'La Tropa' knew nothing of military discipline or tactics, riding through the deserts of northern Mexico with an abandon which Reed found intensely attractive. He was able to prove his masculinity, and therefore his right to be regarded as a *compañero*, one of *los hombres*, by drinking a bottle of Spanish spirits before the men. Henceforth Reed was able to ride with 'La Tropa', and talk with them, as an equal. Captain Fernando asked Reed 'will you sleep with the *compañeros?*' Longinos Güereca, Reed's closest friend among 'La Tropa', seals their friendship no less warmly:

> 'We shall be compadres, eh? . . . We shall sleep in the same blankets, and always be together. And when we get to the Cadena I shall take you to my home, and my father shall make you my brother . . .'[28]

Another close friend was Luis Martinez, with whom Reed spent many hours of intimate conversation. He rode with Güereca, Martinez and 'La Tropa' to La Cadena, where a force of 150 Constitutionalists were to guard a pass against a large force of Federal irregulars, the much-feared *colorados*. This was Reed's first experience of battle. Part of 'La Tropa' was withdrawn from La Cadena and replaced by impoverished and untrained peons – wearing automobile goggles – who ran away in chaotic flight when the *colorados* attacked. Reed heard news of the rout from fleeing soldiers:

> I ran. I wondered what time it was. I wasn't very frightened. Everything still was so unreal, like a page out of Richard Harding Davis. It just seemed to me that if I didn't get away I wouldn't be doing my job well. I kept thinking to myself: 'Well, this is certainly an experience. I'm going to have something to write about.'[29]

His desperate flight and long hike through the desert were indeed an adventure. But when he arrived at the home of his friend Longinos Güereca, Reed was turned away. The Güereca family feared reprisals from the *colorados*. The battle of La Cadena, little more than a minor skirmish, ended disastrously. Reed learned the next day that his friends Martinez and Güereca had both been killed. The idyllic moments of companionship had been swept away by the chaos of battle. The brotherhood which Longinos Güereca hoped would be extended to his *gringo* friend was not the least of the casualties of the war. Some of Reed's certainties about the revolution were shaken by what he saw and heard. Güereca's father, for example, did not share his son's belief in the virtue of the Constitutionalists and the wickedness of the *Federales*: 'Three years ago I had four *riatas* like this. Now I have only one. One the *colorados* took, and the other Urbina's people took, and the last one José Bravo . . . What difference does it make which side robs you?' [30] The old Bulgarian saying – 'Only fools rejoice when governments change' – seems to capture this slice of peasant wisdom. Another soldier, formerly a schoolteacher, remarks to Reed:

> . . . I know that Revoluciones, like Republics are ungrateful. I have fought three years. At the end of the first Revolucion that great man, Father Madero, invited his soldiers to the Capital. He gave us clothes, and food, and bull-fights. We returned to our homes and found the greedy again in power. [31]

The statement which *Insurgent Mexico* makes is, in significant ways, qualified by attitudes such as these. While Reed's position is clear, his book gives a more complex picture of the situation.

Reed's account of the battle of La Cadena was received in New York with intense interest. To many contemporaries it seemed a new kind of war reporting, remote indeed from the hero-worshipping glory stories which gave such a false picture of the Spanish–American War. Walter Lippmann wrote to Reed at the end of March 1914:

> Your first two articles [in *Metropolitan Magazine*] are undoubtedly the finest reporting that's ever been done. Its kind of embarrassing to tell a fellow you know that he's a genius, and you're in a wild country just now. I can't begin to tell you how

good the articles are. If you keep it up we'll all be able to sit comfortably at home and know all that we wanted to know. That's the only immoral thing about your work. You make it unnecessary for the rest of us to stir. You have perfect eyes, and your power of telling leaves nothing to be desired. I want to hug you, Jack.

If all history had been reported as you are doing this, Lord – I say that with Jack Reed reporting begins. Incidently, of course, the stories are literature, but I didn't realize that till afterwards, they were so much alive with Mexico and with you.[32]

(Reed's relationship with Lippmann was rarely as warm and easy after 1914. Political issues, especially the war in Europe, separated them. Reed was critical of Lippmann's relationship to American capitalism.)

Reed's portrait of Pancho Villa is a study of peasant shrewdness, brutality, naïveté and stubbornness. He was by no means an unqualified admirer of the leader of the Division of the North. We first see Villa at the Governor's Palace at Chihuahua, where he is given a medal by his grateful army. The pomposity of the ceremony is nicely balanced by Villa's scruffy dress, his lack of pretention and sly indications of boredom at the ceremony. Villa's entrance into the audience chamber is gloriously theatrical ('It was Napoleonic!') but his behaviour and deflating jokes mock the extravagance of the ceremony. This lack of interest in military rituals endeared Villa to his troops, mainly peasants themselves, no less than to Reed. In this, Villa 'realized something of what the Revolution signified'.

Villa's handling of other matters during the campaign was not so unequivocally praised. His trust in butchers like Rodolfo Fierro, who killed the Englishman William Benton in cold blood, causing an international uproar, and Villa's uncritical support for the Constitutionalist leader Carranza, suggested to Reed the limitations of Villa's judgement. His handling of the currency problem, while bold and fascinating in a crude manner, could not be regarded as anything more than the extension of his career as a bandit. Villa's ruthless policy of expelling all Spaniards and executing captured *colorados* was not explicitly condemned by Reed, but the very absence of comment does not mean that Reed was indifferent to the consequences of such actions. Villa was magnificent, a true man of the people and a military genius; he

was also an arbitrary despot. The revolution which he symbolized
was, as Reed saw it, a struggle of the peons against their
oppressors. Reed was unquestionably on their side, as he had been
on the side of the striking silk-workers at Paterson. The portrait of
Villa in *Insurgent Mexico* expressed Reed's delight at the man's
irreverence but was strongly marked with hinted reservations and
unspoken criticisms. There was more at work here than, as
Rosenstone argues, a simple identification by Reed with his
subject.

If there were things about Mexico which were crude and
violent, he found in the people an instinctive life, a purity of
purpose and sentiment, which, outside the working-class people
in the United States, was largely new to Reed. 'It was a land to
love – this Mexico – a land to fight for.'[33] During the siege of
Gomez Palacio: 'I felt my whole feeling going out to these gentle,
simple people – so lovable they were . . .'[34] He described *rancheros*
he met as 'courteous, loving, patient, poor, so long slaves, so full of
dreams, so soon to be free'.[35] By comparison, the American
mercenaries in Mexico seemed '. . . hard, cold misfits in a
passionate country despising the cause for which they were
fighting, sneering at the gaiety of the irrepressible Mexicans'.[36]
Mexico left Reed with a severe case of primitivism.

He joined the main body of Villa's army at Yermo, and
accompanied the columns of mounted men as they marched
south:

> It was a brilliant day, hot sunshine alternating with big white
> clouds. In two thick columns, one on each side of the train, the
> army was already moving south. As far as the eye could reach, a
> mighty double cloud of dust floated over them; and little
> straggling groups of mounted men jogged along, with every
> now and then a bog Mexican flag. Between slowly moved the
> trains; the pillars of black smoke from their engines, at regular
> intervals growing smaller, until over the northern horizon only
> a dirty mist appeared.[37]

Although refused permission by Villa to accompany the advance
guard of the army, Reed managed to travel ahead of the train
where the reporters were housed and saw the corpses of two dead
rurales:

Something lay huddled around the foot of a telegraph pole –
something infinitely small and shabby, like a pile of old clothes.
The *rurale* was upon his back, twisted sideways from his hips
. . . He had evidently been much bigger when alive, the dead
shrink so. A wild red beard made the pallor of his face
grotesque, until you noticed that under it and the dirt, and the
long lines of sweat of his terrible fight and hard riding, his
mouth was gently and serenely open as if he slept. His brain had
been blown out.[38]

The other corpse had 'the fiercest exultant grin on his face' and
had been shot through the head three times: 'how exasperated
they must have been!' Reed in such passages is learning to look
clearly, and his prose has the cadence and freshness which only
comes from a disciplined precision. The description of the dead
rurales would have merited Reed the envy of a hundred writers.
His impressionistic panoramas of the army on the move are a
further sign of the writerly skills which Reed was developing.
Consider a further passage in which Reed described how the army
prepared for the advance upon Gomez Palacio:

At Santa Clara the massed columns of the army halted and
began to defile left and right, thin lines of troops jogging out
under the checkered sun and shade of the great trees, until six
thousand men were spread in one long single front, to the right
over fields and through ditches, beyond the last cultivated field,
across the desert to the very base of the mountains; to the left
over the roll of the flat world. The bugles blared faintly and
near, and the army moved forward in a mighty line across the
whole country. Above them lifted a five-mile-wide golden
dust-glory. Flags flapped. In the center, level with them, came
the cannon car, and beside that Villa rode with his staff.[39]

In the very best sense, this is pure Cecil B. De Mille.

Gomez Palacio, a railway junction four miles north of Torreón,
astride the north–south railroad line, had been taken and lost by
both sides in the rebellion against Huerta. The junction held the
key to Torreón and the path to Mexico City; neither side could
bypass it. At first excited by the sounds of battle as he approached
by train, and then 'frantic with curiosity and nervousness', Reed
collapses with exhaustion and sleeps soundly through the night.

Waking the next morning, the files of wounded moving through
the dust look like ghosts; the whole scene, the shouting muleteers,
columns of heavy trucks, cursing men and ever-present dust, seem
'an incredible dream'. Dead soldiers in an *arroyo* have an
'unearthly calm' about them. Although this is the morning of the
battle, it seems unreal to Reed. The assault which he witnessed
was made without proper coordination or artillery support. Like
the skirmish at La Cadena, it ended with high casualties and a
rout of Constitutionalist troops. Reed then joined soldiers who
were preparing for a night attack on Federal positions in the
Brittingham Corral. This too was repulsed. 'I soon went back to
camp', he wrote, 'sick with boredom. A battle is the most boring
thing in the world if it lasts any length of time. It is all the
same . . .'[40]

While Reed watched the inconclusive assault on the
Brittingham Corral, a young Englishman, Patrick O'Hea, was
appointed General Manager of the J. F. Brittingham estates in
Gomez Palacio. His perspective on the siege makes a nice contrast
with Reed's. While an undergraduate at Cambridge in 1902,
O'Hea's health broke. He went out to Mexico to recover, and,
finding that he enjoyed the climate, was soon a trusted employee
of large haciendas owned by expatriate Britons. He did not meet
Reed, but in his *Reminiscences of the Mexican Revolution* (1981)
described Villa as an 'Attila', a 'mad dog'. His men were 'savage
for loot and murderous of intent'. The siege turned upon
possession of the Cerro de la Pila, a stone outcropping 200 feet
high which held the emergency water tanks for the city. The death
of the Federal commander of the Cerro opened the way for the
Villistas, but a brave General Velasco 'led a sortie out from
Torreón and, with gunpowder and steel, hurled his opponents
back, leaving the Federals again in possession of the coveted and
bloody eminence'.[41] O'Hea's employees and their families hid in
subterranean stone vaults during the siege, but when the Federals
secretly withdrew he emerged to stop Villa's men from looting the
estate. O'Hea and the British Vice-Consul forced their way into
Villa's presence, persuading him that they should carry a message
to the Federals in Torreón calling upon them to surrender. The
Federals stoutly rejected the offer, but abandoned Torreón to
Villa that night. O'Hea was prepared to undertake whatever
measures of accommodation with the occupiers were necessary,
though he saw nothing in the least romantic in their actions or

demeanor. Villa himself was described by O'Hea as having bloodshot eyes and misfitting clothes. For Reed, indifference to such matters was proof of Villa's iconoclasm. For O'Hea Villa's appearance symbolized the misrule and disorder of the revolution. As may be gathered, O'Hea's *Reminiscences of the Mexican Revolution*, written in the 1950s and 1960s, are a wonderfully preserved example of the late-Victorian British temperament.

His concerns for the protection of property and the maintenance of order were less remote from Reed than might be supposed. In the account of the orgy of looting and drunkenness which followed the entrance of the Villistas into the undefended Gomez Palacio, Reed noted a change in the psychology of the army. His property had hitherto been universally respected. With the sacking of Gomez Palacio it seemed that 'everybody was looting from everybody else'. The Army of the North, which took 1000 killed and 2000 casualties in the siege of Gomez Palacio, suffered a moral collapse on entering the city. Reed felt the army had been 'terribly shattered'. His horse, gun and various other items were stolen. With equal determination, he stole what was needed for his return trip north. (Scenes such as this remind us of the ways in which Reed was unlike Richard Harding Davis and the other great war reporters of that period.) His cable to the New York *World* on 25 March broke the news of the fall of Torreón – a full week before the city actually fell to Villa.

The rest of *Insurgent Mexico* consists of material accumulated before Reed joined Villa's forces at Yermo. He interviewed Carranza at Nogales and wrote an uncannily evocative piece describing the headquarters of the leader of the Constitutionalists. The 'Mexican Nights' sketches dealt with life remote from battle or politics. A cockfight in a provincial village, quarrels over the rules of poker, the performance of a folk play: these things were as much a part of Mexico and its people as the army and its battles which alternately fascinated and bored Reed. Though they seemed remote from the revolution, Reed noted that even in the most distant provinces the 'great seas of modern life' were beginning to touch the lives of ordinary Mexicans. Without trying to understand the revolution in a systematic way, *Insurgent Mexico* showed Reed responding humanely to its energies. Other than several weeks spent in Colorado, he worked on the manuscript until war broke out in Europe.

'I hate soldiers', Reed wrote in *The Masses* in March 1915:

> I hate to see a man with a bayonet fixed on his rifle, who can order me off the street. I hate to belong to an organization that is proud of obeying a caste of superior beings, that is proud of killing free ideas, so that it may the more efficiently kill human beings in cold blood. They will tell you that a conscript army is Democratic, because everybody has to serve; but they won't tell you that military service plants in your blood the germ of blind obedience, of blind irresponsibility, that it produces one class of Commanders in your state and your industries, and accustoms you to do what they tell you even in times of peace.[42]

The militarization of society, the engineering and manipulation of public consent, and the entrenchment of autocratic attitudes, seemed to Reed in 1915 and 1916 the most likely consequences of American entry into the war. The disarray caused by the war in the ranks of the Socialist International, and in particular the enthusiastic support by German socialists for the war, left him with foreboding. He was quite legitimately worried that the same fate awaited the left in America.

Reed made two trips to Europe, both on commissions from the *Metropolitan Magazine*. The first began in August 1914 and ended in February 1915. The second trip lasted from March to October 1915. Reed's efforts as a war correspondent were, by his own admission, largely anticlimatic. No reporter in Europe could expect the latitude or casual informality Reed had experienced in Mexico. His contacts with Pancho Villa, the interview with Carranza, and various experiences of battle, made *Insurgent Mexico* an exciting and vivid panorama of the civil war. On the eastern front, however, Reed was largely restricted to hotel, train and restaurant conversations with the small number of people he met who spoke French or German. He was completely barred, for reasons of language but also due to the nature of the war, from easy contact with ordinary soldiers or civilians. Many of the places he visited were devoid of civilian life altogether, whether through pogroms, typhus or military operations. Outside of the larger towns, the landscapes he saw were empty. There was no group of *compañeros* to welcome him. Reed and the artist Boardman Robinson were able to observe the chaotic state of Eastern Europe, but were neither of them sufficiently knowledgeable to do more than record impressions of the impact of the war. Strolling around the miserable ghettoes of the Pale of Settlement in puttees and broad-brimmed hats made them figures of comedy. In Russia they were taken for spies, repeatedly arrested, lied to by officials, and found the American Embassy in Petrograd resolutely unhelpful. Such experiences dampened their spirits. Reed's notes and Robinson's drawings were confiscated when they left Russia. Some passages in *The War in Eastern Europe*, compiled from Reed's articles in the *Metropolitan*, were written with Reed's customary flair, but the book as a whole lacked the inner involvement which had shaped his experiences in Mexico. What is worse, the book was a commercial failure. Scribner's had only managed to sell 1000 copies in America and 500 in Europe by September 1916.[43] (It is the only Reed title never to have been reprinted.) Some reviews were encouraging, and found a 'new art' of war journalism in Reed's practice:

> Visualization, a presentation to the reader of what the authors themselves have seen – this is the striking quality of the new art. Reed does not rhetorically reconstruct battles in the manner of the past, out of scraps and trifles picked up in the bar of the Ritz in London; nor does Robinson make grandiloquent, melodramatic battle scenes out of Associated Press reports, after the manner of the London and Paris illustrated weeklies.[44]

The dispatches of Philip Gibbs to the *Daily Telegraph*, and 200 other English and American papers, are a little unfairly described as 'bar of the Ritz' reporting, but the contrast with Reed is none the less useful. For Reed it was never 'our' boys, or 'our' side. 'We' were not engaged, and the military virtues which Gibbs, John Buchan in his interminable *Nelson's History of the War*, and many other writers saw constantly on display in the trenches of the western front, were singularly absent in Reed's account. The freedom of his style, so consciously personal and without any of the historian's compunctions to give an account of the fighting, enabled him to write (as he had done about Paterson) personal impressions. Generally speaking, Reed was neither famous enough nor was the eastern front of sufficiently compelling interest for the book to appeal to American readers. Reed witnessed no major battles, and the drawings by Robinson were low key to the point of dullness.

Reed went to Europe an enemy of the war. 'This is not Our War', he wrote in an unsigned article, 'The Traders' War', in the September 1914 *Masses*. Nothing he saw made him any more willing to believe the 'editorial chorus in America which pretends to believe – would have us believe – that the White and Spotless Knight of Modern Democracy is marching against the Unspeakably Vile Monster of Medieval Militarism'.[45] The war seemed to him a confused, ramshackle affair, marked by traditional regional and ethnic hatreds, and conducted with ferocity and great loss of life. (He gives a valuable and not wholly sympathetic picture of the desperate state of the Jewish population in the war zone, and conveys with considerable clarity the intensity of Russian anti-Semitism.) Such a war was remote from the larger principles which President Wilson proclaimed, but Reed, like so many radicals, saw Wilson's promise to keep America out of the war a compelling reason to support him in 1916. He was invited by George Creel to join a 'free gathering of volunteer writers' to support Wilson's re-election.[46] *The War in Eastern Europe*, when it appeared in the summer of 1916, denied that America had any real need to get involved. Within months of Wilson's election, America was in the war. Between Wilson's election and the inauguration a revolution had occurred in Russia – not anticipated by Reed – which altered the political meaning of the war, and changed Reed's life.

Reed returned to America in February 1918 after a five-month stay in Russia. His first political act was to join the Socialist Party. At least since the recall of Bill Haywood from the party's National Executive in 1912 as part of a purge of syndicalists and advocates of direct action and industrial sabotage, he had found the Wobblies more attractive; his criticism of the party's role in Paterson and Colorado was specific and warmly felt. Yet he clung to the hope that the left wing could capture control of the party, at least until the moment in 1919 when Reed and his supporters were expelled from the national convention by police. Despite its many failings, the Socialist Party had roots in the American working class. The foreign-language federations which dominated the National Left Wing Council had no such roots, and within the Communist Labor Party, which Reed founded when they were expelled from the Socialist Party convention in August 1919, he argued repeatedly for a realistic assessment of the American proletariat. (Realistic in this instance meaning pessimistic: Reed was not persuaded that the American working class were on the verge of seizing power.) He also opposed premature merger with the majority within the Left Wing Council, led by Louis Fraina and Charles Ruthenberg, who had simultaneously constituted themselves the Communist Party.

His notebooks and an extensive collection of newspapers, handbills and other documents of the revolution, seized by Federal officials on his return to America, were returned to Reed in November 1918. The manuscript of *Ten Days That Shook the World* was in the hands of the publishers Boni and Liveright by mid-January 1919. Reed was always a quick study. The book was published to generally enthusiastic reviews in March. Given the bitter hostility in America towards radicals (on May Day there were anti-socialist riots by servicemen in various cities across the country), sales were moderately encouraging.[47] Nearly 6000 copies were sold within the first year.[48] Even before the return of his papers Reed had begun, in lectures and articles, to tell the story of the Bolshevik Revolution. On 25 October 1918, Reed spoke at a memorial meeting for Jacob Schwartz, a young man who died during the course of his trial on a charge of distributing leaflets against military intervention in Russia. He recalled the moment nearly a year before when news reached Petrograd that Kerensky's troops and Cossacks were advancing upon the outskirts of the city, and that the military garrisons were divided among themselves whether to remain neutral in the battle or to support the Military Revolutionary Committee of the Petrograd Soviet. Word went out from the Smolny Institute:

'Loose the full power of the proletariat!' The whistles of all the factories blew, and on this day – on the 10th [of November, 28 October Old Style] – the great working class quarters and the slums of Petrograd began to vomit out their hundreds of thousands – men, women and children – some with guns, some with spades, some with axes, and the little children carrying sacks to fill with earth to make barricades against the Cossacks. (applause) During the night of November 10 to 11, the proletariat, the unled, the leaderless, the unorganized proletariat, met at Pulkovo the advance of the Cossacks and met the shock of trained troops and artillery, and rolled and poured over barricades and obliterated the Cossacks! (applause)[49]

When he came to describe this moment in *Ten Days* Reed sharpened the details:

> As we came out [of the Smolny] into the dark and gloomy day all around the grey horizon factory whistles were blowing, a hoarse and nervous sound, full of foreboding. By tens of thousands the working-people poured out, men and women; by tens of thousands the humming slums belched out their dun and miserable hordes. Red Petrograd was in danger! Cossacks! South and south-west they poured through the shabby streets towards the Moskovsky Gate, men, women, and children, with rifles, picks, spades, rolls of wire, cartridge-belts over their working clothes . . . Such an immense, spontaneous outpouring of a city was never seen! They rolled along torrent-like, companies of soldiers borne with them, guns, motor-trucks, wagons – the revolutionary proletariat defending with its breast the capital of the Workers' and Peasants' Republic![50]

The 'little children carrying sacks' have gone; the slums which 'vomited' out the masses now belch out 'their dun and miserable hordes'. But the drama of the scene remains unchanged: the people rolled and 'poured', 'torrent-like', in defence of the Petrograd Soviet and the revolution.

This image, and others associated with it, rely upon analogies with natural processes. They carry an important dimension of Reed's understanding of the Bolshevik insurrection. What Reed learned in Petrograd, he wrote to Boardman Robinson in October 1917, was that 'as long as this world exists, the "working class and the employing class have nothing in common"'.[51] In Reed's view, the workers understood that the revolution was only possible if they made it; it could only succeed if it represented their desires. *Ten Days* was carefully designed to counter smears that the Bolsheviks had staged a *putsch* against the wishes of the peasants and workers, that their revolution was an *unnatural* event, without organic basis. The whole vast apparatus of Reed's imagery was meant to reaffirm the legitimacy of the revolution. No political conspiracy or demagoguery could bring about 'an immense, spontaneous outpouring of a city':

Not by compromise with the propertied classes, or with the other political leaders; not by conciliating the old Government mechanism, did the Bolsheviki conquer the power. Nor by the organized violence of a small clique. If the masses all over Russia had not been ready for insurrection it must have failed. The only reason for Bolshevik success lay in their accomplishing the vast and simple desires of the most profound strata of the people, calling them to the work of tearing down and destroying the old, and afterwards, in the smoke of falling ruins, cooperating with them to erect the framework of the new . . .[52]

What is at stake in Reed's imagery, and in *Ten Days*, is the legitimacy of the revolution itself.

Reed uses geological figures, primarily to convey the larger changes taking place in what was the Tsar's empire. And he uses images drawn from natural processes, such as the sea, to suggest the movement of opinion within the Russian people. In the aftermath of the attempted *putsch* by Kornilov, the Provisional Government and the entire state apparatus created by the March revolution functioned to block elections to the new Congress of Soviets, where the Bolsheviks were rapidly gaining support. With conventional channels obstructed, Reed wrote, 'A ground-swell of revolt heaved and cracked the crust which had been slowly hardening on the surface of revolutionary fires dormant all those months. Only a spontaneous mass movement could bring about the All-Russian Congress of Soviets . . .'[53] After the Bolshevik rising, 'the eddies of insurrection were spreading through Russia with a swiftness surpassing any human agency'.

Vast Russia was in a state of solution. As long ago as 1905 the process had begun; the March revolution had merely hastened it, and giving birth to a sort of forecast of the new order, had ended by merely perpetuating the hollow structure of the old regime. Now, however, the Bolsheviki, in one night, had dissipated it, as one blows away smoke. Old Russia was no more; human society flowed molten in primal heat, and from the tossing sea of flame was emerging the class struggle, stark and pitiless – and the fragile, slowly cooling crust of new planets . . .[54]

(Reed did not live to see the cooling and 'hardening' of the 'crust' of the October Revolution.) Nationalist movements among the Finns, Ukrainians, Caucasians, Siberians and among the Cossacks on the Don meant that 'Old Russia was rapidly breaking up'. Reed does not analyse these events, but visualizes them metaphorically. The images are often highly dramatic.

At one point Reed describes the hall of meetings in the Smolny: it 'was crowded with people roaring like the sea'. The desire for peace swept the Russian armies 'like the sea rising'. At the Jacob Schwartz Memorial Meeting he describes the victory over the Cossacks at Pulkovo occurring when 'the anonymous hordes of the people, gathering in the darkness around the battle, rose like a tide and poured over the enemy'. A similar figure is used in a description in *Ten Days* of a meeting of the armoured car troops at the Mikhailovsky Riding School. Krylenko, People's Commissar for Military Affairs, is pleading with the men to support the Military Revolutionary Committee. If they remained neutral, the city would have no defence against the Cossacks. A vocal claque at the meeting tries to shout down Krylenko as a traitor:

> The whole place seethed and roared. Then it began to move like an avalanche bearing down upon us, great black-browed men forcing their way through.
> 'Who is breaking up our meeting?' they shouted. 'Who is whistling here?' The claque, rudely burst asunder, went flying – nor did they gather again . . .[55]

The armoured car troops hear Krylenko out – and vote to remain loyal to the Military Revolutionary Committee.

No one claims that Reed was writing as a Marxist in *Ten Days*. It is worth reiterating the point, and emphasizing how remote Reed was from the cool and scientific analysis of the revolution which one finds in Trotsky's *History of the Russian Revolution* (1932–3). Indeed, at one point Trotsky complained of the lack of drama which characterized the crucial moments of the Bolshevik insurrection. 'Where is the insurrection?', he asked.

> There is no picture of the insurrection. The events do not form themselves into a picture. A series of small operations, calculated and prepared in advance, remain separated from one another both in space and time. A unity of thought and aim

unites them, but they do not fuse in the struggle itself. There is no action of great masses. There are no dramatic encounters with the troops. There is nothing of all that which imaginations brought up upon the facts of history associate with the idea of insurrection.[56]

(But then Reed, not Trotsky, entered the Winter Palace with the Red Guard.) Trotsky continued:

The bourgeois class had expected barricades, flaming conflagrations, looting, rivers of blood. In reality a silence reigned more terrible than all the thunders of the world. The social ground shifted noiselessly like a revolving stage, bringing forward the popular masses, carrying away to limbo the rulers of yesterday.

We get in Trotsky things which Reed cannot have known. He gives far greater emphasis to the role of the Military Revolutionary Committee in the insurrection, to the point where scholars today see in the struggle of the MRC and the Petrograd Military District for control of the large Petrograd garrison the central event in the seizure of power.[57] What Trotsky explained by careful analysis of the existing balance of forces in Russia, and through a shrewd assessment of the principal figures on all sides, Reed attributed to the subterranean movement of geological strata and natural processes. Trotsky was able to see certain things with shattering clarity – no more frankly than when he wrote that 'Attempts to lead the insurrection directly through the [Bolshevik] party nowhere produced results' – and everywhere attempted scientific objectivity.

Yet finally Trotsky, like Reed, was a poet of the revolution. Trotsky's account of the revolution turns upon a successful act of deception. In the period after the failure of the Kornilov *putsch* at the end of August 1917, the Bolsheviks planned for an insurrection. As chairman of the Petrograd Soviet, Trotsky launched the political attack upon Kerensky and the Provisional Government. At the same time, through the Military Organization of the party, and the MRC of the Soviet, detailed plans were being formulated for the seizure of power. It was necessary to present all preparations, especially those of the MRC, in a purely defensive light. Kerensky had to be deceived about Trotsky's intentions, to prevent their suppression, and Trotsky appreciated that the Executive Committee of the Soviet, which represented the strong Menshevik position earlier in the year, must not be scared off. Even on the eve of the insurrection, he explained,

> There could be no talk of expounding before this caucus [of provincial delegates to the Second Congress of Soviets] the whole plan of the insurrection. Whatever is said at a large meeting inevitably gets abroad. It was still impossible even to throw off the defensive envelope of the attack without creating confusion in the minds of certain units of the garrison.[58]

Trotsky justifies the actions of the MRC to the Smolny as nothing more than 'revolutionary self-defense', and threatens reprisals in kind if Kerensky moves against the Soviet. 'This open threat was at the same time a political screen for the forthcoming night attack.' He was only able to abandon the 'defensive phraseology' on the night of 24 October (Old Style). The 'Art of Insurrection', as Trotsky titled his chapter on the eve of the revolution in his *History*, depended crucially upon disguise and deception. In order to succeed, his performances had to mislead virtually everyone, supporters as well as enemies. Trotsky described how rumours of insurrection were circulated and then denied by the Executive Committee of the party, to keep their enemies off balance. The Soviet was central to the whole stratagem. The Bolsheviks alone commanded a small but intensely loyal following. It was the Soviet, however, which was universally accepted among both workers and soldiers as the true voice and defender of the revolution. Control of the military barracks could only be preserved by uniting all political tendencies under the leadership of the Soviet, and the party leadership recognized that the Soviet was an indispensable part of the deception. (Reed, of course, knew nothing of Trotsky's deception, and saw spontaneous agreement where Trotsky presents careful planning and realistic manipulation.) It is entirely possible that Trotsky seriously over-estimated the importance of the Bolsheviks' conspiratorial planning, towards which his own efforts were directed during the revolution. Nevertheless, the image of the final stages of the revolution in Trotsky's *History* is of events occurring out of sight, of a plan fully elaborated and put underway, yet which remained invisible until that 'series of small operations' was revealed and Trotsky could at last stand before the delegates to the Soviet at the Smolny and speak openly of what he was doing.

This formal acknowledgement of the shifting 'social ground' was expressed by Trotsky in terms of roles reversed by the revolution. The Provisional Government was replaced by the Council of People's Commissars. With that transformation the workers, formerly the exploited victims of capitalism, had to defend the new state by protecting the very machines and factories which had been instruments of their oppression. 'Sabotage on the part of the property owners and administrators', Trotsky wrote,

> shifted to the workers the task of protecting the plants – the machines, stores, reserves of coal and raw material. Roles were here interchanged: the worker would tightly grip his rifle in defense of the factory in which he saw the source of his power.[59]

Other kinds of transformation were occurring. The MRC, as the crisis in Petrograd developed, 'occupied in relation to the troops the position of a governmental headquarters, not the headquarters of conspirators'. The Bolsheviks appointed 'ministers' or commissars who, in the name of the Soviet, gradually usurped the functions of the Provisional Government. The revolution made criminals out of ministers, and ministers out of Bolsheviks who only months before had been under arrest or in hiding. Lenin fled in disguise in July; Kerensky's turn came in October. The disaster of the 'July Days' saw the collapse of public support for the Bolsheviks. By October it was the Provisional Government which was in a state of collapse. As Martov said, the Bolsheviks found power in the street and picked it up. Trotsky's *History* is alive to the profound ironies consequent upon the sudden reversal in the fortunes of the Bolsheviks. From the perspective granted by a dozen years after the revolution, Trotsky's viewpoint was sometimes savagely and comically ironic. His text is alive with almost incandescent energies. A knowledge of the subsequent history of the revolution adds yet further layers of ironic meaning. Under the Tsars all radicals were liable to imprisonment in the Peter and Paul fortress. Under the Provisional Government, socialist ministers imprisoned Bolsheviks. During the insurrection these same socialist ministers were themselves imprisoned by their Bolshevik successors.

Trotsky defended such acts by reference to the behaviour of socialists in July. Though he does not say so, we know, and so did Trotsky's readers in the early 1930s, that within four or five years it was Trotsky's supporters who filled the Peter and Paul, and many other prisons, as the wheel of revolutionary fortune turned yet again.[60] Trotsky's ironies have the larger sweep of history behind them. No matter which side was in power, the Peter and Paul was needed.

Reed's ironies, on the other hand, were often local and specific. He was travelling to Tsarskoye Selo, while the sound of Kerensky's cannons could be heard in Petrograd, in the hope of seeing the decisive military confrontation. The truck in which he was riding carried Red Guards, a small cannon, and corrugated-iron bombs which rolled back and forth as they swayed from side to side. Patrols tried to stop them, but were brushed aside. It soon became clear that no one knew precisely where the front was. They stopped and asked a sailor, but he scratched his head and admitted that he'd also been trying to find it. Firing was heard ahead to the left. Reed and the soldiers spread out and stealthily entered the forest: 'It was silent in the woods. The leaves were gone, and the tree-trunks were a pale wan color in the low, sickly autumn sun. Not a thing moved, except the ice of little woodland pools shivering under our feet. Was it an ambush?'[61] They found three soldiers sitting obliviously around a small fire: ' "What was the shooting going on around here?" One of the soldiers answered, looking relieved, "Why, we were just shooting a rabbit or two, comrade . . ." ' Such moments, which in their small way reveal the state of mind of a reporter who was anxiously looking for a big story, do not occur in Trotsky's narrative. They give a distinctive flavour to *Ten Days*. Even with scenes not directly involving himself, Reed appreciated ironies in whatever form they came. A scene he witnessed in the barracks of the Second Tsarskoye Selo Rifles embodied for Reed one of the essential meanings of the revolution. After dining in what looked to Reed like any officers' mess in Europe, the colonel spread out a map indicating the positions occupied by the company that morning. Then the chairman of the regimental committee entered. The colonel explained that he did not feel it necessary to take up advanced positions, but the regimental committee thought otherwise and demanded that they engage the Cossacks near Gatchina in the morning. As Reed describes the scene, the colonel returned to the map and issued orders for the advance. When ready, the orders were signed by the chairman of the regimental committee and presented to the colonel. 'Here was the Revolution!'[62]

Like various scenes in Trotsky's *History*, the reversal of roles between the soldiers and the officers expressed in miniature the larger reversals which the revolution was making possible. Reed captured another such moment when he described the opening session of the Second Congress of the All-Russian Soviets, which met at the Smolny late in the evening of 24 October (Old Style). The opening had been delayed for hours while the MRC desperately waited for news that the Winter Palace had been taken. The leaders of the old Central Executive Committee (as Reed names it, the 'Tsay-ee-kah'), with the exception of those like Kerensky who had joined the Provisional Government, took their place on the platform. They included Gotz, Dan and Lieber, leading Mensheviks who appeared to Reed 'white-faced, hollow-eyed and indignant'. The Soviet at once elected a new 'Tsay-ee-kah' dominated by the Bolsheviks. The Mensheviks rose and left the platform, to be replaced by Trotsky, Kamenev, Lunacharsky and the others. 'How far they had soared, these Bolsheviki, from a despised and hunted sect less than four months ago, to this supreme place, the helm of great Russia in full tide of insurrection!'[63]

The scene in the Tsarskoye Selo Barracks and that which he witnessed in the Smolny on 24 October were connected to each other not only by Reed's role as observer, but by the deeper geologic processes of the revolution itself. Such long-term changes had as well to be explained in terms of their moment-by-moment expression. Reed portrays the MRC as a Catherine-wheel, 'throwing off orders, appeals, decrees, like sparks . . .'[64] The soldiers and workers pouring into the Smolny were 'Men literally out of themselves, living prodigies of sleeplessness and work – men unshaven, filthy, with burning eyes who drove upon their fixed purpose full speed on engines of exaltation'.[65] These are men who have become instruments of their will. On the day before the insurrection was scheduled to begin, Reed noted that the MRC in the Smolny 'flashed baleful fire, pounding like an overloaded dynamo . . .'[66] The next morning Reed turned back and saw the Smolny 'bright with lights'. It hummed 'like a gigantic hive'.[67] (By comparison, no voice from the 'rough world outside' could penetrate the high, cold hall in the Mariinsky Palace where the

Council of the Republic met.) The revolution was a Catherine-wheel, an engine and a dynamo, transforming all those who touched it:

> On the top floor [of the Smolny] the Military Revolutionary Committee was in full blast, striking and slacking not. Men went in, fresh and vigorous; night and day and night and day they threw themselves into the terrible machine; and came out limp, blind with fatigue, hoarse and filthy, to fall on the floor and sleep . . .[68]

During the most exciting moments of the revolution Reed found sleeping men all over the Smolny:

> Inside, the long, gloomy halls and bleak rooms seemed deserted. No one moved in all the enormous pile. A deep, uneasy sound came to my ears, and looking around, I noticed that everywhere on the floor, along the walls, men were sleeping. Rough, dirty men, workers and soldiers, spattered and caked with mud, sprawled alone or in heaps in the careless attitudes of death. Some wore ragged bandages marked with blood. Guns and cartridge-belts were scattered about . . . The victorious proletarian army![69]

(Even here Reed cannot resist a final ironic exclamation.) The inner symbolic form of the revolution in *Ten Days That Shook the World* is that of transformation: men made into machines, and then, exhausted, collapsing into sleep. Such experiences did not depend upon personal conversion. One looks in vain in Reed's book for true political dialogue. The opposing sides are too bitterly entrenched, their hostility too little capable of compromise or reconciliation. This was part of what Reed learned in Petrograd in October 1917, and this absence of common ground was one of the fundamental assumptions which linked Reed to the Bolsheviks.

Reed's book marks a decisive break with the literary radicalism of his generation. The break was caused by the Bolshevik Revolution itself, though Reed showed himself in Colorado to be ready for it. American involvement in the First World War divided the Socialist Party. The Bolshevik Revolution divided it again. Afterwards, the nature of the appeal which the Communist Party made depended far less on personal experience or conversion testimony, than on the achievements and ideals of the revolution in Russia. The Socialist Party never regained the dominant place it formerly occupied on the American left. The conversion experience, so central to the way socialists imagined socialists could be made, faded away. So, too, faded the literature which gave imaginative expression to these hopes.

Ten Days That Shook the World ended with the Congress of Peasants' Soviets which was summoned to Petrograd by the Government of People's Commissars. The Social Revolutionaries, traditionally the party of the peasants, dominated the Peasants' Soviet and were strongly critical of the unbending policy of the Bolsheviks. Secret negotiations were underway to bring the Left Social Revolutionaries (who accepted most of the Bolshevik programme) into the 'Tsay-ee-kah' of the Soviet. This depended upon the peasants accepting the Land Decree, by which the great estates were broken up and private property in land forbidden. When an agreement was announced, a joint session of the two soviets confirmed the triumphant conclusion of this first phase of the revolution. It was an appropriate moment to end the book. In the course of Reed's final chapter he quotes from Lenin's courageous speech before the Peasants' Soviet. Differences between the Left Social Revolutionaries and the Bolsheviks were highlighted by earlier speeches, and no less firmly expressed by Lenin. 'The mistake of the Left Social Revolutionaries', he explained,

> lies in the fact that at that time when they supported the Provisional Government they did not oppose the policy of compromise, because they held the theory that the consciousness of the masses was not yet fully developed . . .
>
> *If Socialism can only be realized when the intellectual development of all the people permits it, then we shall not see Socialism for at least five hundred years* . . . The Socialist political party – this is the vanguard of the working class; it must not allow itself to be halted by the lack of education of the mass average, but it must lead the masses, using the Soviets as organs of revolutionary initiative . . .[70]

Trotsky noted in his *History* that 'Lenin did not for one moment bow down to any "sacred" spontaneousness of the masses'.[71] In an address to the Petrograd Bolsheviks, Lenin said that 'We cannot be guided by the mood of the masses: that is changeable and unaccountable. We must be guided by an objective analysis and estimate of the revolution.'[72] There could be no misunderstanding Lenin's attitude on this matter. Reed quoted Lenin's speech at the Peasants' Congress in *The Revolutionary Age* of 18 January 1919. Yet the whole of the article ('A New Appeal') was a criticism, by implication, of the Leninist position. Reed was far more pessimistic than Fraina, Ruthenberg or the leaders of the foreign language federations about the revolutionary mood of the American proletariat. In an earlier article ('Bolshevism in America') in *The Revolutionary Age* of 18 December 1918, Reed wrote that

> The American working class is politically and economically the most uneducated working class in the world. It believes what it reads in the capitalist press. It believes that the wage-system is ordained by God . . . It believes that Samuel Gompers and the American Federation of Labor will protect it as much as it can be protected. It believes that under our system of Government the Millennium is possible. When the Democrats are in power it believes the promises of the Republicans, and vice versa. It believes that Labor laws mean what they say. It is prejudiced against Socialism . . . In America for a long time there has been no free land, nor opportunity for workers to become millionaires. The working class does not yet know this.

A month later he returned to the historic and economic factors which shaped the consciousness of the American working class. Economic growth, natural resources and 'the fluidity of social boundaries' encouraged the American worker to believe, 'consciously or unconsciously, that he can become a millionaire or an eminent statesman'. Failing to understand that 'the day of universal opportunity' had passed, American workers remained impervious to the appeal of socialism. Reed wrote that the American worker 'does not see that *the whole complex structure of our civilization is corrupt from top to bottom* . . .' (my italics).

Reed interpreted the traditional propaganda of the Socialist Party in America as being essentially reformist:

The idea seems to be, 'First make a Liberal, and then convert him to Socialism.' This is my interpretation of Socialist campaign literature, and Socialist speakers at election time. Fully a third of the Socialist votes in normal times are, I think, cast by middleclass persons who think that Karl Marx wrote a good Anti-Trust Law . . .

Doubting whether such appeals actually worked, Reed explained his own way of making socialists:

My idea is to make Socialists, and there is only one way of doing that – by teaching Socialism, straight Socialism, revolutionary Socialism, international Socialism. This is what the Russian Bolsheviki did; this is what the German Spartacus group did. They approached not Socialists, but *people*: workers, peasants, soldiers who did not know what Socialism was. First, they found out from the working people what they wanted most. Then they made those wants into an immediate program, and explained how they were related to the other demands of the complete Social Revolution. And they explained, explained, eternally explained . . .

Reed advised those on the National Left Wing Council to 'find out from the American workers what they want . . . and they must make the workers want more – make them want the whole Revolution. They must do this in words which can be understood immediately by the workers, in terms of their own lives . . .'

In the context of European socialism, Reed was a Leninist. But in the domestic context one can see the heresy of American 'exceptionalism' taking root in his attempt to persuade his colleagues on the left wing to address resolutely the specific conditions and mentality of the American working class.[73] (In the mid-1920s the Communist Party faction led by Jay Lovestone, who looked to Bukharin for support within the Communist International, claimed the specific and exceptional features of American economic and political life largely exempted America from the Comintern theses on the imminent collapse of capitalism in the West.) Reed believed that the Russian Revolution had been made by the people. He was no less convinced that a socialist revolution in America could only occur if the vanguard party reached the masses and listened to them. Reed believed that only a 'practical' socialism could succeed. This helps to explain why Reed argued so strenuously that the left wing should stay within the Socialist Party.[74] Reed's politics were in this central respect closer to the Left Social Revolutionaries than to the Bolsheviks. He was a genuine revolutionary; but he was also an American. Although he had little intimate contact with Socialist Party politics, and was often critical of the party's policies and actions, he was, no less than the other Socialist Party writers of his generation, steeped in assumptions which were as much populist, syndicalist and democratic as they were Leninist. He believed that a major task of socialists lay in the making of more socialists. In this he was closer to William Morris than to Lenin. In other respects he accepted the lessons of the Bolshevik Revolution, and loyally defended its policies. But he seems to me a figure more comfortable on the left wing of the Socialist Party than one of the many former socialists gingerly trying to make their way through the minefield of the Comintern; he would not have prospered under Stalin.[75]

5 Proletarian Literature and the John Reed Clubs

In February 1921 Irwin Granich, not yet transformed into 'Michael Gold', published 'Towards Proletarian Art' in *The Liberator*.[1] This essay has been described as 'the first significant call in this country [the United States] for the creation of a distinctly and militantly working-class culture'.[2] What Gold meant by 'proletarian art' remains unclear. He uses 'proletarian' interchangeably with 'masses', and suggests that Walt Whitman was the discoverer, without quite realizing it, of proletarian art in America. The proletariat for Gold were nothing less than heroic possessors of Life – 'The masses know what Life is, and they live on in gusto and joy' – who have been thwarted by society from the full realization of their artistic and cultural heritage. Gold's thought was dominated by a lyrical and mystical celebration of the modern industrial worker, tinged by frustration at the bitter waste of human potential under capitalism. The only serious attempt anywhere in the world to encourage proletarian culture, Gold concluded, was being made by the Proletcult in Russia, where there was an 'organized attempt to remove the economic barriers and social degradation that repressed . . . proletarian instinct during the centuries'. A month later, writing again in *The Liberator*, Gold referred to the Proletcult as 'the evocation from the masses of the art and science latent in them, the creation of the workers' culture, based on human brotherhood and not on egotistic beauty-seeking in art'. Regular readers of *The Liberator* might have recognized the journal's handsome editor, Max Eastman, impaled by Gold's final phrase. Ironically, when Gold discovered the Proletcult, that organization had just lost its independence, and its leading ideologist, A. A. Bogdanov, had been summarily driven from political life by Lenin.[3] Not for the last time, Americans were poorly informed about events in the

Soviet Union and found themselves enthusiastically supporting positions which were being abandoned there.[4]

The principal sources of information in the West about the Proletcult were White Russian *émigrés* and their conservative sympathizers. John Cournos, writing on 'Proletarian Culture' in *The New Europe* (October and November 1919), was among the first to document the activities of the Proletcult. He made little pretence at objectivity, and had a sharp eye for the most extreme and damaging illustration. The Russian Liberation Committee in London, whose aim was 'the overthrow of Bolshevism, the restoration of order in and the regeneration of Russia', issued a pamphlet, *circa* 1919, entitled *Proletarian Culture*, by the distinguished historian M. I. Rostovtsev. His purpose, openly stated, was to denounce the 'total impotence in [Bolshevik] creative work' and the 'sickly, contradictory, reactionary class-ideology' of the Bolsheviks. *The Plebs*, journal of the Plebs League and voice of radical independent workers' education in Britain, one of the few journals actively sympathetic to the Proletcult, published articles by Lunacharsky, an old ally of Bogdanov, in October and November 1920.[5] The first detailed account of the thought of Lunacharsky, Poliansky and Bogdanov in English was by Eden and Cedar Paul in *Proletcult* (1921). The Pauls' perspective was closer to Ruskin College than to the Bolsheviks, and they were not very well informed of events in the Soviet Union, but they offered an account of some of the major ideas of the Proletcult.[6] Gold did not mention the Pauls' book,[7] but he seems to have shared their assumption that the Proletcult represented an extension of Western concerns with workers' education. On his first trip to Russia in 1924 Gold stopped off in England and attended the Bispham Summer School, where he met the editors of *The Plebs*. This was a fraternal call, since Gold was in 1924 one of the editors of *The Liberator*. *The Plebs* subsequently published a long poem by Gold in October 1924, which was accompanied by an editorial note mentioning his visit. This was not the only American connection with *The Plebs*. Maurice H. Dobb published a substantial essay on Thorstein Veblen in March 1925. A 'Response to Trotsky' by Max Eastman appeared in October, and in November a speech by H. W. L. Dana of Boston Trades Union College was published. Dana's topic was 'The Place of Literature in Workers' Education'.

Proletarian literature or culture occupies an uncertain place in socialist thought. It has no place in the scattered comments on literature of Marx and Engels, although it is directly related to the determination of the cultural and ideological superstructure by the means of production (the 'base') in Marxist theory. Nor does it appear in Plekhanov's *Art and Social Life* (1912–13). Lenin was opposed to it, as was Trotsky, whose brilliant polemic *Literature and Revolution* (1925) is in part directed against the idea. Bukharin, at first sympathetic towards proletarian cultural activity, became increasingly doubtful of the claim of any single group for dominance in cultural or literary fields. Among the leading Bolsheviks, only Lunacharsky was seriously interested in the question. Despite this formidable array of opponents, the concept of proletarian literature was at the heart of every major literary debate in the Soviet Union between 1918 and 1932. It emerged in the Communist literary movements in Europe and America at about the same time, and has remained a persistent element of left ideology to this day. The history of the concept has more than merely historical importance.

When Lenin thought of proletarian culture, it was mainly in terms of the need to raise the general cultural level of the Russian peasantry. The leading theoretician of proletarian culture, A. A. Bogdanov (1873–1928), was a disciple of Mach, and one of the leading 'Otzovists', who opposed participation in the Duma after the failed revolution of 1905, and for whom 'legal Marxism' was a contradiction in terms. Bogdanov's 'leftism', to use Lenin's word, had a philosopic basis of which it is perhaps sufficient to indicate that it drew him into bitter conflicts with Plekhanov (who directed *Materialismus Militans* in 1908–10 against Bogdanovism and philosophical idealism), and Lenin (*Materialism and Empiriocriticism*, 1909). Dominique Lecourt has argued that Bogdanov's ideas were regarded with considerable favour among Bolshevik intellectuals, and had a subterranean life in subsequent Soviet ideology.[8] Lecourt associates Bogdanovism with a disappointed populism, and suggests that it enabled Bolsheviks to justify an anti-peasant policy. After years of exile, Bogdanov returned to Russia in 1917 and founded Proletarian Culture, or Proletcult, with the express aim of extending the class war to every phase of Russian culture. His primary instruments for this were literary studios. By 1920 the Proletcult had become a mass movement, with some 450 000 members.[9] By any standards this was important revolutionary activity, and it was being conducted outside party direction, and in an area in which there was no official party policy. Bogdanov strongly asserted the independence of Proletcult from the party. However, what the Proletcult meant by the class war in cultural life is best seen in its hostility towards 'bourgeois specialists', the writers who had established themselves under Tsarist rule. Many of the leading figures of the Proletcult were not themselves of proletarian origin, and Bogdanov, in a lecture reprinted in *Labour Monthly* in September 1924, defended the value of the art of the past for the proletariat of the present day ('it should serve as a means to deepen and enlighten them, to extend their field over all the life of humanity, along all its path of toil . . .'). But the basic contradiction was plainly visible; what was the point of basing literary education in a socialist society upon the aristocratic and bourgeois writings of the past? It was strongly felt at the grassroots level of the Proletcult that a complete break with the culture of the past was necessary. There were also intellectuals saying this – e.g. the Futurists, led by Mayakovsky. It was a view enthusiastically expressed at the All-Russian Proletcult Congress held in Moscow in 1918: 'We are entering the new life with a load of proletarian consciousness. They went to load us with another excessive burden – the achievements of bourgeois culture. In that case we will be like an overloaded camel, unable to go any further. Let us throw away bourgeois culture entirely as old rubbish.'[10] There were humanistic and bourgeois arguments to place against this view, but it was harder to find Marxist ones.

Operating with the support of Lunacharsky in the Commissariat for Education, and of Bukharin in the pages of *Pravda*, the Proletcult was patronized by Zinoviev, Radek, and by the left wing of the Central Committee of the party. But Lenin's wife Krupskaya, who worked with Lunacharsky, strongly opposed the independence of the Proletcult and Lenin shared her suspicion, not only because Bogdanov was an old political and philosophical enemy, but because he doubted whether a culture could be created in this mechanical and arbitrary fashion. A more immediate cause for Lenin's attitude, however, may have been the attempt to form a Proletcult International in 1920. A small number of foreign delegates present in Moscow that summer for the second congress of the Communist International were invited to form a Central Bureau, and to issue a call for Proletcults to be formed throughout the world. For various reasons, the idea never got off the ground. The French delegate, for example, died in an accident on the way home. Yet the ambitions of Bogdanov and the Proletcult were plainly declared. In October 1920, with a dramatic intervention, Lenin brought the Proletcult under the control of the Commissariat for Education, and obtained Bogdanov's resignation.[11] In doing so, Lenin set a fateful precedent. Increasingly, attention was paid to a brief essay he wrote in 1905 on 'Party Organization and Party Literature'. In this ambiguous document Lenin asserted the need for strict control of party literature, by which he meant the political papers, magazines and other vehicles for party propaganda and debate which were being published legally in Russia for the first time. Although he was not laying down a policy for imaginative literature (something which runs against the grain of everything we know about Lenin), this essay was frequently cited by Stalinist functionaries, in an act one historian describes as a deliberate misreading, to justify party control over the whole range of imaginative literature.[12] Towards the end of her life Krupskaya stated that 'Party Organization and Party Literature', and other of Lenin's articles on the same topic from that period, 'do not concern literature as a fine art'.[13]

The ideas of Bogdanov survived in a distorted form in Russia, being taken up by various groups of young Komsomols and by writers and critics within the party. And the idea of literary studios and worker–correspondents remained with Mike Gold, and was later to serve as a model for a proletarian literary movement in America.

Gold tried to introduce worker–correspondents into the *New Masses*. The John Reed Clubs were an attempt to apply the Proletcult notion of literary studios to America. The idea of worker–correspondents, abbreviated 'worcorr' in the *Daily Worker* in emulation of the Russian 'Rabcor', came naturally to Gold. Literacy and education were matters of great importance within the Jewish ghetto in the lower East Side in New York, where Gold grew up. As well as there being a tradition of religious study and scholarship in the ghetto, workers' circles and educational alliances, groups sponsored by unions, Zionists, uptown German Jews, and by the innumerable *landsmannschaftn* (fraternal associations of emigrants from a particular village or province) competed to provide cultural and educational facilities for the newly arrived Jew. It was widely believed that education was essential if Jews were to prosper in America. Gold based his hope for a proletarian literary movement in America upon his experience of the Jewish proletariat in New York.[14] But the Jewish worker was not typical of other immigrants, nor of the native American working class. In any case, the creation of a proletarian culture in America was inconceivable in 1921, when the left was in total disarray. The deportations, police raids and sweeping prosecutions which followed the war effectively destroyed the socialists as even a modest political force. The Communists were an underground party, deeply divided by sectarianism.[15] Gold was not, one concludes, thinking about a proletarian literary movement in the left as it was in 1921.

The position of the American Communist Party, isolated from the trade unions and with little support from the native working class, seriously influenced the development of Marxist theoretical work. It was a party of immigrants, not of intellectuals. Little thought was given to the question of attracting such people to the party, though by the end of the 1920s events such as the defence of Sacco and Vanzetti brought figures like Dos Passos into sustained collaboration with the party. The leading American Marxist critic, V. F. Calverton, remained outside the party. Calverton's *The Newer Spirit* (1925) argued the fundamental materialist point that the economic 'base' determined the cultural and literary 'superstructure'. Thus Emerson was seen as 'the accurate manifestation of the sociology of the period'. Like Gold, Calverton regarded Whitman as the first American writer to 'put the muffled music of the swelling proletariat into poetry'.[16] There is a chapter on proletarian art in his *The Newer Spirit*, but it is all too typical of Calverton's taste for meaningless rhetoric and vague generalization. In the late 1920s he published long, pseudo-scholarly articles on 'Labor and Literature' and 'Literature and Economics' in party journals, in which he extended and documented a mechanical and reductive argument that literature is determined by social and economic factors.[17] Alfred Kazin, in a sympathetic portrait of Calverton, describes him as 'a remarkably unsubtle Marxist critic'.[18] Unlike Mike Gold, Calverton did not believe that a proletarian literature could be created *tout court*. By 1932, after he had broken with the Stalinists, Calverton somewhat disingenuously expressed doubts about whether the term 'proletarian' had any meaning in the context of American literature. Five years later, in an article appropriately entitled

'Proletarianitis', he had moved closer to Trotsky's sceptical position on this question.[19] Calverton's *The Liberation of American Literature* (1932) was not a book of notable critical discrimination. Lacking that, the substantial framework of economic and historical analysis served no useful purpose in the development of a Marxist critical theory. His periodical, *The Modern Monthly*, close in spirit to Eastman's *Masses* (it was one of the few periodicals on the left which remained open to Eastman in the 1930s), was perhaps his most important contribution to the left.

The bitter struggles in Russia over proletarianism made a belated appearance in America in 1925, with the publication of Rose Strunsky's translation of Trotsky's *Literature and Revolution*. Given Trotsky's position in Russia at that time, it received surprisingly enthusiastic reviews in the party press. Gold, in an otherwise rhapsodic notice in the *New Masses* in October 1926, politely disagreed with Trotsky over the question of whether the proletariat could expect to create a culture of its own. Later in 1925 the *Daily Worker* published an account of the conference of proletarian writers held in Moscow in January. (This article may have introduced the notion of 'literary Trotskyism' to American readers.) It was followed by an article by Robin E. Dunbar which was the first example on the American left of the spirit of the Proletcult.[20] Dunbar expressed nothing but contempt for bourgeois art, 'corrupted by sycofancy [*sic*], parasitism and class collaboration', which was only rivalled by his hatred of bohemians, 'lounge lizards and jazz hounds and sex degenerates'. The bitter tone, and priggishness, were equally characteristic of leftism in the 1920s. Calverton's urbane scholarship could not appear further removed in spirit than this. Dunbar goes on to give the Calvertons of the left a piece of advice: he had 'better turn common laborer, join the union, quit talking about art, and do a little work for Communism, if he wants to be remembered along with the blessed, like John Reed, Joseph Dietzgen and Daniel De Leon . . .'

The *New Masses*, founded in 1926, was initially open to all sorts of writers, many not on the left at all. Contributors included D. H. Lawrence, Robinson Jeffers and Allen Tate. The general tone of the *New Masses* was radical, of course, but not doctrinaire, and in this it proclaimed its descent from Eastman's *Masses*. A financial crisis in the late 1920s brought about a realignment of the editorial board. Mike Gold was briefly deposed as editor, but with Joseph

Freeman's proxy vote (sent from Moscow) he returned to transform the *New Masses* into a magazine of proletarian writing.[21] In an editorial Gold invited contributions from 'worker–correspondents':

> Confessions – diaries – documents
> Letters from hoboes, peddlers, small town atheists, unfrocked clergymen and schoolteachers –
> Revelations by rebel chambermaids and night club waiters –
> The sobs of driven stenographers –
> The poetry of steelworkers –
> The wrath of miners – the laughter of sailors –
> Strike stories, prison stories, work stories –
> Stories by Communist, I.W.W. and other revolutionary workers.[22]

This was the American equivalent of the call in Russia during the first Five Year Plan for 'a type of author–fighter who can take part simultaneously in production at his bench and in literary struggles, fighting pen in hand'.[23] Writers were strongly encouraged to write novels on *kolkhoz* life. Shock brigades of writers descended on far-flung construction sites, like the White Sea canal, and produced in record time massive documentary accounts. In America, Gold's appeal was both sentimental and populist – a combination perhaps unique in the worldwide Communist literary movement – and was aimed at young and unprofessional writers. Gold seems to have understood very little of what emerged from the sixth World Congress of the Comintern, held in Moscow during the summer of 1928. The official analysis concluded that the capitalist West was on the verge of a revolutionary crisis. Unceasing struggle was demanded against the 'mis-leaders' of the social democratic unions. Socialists were denounced as 'social fascists'.[24] Communist Party tactics became increasingly rigid and sectarian. On the literary front, the rise of the RAPP group of proletarian writers and critics was an unmistakable sign of the shift to the left.

Thus in Russia, in the aftermath of Lenin's move against the Proletcult in 1920, there were numerous groups competing for power in literary circles. The most radical of these identified themselves with a version of proletarianism which sought to transform all literary activity into class warfare. They launched a violent attack on the fellow travellers, their journal *Krasnaya Nov* (*Red Virgin Soil*), and its editor Alexander Voronskii, who was suspicious of attempts to inject party ideology into creative literature, emphasizing instead the cognitive value of art as a form of knowledge. Voronskii advocated a policy of collaboration with bourgeois literary 'specialists', and became a symbol of Lenin's New Economic Policy in Soviet culture.[25] The attacks on Voronskii and the fellow travellers reached such a scandalous level that an attempt was made to ease matters by a debate held in the Press Division of the Central Committee in May 1924. The final resolution, written by Bukharin and accepted as party policy a year later, reflected the NEP spirit of reconciliation. The debate and resolution was a striking example of 'NEP culture'.[26] On paper at least, Voronskii was vindicated. The proletarians' aggressive attempt to dominate Soviet literature was rebuked. While the party generally supported their aims, there could be no official support for the proletarians or any other literary group. The resolution called for open competition. In practice, the attacks on Voronskii and the fellow travellers such as Pilnyak and Zamyatin continued unabated. The proletarians, reorganized under a new name (VAPP, then RAPP), and a new leader (Leopold Averbakh), continued their aggressive polemics. The fall of Trotsky in 1927 made possible a concerted move against Voronskii, who was removed from the editorship of his magazine, expelled from the party as a Trotskyite, and exiled to Siberia.

Thus after three years of 'open competition', when the first Five Year Plan began in 1928 the proletarians of RAPP were the only surviving group. Fellow travellers and others were ruthlessly hounded, and RAPP became synonymous with an aggressive pursuit of the literary class war. Western critics have suggested that, for reasons not wholly clear at the time, the RAPP leadership was slightly less than enthusiastic about fulfilling the party's wish to integrate literature into the Five Year Plan by sending writers on tours of factories and collective farms.[27] At the moment when the RAPP leadership staged a brilliantly successful international congress of revolutionary writers at Kharkov in 1930, and to all appearances were unchallengeable in Soviet literary life, attacks began to appear in the press which culminated in Stalin's decree in April 1932 which abolished RAPP and all other existing literary groups in preparation for their eventual replacement by a single writers' union. Averbakh, who epitomized the sectarianism of the period from 1927 to 1932, was sent off to the Urals and disappeared from history. Few tears were shed on his behalf.[28] Western correspondents in Moscow, who saw this development in the light of other moves by Stalin in 1931 to improve the regime's relations with the intelligentsia, hailed the fall of RAPP as a major act of liberalization. There was, according to Louis Fischer, 'a new air of tolerance in intellectual fields'.[29]

The transformation of the *New Masses* into a Proletcult journal was a belated reflection of Stalin's shift to the left in 1928. In Soviet terms this involved a comprehensive politicization of literature. Gold, however, whose roots were in populist forms of cultural radicalism and whose career as a radical began with the anarchists, looked no further than the Proletcult ideal of tapping the genuine reservoir of literary hunger among elements of the American working class. Contributions came from a silk weaver in New Jersey (Martin Russak), a lumberman in Minnesota (Joseph Kalar), a taxi driver in New York (Herman Spector), and a farm labourer in the Midwest (Jack Conroy).[30] Many of the new contributors were unemployed. All of them were young. Those who had published already were likely to have appeared in small radical magazines or college papers. The irony was that under party tutelage a rough, unspoiled proletarian literature along the lines of the Proletcult began to take shape – approximately eight years after the Proletcult had been banned in Russia.

Between 1928 and 1930 the *New Masses* was a Proletcult magazine. But such was economic 'reality' in capitalist America that it became abundantly clear that the magazine could not survive as it was. In hindsight it may have been following an interesting direction, but it was not particularly attractive to the typical readers of literary magazines. The magazine could only be saved from bankruptcy if it returned to the publication of established writers. In November 1929 the editorial board formed the John Reed Club in New York, for younger writers. This in turn freed the *New Masses* for a more commercial editorial policy.

The foundation of the John Reed Club (JRC) was an important moment in the history of the left in American literature.[31] What the club represented is best understood through its slogan 'Art is a Class Weapon'. This emphasized a comprehensive rejection of 'Art for Art's Sake'. It also denied the idealist tradition in aesthetics, which sought to portray art in terms of its inner nature and forms. Behind the John Reed Club was the basic Marxist tenet that culture, in the last instance, is always class culture. By denying any transcendent meaning to art, the critics and writers in the club sought to regard it as an instrument in the struggle for social liberation. It was not neutral in the class struggle, and artists could no longer remain above the battle. Ultimately the JRC slogan promised to heal the separation of art and society which has become so characteristic in twentieth-century Western culture. Artists were offered a way to reintegrate themselves into society by committing themselves to the cause of the proletariat. Even more than a demand for social responsibility in art, it was a call for secular redemption. The appeals to wavering bourgeois writers in the *New Masses* had, between the lines, a clear message: sinners, save yourselves.

John Reed's name was an inspired choice, although Reed's mother Mary protested to Lincoln Steffens at its use for the club.[32] Reed was an intriguing and heroic figure on the American left, poet, journalist and revolutionary, and author of *Ten Days That Shook the World*. Reed was also one of the founding members of the Communist Party in America. The club's independence of the party was merely a polite fiction: Richard Wright received a small weekly salary from the party to act as organizer of the John Reed Club in Chicago.[33] (In 1932 Mike Gold referred to the clubs as having sprung up 'almost spontaneously'.[34]) It is doubtful whether there was a majority of party members within the clubs, though the party cell, or 'unit' as it was called, whether known to be party members or not, usually played a dominant role. The JRC appealed to writers who were socially conscious, but not necessarily only those who were Communists. There was a potential source of friction between the party faction who, we can assume, were mainly interested in using the JRC for political work, and those who were more interested in literature. The process of self-selection among the members probably worked strongly in favour of political commitment.

By any standards the growth of the clubs was remarkable. At the time of the national convention of the JRC in 1934, there were thirty clubs with over 1200 members. The national office was in New York. There was a *J.R.C. Bulletin*, first published in April 1934, and numerous literary magazines issued by the various clubs. The most prestigious was the *Partisan Review*, founded by two young members of the JRC in New York (Philip Rahv and 'Wallace Phelps' [William Phillips]). Outside New York, the JRC magazines tended to be rather modest, except in places like Los Angeles and Chicago, where literary talent was somewhat thicker on the ground.[35] The JRC in Carmel, California, to which Ella Winter belonged, was formed by young radicals who were mainly interested in defending migratory agricultural workers. In 1932 the JRC in Carmel had nine members, but an audience of 120 attended a talk by Lincoln Steffens on 'Why Communists Have to Be Blankety-Blanks'.[36] In New York the JRC organized a writers' school with courses on Marxism and literature taught by Joshua Kunitz, on poetry by Horace Gregory, on fiction by Edward Dahlberg, and on English prose by Kenneth Burke. A course on literary criticism was led by Philip Rahv, Jerre Mangione and 'Wallace Phelps'. The classes met on Monday nights, from 7.30 to 9.00. There were regular Sunday night discussions and lectures. John Chamberlain, Dahlberg, Burke and Kunitz took part in a panel discussion of 'Bourgeois and Proletarian Types in World Literature' held on 28 January 1934. Samuel Putnam gave a lecture on 18 February 1934 entitled 'From Dada to Revolution'. John Howard Lawson addressed the JRC Forum on 'The Fellow Traveller and Marxian Criticism'. Sender Garlin lectured on 'The Evolution of Theodore Dreiser' at the Philadelphia JRC. The Mexican muralist David A. Siqueiros spoke on 'The Road the American Artist Should Follow' on 30 May 1934. Located at 430 Sixth Avenue, the JRC was a meeting point for younger writers. The finances of the club were always uncertain. Money to launch the *Partisan Review* was raised by a public lecture on 'Literature and Fascism' by the English Marxist John Strachey.[37]

In addition to specifically literary activities, the JRC organized meetings to protest against war preparations, and to oppose the Dies Bill which threatened to deport aliens who were members of the Communist Party. The JRC countered anti-Soviet slanders, and contingents from the club participated in picket lines in New York, and marched behind a club banner, in May Day parades. But it is necessary to get the size of the club in perspective. At the Regional Conference of the JRC of the East, held in New York on 29 July 1933, Alan Calmer gave a report on the activities of the Writers' Club. He said there were 141 writer–members, of whom 80 were very active. Of the 100 members of the club who participated in the 1933 May Day parade, 60 were members of the Communist Party, of whom 20 were regarded as being very active in the organization. Calmer noted that although there was an expectation that manuscripts by members would be brought before the club for discussion before publication (Hicks's 'Toward a Proletarian Literature' was so treated), 'The most interesting manuscripts haven't been brought before the club, and as a result the inner life of the writers group organizationally is very weak.' His account of the political level was similarly pessimistic:

> We haven't in the club any organized opposition to Party leadership. I think that the club follows the Party leadership in a somewhat mechanical way, it follows its campaigns, doesn't raise any ideological questions. The club follows the Party leadership without much discussion of why the party has this particular point of view.[38]

For connoisseurs of such organizations, a comment by Conrad Komorowski, a left-wing Communist and official in the JRC, is worth savoring: 'There are no bourgeois writers in Kalamazoo, but neither are there proletarian writers . . .'

The artists' sections were equally active. Ivan Albright, Mitchell Siporin and many others contributed to annual 'proletarian art' exhibits in Chicago. An exhibit, 'The Social Viewpoint in Art', was held in New York in February 1933. Later that year the JRC in Chicago organized an exhibit of anti-war paintings and graphic art which was displayed outside the World's Fair. The Chicago Club also organized a showing of Käthe Kollwitz's drawings. An exhibition of work by black painters in support of the Scottsboro Boys, brought together by D. A. Siqueiros and the JRC in Los Angeles, was broken up by the Red Squad of the Los Angeles Police Department. Similar raids took place on the JRC in Philadelphia and elsewhere.[39] By 1934 the Artists' Union of the JRC was reported to have 750 members.[40]

Although the JRC was founded by members of the Communist Party, the club at first received no institutional recognition from the party itself. Nor was it affiliated to any of the left-wing organizations created within the Comintern, such as the International Organization of Revolutionary Literature (IORL), established in Moscow in 1927 when various writers were present in Russia to celebrate the tenth anniversary of the revolution.[41] A bureau was formed, with Bela Illes, a Hungarian Comintern functionary, as General Secretary. Henri Barbusse and Johannes Becher were on the executive. Illes was the editor of a journal entitled (in Russian) *Magazine of Foreign Literature.* The minimum programme for affiliation, as formulated in 1927, had little to do with literature, and a great deal to do with Soviet fears of an attack by the capitalist West. Writers were expected to call for a continued struggle against imperialist wars, and to oppose fascism and the White terror. The IORL transformed itself into an International Union of Revolutionary Writers (IURW) in 1928. Ludwig Renn indicated that it began with a membership of 300, which had increased to 350 at the time of the Kharkov congress in 1930. Affiliation to the IURW was on an individual basis, since there were no mass proletarian cultural organizations in the West in the 1920s. In consequence the IURW and the International Bureau of Revolutionary Literature (IBRL), its governing body, became accustomed to dealing with individual writers. This was to be a considerable source of friction between the bureau and the American delegation at Kharkov.

If the John Reed Clubs were seriously committed to a revolutionary cultural line, affiliation with the IURW was essential. The second congress of the union met at Kharkov in November 1930.[42] The American delegation, which was invited to the congress, represented the John Reed Clubs and the *New Masses.* It consisted of Fred Ellis, Michael Gold, William Gropper, Joshua Kunitz, A. B. Magil and Harry Alan Potamkin. The question of affiliation was of primary concern. The Americans complained that the bureau, by dealing directly with prominent American radicals like Upton Sinclair and Theodore Dreiser, prevented the creation of a mass organization of revolutionary writers. Their hope was that the John Reed Club would be recognized as an official section of the IURW in America. In speeches by Magil, Potamkin and Gropper, a vigorous though perhaps slightly optimistic picture was given of the activities of the JRC and the *New Masses.* These claims were received by other delegates with some derision. One speaker described the *New Masses* as 'the magazine of the left-wing "fellow travellers literature"'. Alexander Fadieev, speaking on behalf of RAPP, pointed out that the American criticism of the bureau was 'quite strange and empty' in the absence of any mass proletarian movement in America. In the next session Potamkin made a telling attack on the bureau: 'in France, where the mass movement is weak, the IBRL maintained connections with only one comrade – Barbusse: the results are well-known. In Rumania the IBRL relied upon Panait Istrati . . .' At Kharkov both Barbusse and Istrati were portrayed as notorious backsliders. Barbusse's conduct of the literary pages of *l'Humanité* and *Monde* came in for pointed criticism in the conference resolutions. He was the only individual to be singled out in this fashion. Potamkin opposed the admission of Upton Sinclair to membership of the bureau (an argument, given the relative importance of Sinclair and Potamkin, which was not likely to carry much weight), but his general point concerned ineffective communications:

> Hitherto all the relations between the IBRL and the USA have taken place through comrade Joseph Freeman and the [John Reed] Club had almost no knowledge even about the existence of the IBRL; its information was gathered from the press and not through direct relations.

The debate at this point drifted off to the situation in the Ukraine.

At the next session Michael Gold referred to his attempt 'to make the ideology of this journal [*New Masses*] distinctly proletarian'. Joseph Freeman describes this attempt as having taken place in 1927, when Gold was briefly removed from the editorial board for inefficiency.[43] To Freeman, then living in Moscow, this seemed 'objectively a vote for playboyism [i.e. Eastmanism?] in literature and politics'. He sent Gold his proxy support. As has been indicated, the reorientation of the *New Masses* which occurred in 1928 turned the periodical strongly towards a proletarian line. Freeman returned from Moscow in 1927, but we know little of his role as IBRL representative in America, other than the fact that young sectarians such as Potamkin seem to have resented Freeman's curiously free-floating authority on cultural matters. It would also be nice to know why Freeman was not invited by the Bureau of the IURW to attend the Kharkov conference.

There was surprisingly little attention paid at Kharkov to the meaning of the term 'proletarian literature'. In the West the term was used interchangeably for literature by proletarians, or literature for proletarians, or literature about the proletariat. For the party, the problem with the first definition was that it placed far too strong an emphasis on the class of the writer, and would, if strictly taken, exclude all writers of bourgeois origin. The second usage described an intended readership, and the third was a subject-matter. At Kharkov the term was used without great precision, and usually meant literature written in explicit commitment to the policies of the vanguard party of the proletariat. The definition of 'proletarian literature' in party usage corresponded to none of the common meanings of the phrase. It meant, quite explicitly, literature written in conscious alignment with Communist Party policy. The Kharkov programme has been summarized by Max Eastman in *Artists in Uniform* (1934):

1. Art is a class weapon . . .
2. Artists are to abandon 'individualism' and the fear of strict 'discipline' as petty bourgeois attitudes.
3. Artistic creation is to be systematized, organized, 'collectivized', and carried out according to the plans of a central staff like any other soldierly work.
4. This is to be done under the 'careful and yet firm guidance' of the Communist Party.
5. Writers and artists of the rest of the world are to learn how to make proletarian art by studying the experience of the Soviet Union.
6. 'Every proletarian artist must be a dialectical materialist. The method of creative art is the method of dialectical materialism.'
7. 'Proletarian literature is not necessarily created by the proletariat, it can also be created by writers from the petty bourgeoisie', and one of the chief duties of proletarian writers is to help these non-proletarian writers 'overcome their petty bourgeois character and accept the view-point of the proletariat'.[44]

Artists in Uniform was and is a powerful book, perhaps Eastman's best. The indictment he makes of Soviet cultural policy has been confirmed by many scholars in the West. Eastman was, of course, reviled as a Trotskyite and renegade by party critics. It is not necessary to accept this perspective on Eastman to point out that his account of the Kharkov programme is seriously damaged by distortions and fabrications. In the 'Resolution on Questions of

International Proletarian and Revolutionary Literature', printed in the special number of *Literature of the World Revolution* in 1931, many of the words and phrases used by Eastman are not to be found. The implication of his account is that the Kharkov programme was virulently leftist. Yet in the printed text, making allowance for the condensation of speeches and other material and awkward translations, the political line is cautious, whereas Eastman presents it as headstrong. There is no mention, for example, of 'collectivized' artistic creation. The second item is simply not part of the Kharkov programme as it appears in the printed text. Nor is the party's role spelled out as Eastman suggests in the fourth item. Equally serious are the distortions caused by removing a phrase from its context. Eastman prints 'Art is a class weapon' (in fact, the slogan of the John Reed Clubs), where the printed resolution reads 'Proletarian literature is nothing more than a weapon in the class struggle': what was appropriately qualified at Kharkov appears as a universal in Eastman. His sixth item is formed by a similar process. The Kharkov resolution reads 'every proletarian artist must be a dialectic materialist. The creative method of proletarian literature is the method of dialectic materialism.' Eastman drops the qualifying 'proletarian' in the second sentence, so it reads 'The method of creative art is the method of dialectical materialism.' Eastman's version is cruder than the original, but, from his point of view, a great deal more useful for his anti-Stalinist polemics. The Kharkov programme was, to be sure, Stalinist, but it was neither as grotesquely ominous nor as totalitarian as portrayed by Eastman. He presents a leftist caricature of Kharkov.

There were, in fact, some interesting things said at Kharkov which Eastman ignored. The speeches by Aragon and the Letter from Barbusse attempted to inject an element of realism into the Soviet picture of the literary situation in Western Europe. The long address by Becher on war danger and the proletarian writer points out that despite being a 'literature of the masses', the work of proletarian writers had failed to attract a mass readership. The thought of what actually constituted popular reading in Germany, that 'black abyss', left Becher momentarily speechless. This dizzying glimpse of the true depths of popular taste reminds us of a persistent absence in Marxist writing between the wars: 'popular culture', for obvious ideological reasons, was ignored when it was not simply dismissed. It was a major weakness in the

Marxist analysis of capitalist culture that the crucial phenomenon of mass reading and entertainment was of so little interest.

Kharkov was dominated by RAPP, and by the RAPP concern that proletarian literature be regarded in terms of content and ideology and not in terms of class. The constant reference to the need to win over fellow travellers may have sounded implausible from an Averbakh, but it corresponded to the needs of Western groups. The alternative, constantly denounced, implied a leftist exclusivism. It was in this area that the American delegation disagreed with the conference position. In the American resolution there was a shift of emphasis, which called for an extension of the proletarian base of the *New Masses*.[45] This was later to be described as an example of 'ultra-left sectarianism' by one of the participants.[46] The John Reed Club delegation in effect proposed to proletarianize the *New Masses* at the moment when IURW was reemphasizing the need to win over progressive elements of the bourgeoisie. Though this was not yet the appeal of the popular front, and the struggle of 'class against class' (another Comintern slogan from this period) was intensifying, at least in party polemic, it was still necessary for the General Secretary to rebuke the 'feverish radicalism' of Harry Allan Potamkin from the JRC delegation.

Michael Gold led the minority of the US delegation which favoured strict adherence to the IURW line.[47] The majority, led by A. B. Magil, were leftists.[48] This split was carefully concealed in the conference report which appeared in the *New Masses* in February 1931, and was flatly denied by Magil in 1934. The split accurately reflected divisions within the John Reed Clubs, particularly over the proper attitude towards fellow travellers. Philip Rahv, at the age of 24, was the voice of leftism: 'A more definite frontier between the proletarian and the bourgeois in letters should be established.' Compare this with S. Gopner, speaking for the Executive Committee of the Comintern, at Kharkov: 'The organization of revolutionary writers must not erect a superfluous barrier between itself and those whose revolutionary instinct is greatly developed, but who have not succeeded as yet to come to any definite standpoint, who have not yet acquired firm Marxist views.' A weighty reply from within the party, accusing Rahv of 'abstract schematism and formalism', quickly followed.[49] On the left of the JRCs there was little patience with fellow travellers. Even Dos Passos was criticized within the JRC for publishing in the liberal journal *Common Sense*.[50] Mike Gold, willy-nilly on the left and right of the JRC, gave a hint of the new mood in an aggressive and insulting piece on Thornton Wilder, who was no fellow traveller but an eminently bourgeois writer. It was followed by a review, in which Gold described Archibald MacLeish as an 'unconscious fascist'.[51] The right in the JRCs, which contained most of the talented writers and critics, wanted a more flexible and sophisticated approach to the party's handling of doctrine. Thinking of the impact of crudely sectarian attacks upon bourgeois intellectuals, they favoured a more tactful tone. On issue after issue the sides divided, although the composition of right and left within the clubs altered and was always likely to be influenced by personal and subjective factors which never appeared in print. It is sometimes theory which underlies this political split, but also a judgement of tone and tactics.

A year after Kharkov the IURW published a survey of the performance of the *New Masses*.[52] One student described the criticism as 'harsh and microscopic'.[53] The journal was accused of having no plan or strategy for action against the class enemy in literature. Its struggle against fascism was inadequate. There had been silence over the social fascists Max Eastman and V. F. Calverton which the IURW felt could no longer be tolerated. Insufficient attention was paid to the achievements of socialist reconstruction in the Soviet Union. There was a 'general theoretical backwardness' evident in the pages of the *New Masses* which revealed confusion over 'the most fundamental questions of proletarian literary theory'. At the root of these errors and shortcomings lay 'the insufficient politization of the whole work of the *New Masses*'. In an examination of another American left-wing literary magazine, the IURW concluded that the flaws of the *New Masses* were characteristic of American revolutionary literature as a whole.[54] There was an 'inadequate mastery of the militant Marxist–Leninist outlook' demonstrated in the American tendency towards 'an empirical recording of events . . . without outlining the ways of their revolutionary transformation'. The IURW text was summarized in the *New Masses* in September 1932, after a nine-month silence which can best be interpreted as a sign of a major struggle within the editorial board. The dimensions of that struggle may be hinted at in Joseph Freeman's account of his attempt in 1931 and 1932 to reorganize the *New*

Masses, replace the party hacks, and create a magazine 'which a trained mind would listen to with respect and with intellectual profit'.[55] Freeman regarded the whole of the existing Marxist criticism in America as 'mechanical and childish', and called for writers and artists to be released from routine party chores. (Was he thinking of the request the party made to Richard Wright to abandon a novel in progress and organize a committee to study the cost of living?) This was a move, a *putsch*, against leftism within the John Reed Clubs. In 1932 such a policy was premature. Even the right, one suspects, could not see that the logic of their position ultimately required a different analysis of the state of capitalism in America than that which was put forward by the Comintern. This would lead to a split within the party, and a return to the Lovestoneite thesis of 'American Exceptionalism' which had been defeated within the party, at Stalin's insistence, in 1929.[56]

In the end the IURW criticisms were accepted. Old friends and former collaborators of Calverton broke off relations, and a massive attack on him appeared in the *New Masses*. The 'draft manifesto' of the John Reed Clubs, published in the *New Masses* in June 1932, placed great stress upon adherence to the Kharkov line:

Today there are thirteen John Reed Clubs throughout the country. These organizations are open to writers and artists whatever their social origin, who subscribe to the fundamental program adopted by the international conference of revolutionary writers and artists which met at Kharkov, in November 1930. The program contains six points . . .
(1) Fight against imperialist war, defend the Soviet Union against capitalist aggression;
(2) Fight against fascism, whether open, or concealed, like social-fascism;
(3) Fight for the development and strengthening of the revolutionary labor movement;
(4) Fight against white chauvinism (against all forms of Negro discrimination or persecution) and against the persecution of the foreign born;
(5) Fight against the influence of middle-class ideas in the work of revolutionary writers and artists;
(6) Fight against the imprisonment of revolutionary writers and artists, as well as other class-war prisoners throughout the world.

It is perhaps in response to the IURW criticism of 'insufficient politization' in the work of the American comrades that the entire literary dimension of the John Reed Clubs has been replaced by political imperatives. This is the most striking consequence of Kharkov on the American left.

The second national convention of the John Reed Clubs met in Chicago in 1934.[57] The warfare between right and left continued, but there was a perceptible move towards the right by the party leadership. A resolution condemning 'sloganized tracts disguised as poetry and fiction' was passed. Alexander Trachtenberg, director of the party's publishing house and the link between the Central Committee and the JRCs, spoke at length against sectarianism. He proposed that the clubs organize a national congress of writers. Such a gesture was an open hand extended towards the bourgeois literary world. The implication was that it was time to move away from the specifically proletarian and political concerns of the JRC, as outlined in the 'draft manifesto'. Apparently few delegates saw this in Trachtenberg's proposal. At a hotel in Chicago that night the full meaning was spelled out. The party was shifting towards a people's front, and the John Reed Clubs, which had been the instrument of the sectarian policy of 'class against class', were to be dissolved. The younger writers would have no role in the new organization, to be called the League of American Writers. And so the John Reed Clubs disappeared with little fuss. Leon Dennen pointedly observed that it was undemocratic to disband an organization without consulting its membership. For this protest Dennen was excluded from the 'call' for the League when it was published in 1935. Five years after Kharkov, the entire literary strategy of the party was abandoned.

From 1921, when Mike Gold issued his call for a proletarian literature, until 1930, when the 'correct' line was established at Kharkov, the example of the Proletcult was the dominant influence on the American literary left. In this period Gold, at first almost single-handedly and then in the *New Masses*, sought to create an American proletarian literature. Between 1930 and 1934 the IURW, following the left turn of the Comintern, emphasized a policy which wholly integrated literature within the class struggle. The John Reed Clubs were created for this purpose, but the literary dimension of JRC activities progressively withered under party and IURW pressure. From 1935 the party's attempt to create a people's front was accompanied by a substantial move to the right. Leftism and sectarian attitudes were to be avoided. The JRCs were dissolved and the term 'proletarian literature' disappeared from the pages of the *New Masses*. Interest in a specifically proleterian or Communist or revolutionary literature was replaced by the more immediate need to establish good working relations with writers like Archibald MacLeish and Ernest Hemingway, figures who had been bitterly attacked by party critics just a year or two before. Big names, prominent bourgeois writers, were now at the centre of party policy, for which the League of American Writers was the main vehicle. At each stage of its brief career, proletarian literature followed as closely as possible the current Soviet line. This attempt is so obvious that the experience of the left in American literature is scarcely comprehensible without a firm grasp of the ways in which Soviet literary policy was emulated.[58] The call for the League of American Writers followed closely on the heavily-publicized meeting of the All-Russian Congress of Writers in the summer of 1934, so closely in fact that the similarity was widely noticed. The emulation goes even further. What else could Earl Browder and Alexander Trachtenberg, the General Secretary and the literary commissar of the Communist Party, have been thinking when they stepped in to dissolve the John Reed Clubs in 1934, other than Lenin's move against the Proletcult in 1920, and Stalin's summary dissolution of RAPP in 1932?

6 Edmund Wilson Turns Left

The 1920s ended on a mixed note for Edmund Wilson. His first book of literary criticism, *Axel's Castle*, was nearing completion, in which he suggested the end of an era: 'though we shall continue to admire them as masters, [Proust, Valéry, Joyce, Eliot and Stein] will no longer serve us as guides'.[1] He was busy divorcing his wife Mary and had decided to marry Margaret Canby. Wilson's working-class mistress, Anna, would obviously have to be told. Her parting words were recorded in his journals from the 1920s: '"Well," she said sadly, "I'll have to look for another lover."' Anna advised him not to cheat on his new wife. 'Goodbye, be good to Margaret', she advised. (Their affair was resumed a year and a half later while Margaret was in California.) That evening Wilson discovered that Anna had infested him with crabs, 'a whole community in various stages of development'. He soon learned that she had also given him gonorrhea: 'After we parted and I had discovered crabs, she began to fade into the dinginess of some of my first impressions of her, to blend with and disappear in the grayness of the winter pavements.'[2]

That was the trouble with 'de Voikus' (as Malcolm Cowley sardonically described the working classes). Every time you got close to them, they faded into the 'dinginess' of urban life, or gave you cause for fear or regret. While in Pineville, Kentucky, where Wilson had gone in 1932 as part of a delegation to publicize the plight of striking miners, he noted a 'feeling of gloomy distaste' for those at a protest meeting. Wilson wrote in his diary that he 'didn't know the people and didn't like them much', and those he knew were like himself, people who had gone in for the thing 'out of curiosity, exhibitionism, or desire for drama'. The rest were 'queer equivocal anomalous people – Mongrel Negroes and Jews, thyroid women'.[3] Having been to an exclusive private school, and

141

then Princeton, Wilson had little contact with the 'masses', and nothing had happened to prepare him for life in the US army:

> You have no idea, seriously [he wrote to Stanley Dell in 1917], how isolated and inward you become, surrounded by and dealing with people with whom you cannot talk the real language, whose habits and manners you detest, and with whom the only qualities which you have in common are the qualities which you would most willingly destroy forever . . . This is not the absence of charity on my part, it is only the reaction of intelligence.[4]

These sentiments will have to be kept in mind as we trace Wilson's political evolution in the 1930s. He was not one of nature's democrats. He registered the working class as an alien, threatening presence. While travelling through Brooklyn, at the height of his period as a Marxist in 1932, he observed the 'sordid roofs packed for miles' and was 'moved for a moment by a vision of that immensity of anonymous life'.[5] Returning from Provincetown in 1934, Wilson described himself as feeling that 'the people in the streets looked like sinister specters – I was almost afraid of them, looked askance at them uneasily as if they might be going to bite or slug me.'[6]

When he described his affair with Anna in 'The Princess with the Golden Hair', the longest story in *Memoirs of Hecate County* (1946), class-consciousness coloured Wilson's account of their relationship, from the narrator's instinctive distaste of Anna's crudities to his transformation of her into a symbol of proletarian-organic life. The stories she told him about her work as a waitress gave new meaning to the indignation he felt while reading the 'hideous industrial chapters' of *Das Kapital*. She helped him escape from the 'prison of the social compartments':

> it was Anna who had made it possible for *me* to recreate the actuality; who had given me that life of the people which had before been but prices and wages, legislation and technical progress, that new Europe of the West Side and Brooklyn for which there was provided no guidebook.[7]

(And perhaps it was Anna who enabled Wilson to write so

sympathetically of Engels, and his Irish working-class mistress Mary Burns, in *To the Finland Station*.)

By the end of the 1920s, Wilson noted that a few writers in America were beginning to provide that 'guidebook' to the life of the people. He praised John Dos Passos for trying to 'take the social organism seriously'.[8] In 1930, while completing the last chapter of *Axel's Castle*, Wilson reviewed Edward Dahlberg's *Bottom Dogs*, a novel set amidst the orphanages, barber shops, bakeries and dance-halls of the proletarian Middle West. Wilson liked Dahlberg's language, describing it as 'hard, vivid, exact and racy, and with an odd kind of street-lighted glamor'. And he was struck by the way Dahlberg transmuted 'the rawest, the cheapest, the most commonplace American material' into fiction. The distaste he felt in 1917 for those who did not speak the 'real language' had now given way before a new interest in 'commonplace America material', but in other respects Wilson in 1930 was still the same person. He concluded that Dahlberg's book, and the current American crisis, had a wider meaning for intellectuals:

> The task of the intellectual is not merely to study the common life but to make his thoughts and symbols *seem* relevant to it – that is, to express them in terms of the actual American world without either cheapening them or rendering them vapid.[9]

For the 'thoughts and symbols' to *be* relevant, as opposed to merely seeming to be so, would suggest a different role for the intellectual. But in 1930, direct commitment to socialism or to the class struggle was far from what he had in mind. The assumption here is that the writer will impose his 'thoughts and symbols' most successfully by expressing them in terms of the common life. It was more a matter of 'intelligence' deftly adjusting approach and style than seriously challenging the function of the artist in bourgeois society. What was at least new in all this, for Wilson as for his generation, was the conscious desire to grasp the 'actual American world'. It was closing time in Axel's castle; 'the private imagination in isolation from the life of society seems to have been exploited and explored as far as for the present is possible'.[10]

The 1930s was a brilliant period for political journalism,

reportage and travel writing. Sociologists in America were producing close, empirical studies of smalltown life and of ethnic subcultures. Documentary films and photographs, social-realist paintings and murals and 'proletarian' novels all attest to the growing concern to see and record the actual. The major work of the Federal Writers' Project was a massive series of guidebooks and histories of the 48 states. Wilson played a part in clearing the way for what became the central political–aesthetic style of the decade, when he published *The American Jitters: A Year of the Slump* in 1932. Wilson was a tireless recorder of conversations, momentous or trivial, and wrote vividly of the look of American landscapes and cities. In the 1930s, he was a man with a notebook, scribbling away on a train, in Chicago, Kentucky or Moscow, a man alive to the main currents of his time. Dos Passos's journalist in *The Big Money* (1936) was such a man: 'pencil scrawls in my notebook the scraps of recollection the broken halfphrases the effort to intersect word with word to dovetail clause with clause to rebuild out of mangled memories unshakably (Old Pontius Pilate) the truth'.[11]

Wilson was too level-headed, too well-launched on a literary career in the 1920s, to share the cultural despair of the expatriates. He had hopes of New York as a 'cultural center': 'it seems to me that there is a lot doing intellectually in America just now [1921] – America seems to be actually beginning to express herself in something like an idiom of her own.'[12] As late as 1929, while praising Dos Passos's attempt to deal with the 'social organism', Wilson found his friend's pessimism excessive, his picture of America too melodramatic and biased. He felt there were essential things which transcended politics: 'Under however an unequal distribution of wealth, human beings are still capable of enjoyment, affection and enthusiasm – even of integrity and courage.'[13] At the moment when the John Reed Club was being founded in New York, the liberal agenda was still essentially intact for Wilson, at least until the collapse of the stock market in 1929 and the depression which followed.[14] Looking back on that period years later, he picked out two events which had shaken the faith of liberals even before the collapse: the execution of Sacco and Vanzetti in August 1927, and the impotance of liberals before the bitter labour conflict in Gastonia, North Carolina, in 1929. But for Wilson himself, the stroke which removed Herbert Croly from active participation in the political direction of *The*

New Republic in the late 1920s enabled Wilson to write on politics. When Croly died in May 1930, the editorial collective allowed him even further scope to explore his discontents with American life. 'Politically I am going further and further to the left', he wrote to Allen Tate in May 1930, 'and have moments of trying to become converted to American Communism . . .'[15]

That summer in Provincetown Wilson talked endlessly with John Dos Passos about the political situation. Agreeing that 'the Communist Party with its pedantic Marxism is impossible', Dos Passos half-seriously wondered whether a 'radical millionaire' could be persuaded to hire a publicity expert like Ivy Lee (who did such impressive work on behalf of Rockefeller in Colorado in 1914) 'to use American publicity methods to convert the Americans to Communism'.[16] The need to Americanize Communism, an old theme of John Reed's, was repeatedly hammered home by Dos Passos: 'the extraordinary thing about Americans', he wrote to Wilson in January 1931, 'is that while they strain at a gnat of doctrine, they'll swallow an elephant of experiment – the first problem is to find a new phraseology that we'll be at home with to organize mentally what is really happening now . . .'[17]

Wilson's first major political intervention was 'An Appeal to Progressives' in the *New Republic* on 14 January 1931. He argued that the unfolding economic disaster had caught out liberals and progressives who had been counting on a 'benevolent and intelligent capitalism' to act as the motor of social change. It was a charge that was effective and accurate: 'we . . . have been betting on capitalism' and have lost and have nothing in its place. 'The future is as blank in the United States today as the situation is desperate . . .'[18] Recognizing that even though radicals and progressives in America repudiated Marxist dogma and the strategy of the Communist Party, Wilson urged that they must, to save liberalism itself, 'take Communism away from the Communists and take it without ambiguities'. The American 'traditional idealism' and 'genius for organization' may, now that the full meaninglessness of life under capitalism has been revealed by the depression, turn to a more radical social experiment. 'An Appeal to Progressives' sets out an interpretation of the current situation, and a tactic enabling liberals to '*seem* relevant' to the common life. American liberals, since the heyday of Herbert Croly, had rejected the Marxist expectation of increasing class conflict, but Wilson, as he observed President Hoover, and listened to the President's hopeful reiteration that the nation only needed 'confidence' to get back on its feet, concluded that something more drastic was required. Wilson's loathing of Hoover reached a low, or high, point in the summer of 1932 when the Bonus Marchers were driven out of Washington. In a letter to Waldo Frank he described Hoover as 'something hardly human which has emanated from the primary sordid substratum of the life of the commercial-industrial era, an amoeba with nothing but self-nourishing and self-protecting instincts'.[19] While emphasizing the need for social control and economic planning, Wilson was writing from within American liberal thought and to a liberal readership. But his message was that liberal nostrums were not enough. The country's ills could only be cured, he thought, by the application of radical measures. The editors of the *New Republic* sent a proof of Wilson's article to Stuart Chase and printed Chase's reply, a spirited personal defence. Other liberals were not quite the supine figures of Wilson's imaginings. Charles A. Beard's 'The Myth of Rugged American Individualism' appeared in *Harper's Magazine* in December 1931, in which Beard showed how little the business community, anxious for subsidies and import restrictions as their markets collapsed, acted in accordance with traditional American beliefs in individualism.

Wilson read Karl Marx during the bleak winter of 1931–2, and launched an even more pointed attack on Chase, Beard and Walter Lippmann, prophets of liberalism:

> Who today in any camp on the left can have the optimism to believe that capitalism is capable of reforming itself? And who today can look forward with confidence to any outcome from the present chaos short of the establishment of a socialistic society – not like the Russian: how could it be? America is not Russia – but with this in common with Russia: that it shall aim to abolish all social classes and private enterprise for private profit.[20]

At every stage in his radicalization (except for a brief moment after he went to Moscow in 1935), the firm distinction Wilson drew between the Russians and the Americans was emphasized. It was, in a sense, a signal to uncertain liberals that he had not gone naive about the two countries. At another level, it is possible that it provided him with a structure of comparisons, a way of understanding both societies through their uniquenesses. However bleak things in America seemed, he tried to keep the many and profound differences in view which separated the two societies. Converts to Marxism customarily emphasized the similarities, sometimes to the point of wild overexaggeration; Wilson tried to keep his historical judgements clear of such wishful thinking.

In February 1932 Wilson joined a party of 'liberals' led by Waldo Frank which travelled to Bell County, Kentucky, under the auspices of International Labor Defense, to examine labour conditions. Theodore Dreiser had led an earlier group (which included Dos Passos) which visited Kentucky in November 1931. Their report, entitled *Harlan Miners Speak*, and the publicity surrounding their trip, did much to rouse liberal interest in the conditions of striking coal miners. Wilson seems to have retained his sense of humour about the people and events in Kentucky, but referred to them in his account of Russia in *Travels in Two Democracies* in a passage which helps us understand what it meant to be a fellow-traveller in the 1930s:

> I always find that Americans who become bitter over espionage in Russia have never had any experience of what may happen in the United States in any industrial center. These people have never been made uncomfortable at home, because they have never been suspected of supporting the interests of labor against the interests of the employing class. So I was not made uncomfortable in Russia, because I was a visiting journalist known to be sympathetic with the Soviet regime. In America, the visiting journalist whose sympathies are not known, though he may be merely reporting strikes or even merely looking at factories, soon finds the police and the officials checking up on his lodgings and his movements; and in the ruder and more remote communities, he is likely to be confronted with the gun-thugs who threaten to run him out of town. If he is known to be engaged in pro-labor work, he may be followed on the train by a detective and very likely *will* be run out.[21]

But he would be not executed, or given a 20-year sentence to Kolyma or the Lena River. The differences between the two societies were dishonestly being obscured in such passages, but they are comparatively small in number and importance. There is another point worth emphasizing about Wilson's visit to Kentucky in 1932. Where John Reed and Max Eastman travelled independently to Colorado in 1914 as working journalists, and where Sinclair went as an individual, the groups led by Dreiser and Frank in 1931–2 were, as it became clear later, pawns in an orchestrated political campaign. Wilson sensed something of this. Although he joined the National Committee for the Defense of Political Prisoners, along with Dos Passos, on his return to New York, he wrote to the novelist that he planned to stay clear of similarly manipulated occasions: 'if the literati want to engage in radical activities they ought to organize or something independently – so that they can back other people besides the comrades and so that the comrades can't play them for suckers . . .'[22] On the face of it, Wilson and Dos Passos were willing fellow-travellers, but it is already clear that they both were increasingly anxious to separate their interest in Marxism, and sympathy for the Soviet Union, from their attitudes towards Communists in America. Dos Passos's point had stuck firm. Wilson's admiring words in *The American Jitters* about the leading Bolsheviks ('they are men of superior brains who have triumphed over the ignorance, the stupidity and the shortsighted selfishness of the masses, who have imposed on them better methods and ideas than they could ever have arrived at by themselves')[23] did not extend to the 'comrades' in America.

On his return from Kentucky, Wilson drew up in conjunction with Dos Passos, Lewis Mumford, Waldo Frank and Sherwood Anderson a 'Manifesto' which they proposed to circulate to other writers. The main points of agreement were that a 'new social-economic order' was needed, in which economic rivalry and private profit would be barred; that the ruling class must be expelled from its present position of power; that there was a 'fundamental identity of interest' between writers, workers and farmers; that 'a temporary dictatorship of the class-conscious workers' was needed to abolish classes based on private property; and that the ultimate aim of the revolution was 'a new human culture based on common material possessions'.[24] While willing to sign the 'Manifesto', Dos Passos was sceptical about its language and sincerely doubted that it would 'cause any bankers to jump out of fiftieth storey windows'.[25] He told Wilson that the language of the 'Manifesto' showed too many signs of Communist Party influence. 'I think the only useful function people like us can perform anyway is introduce a more native lingo into the business –',[26] a theme which reappears several times in *The Big Money*, especially in the grim scene in which Mary French waits for Don Stevens: 'She was too sleepy to follow what they were talking about, but every now and then the words centralcommittee, expulsions, oppositionists, splitters rasped in her ears.'[27] In 'The Camera Eye (49)' Dos Passos had written of the need to 'rebuild the ruined words worn slimy',[28] but his suggested alterations seemed to Wilson 'incomplete and lack[ing] concision' although he agreed that the 'manifesto' would have a broader appeal if they were adopted.[29]

News of Wilson's move to the left rippled across the literary community. Hemingway heard in Key West of Wilson's conversion and wrote asking Scott Fitzgerald if he, too, had become a Communist.[30] News that Wilson had been teaching a mutual friend the fundamentals of Marxism and Leninism struck Fitzgerald with 'amazement'. He advised Wilson to go 'Back to Mallarmé'.[31] After visiting Wilson in New York, Fitzgerald wrote to Max Perkins that he looked 'gloomy': 'A decision to adopt Communism definitely, no matter how good for the soul, must of necessity be a saddening process for anyone who has ever tasted the intellectual pleasures of the world we live in.'[32] Archibald MacLeish, no admirer of Wilson, linked his conversion to Communism with Ezra Pound's new interest in economic theory as further signs of an 'arid industrialism' in American letters.[33] When the second part of Wilson's 'Literary Class War' appeared in the *New Republic* (11 May 1932), with its suggestion that 'nine-tenths of our writers would be much better off writing propaganda for Communism than doing what they are at present: that is, writing propaganda for capitalism . . . I wish we had a Magnitogorsk and that they could all be sent there',[34] Hemingway lost his temper:

Wilson writing he would send us other writers to write patriotism about some bloody factory – (He knows what's good for people) – Like hell he would. He wouldn't send me anywhere.

If things were like that I would kill him so damned quick – oh hell what's the use of talking like that –[35]

The perception of Wilson on the left took place in a remarkably different context, of which two examples may be suggested. The John Reed Club was in the midst of a bitter debate in 1932 about the correct policy towards non-party radicals and intellectuals. There were signs of strong left-wing sentiment on periodicals such as the *Menorah Journal*, where a group led by Herbert Solow, Elliot Cohen, Felix Morrow and Lionel Trilling were struggling against an entrenched bourgeois editorial board. During this fight, in which they attempted to open the pages of the *Journal* to radicals such as Levy, Magil, Gold and Potamkin, an approach was made to the Executive Committee of the John Reed Club for support and solidarity. At first encouraged to split, in the best Leninist fashion, Solow and Cohen were then denounced by the JRC as 'rotten bourgeoisie' and 'hopeless confusionists'.[36] Solow compared his position with that of other left-wing elements in their relation to the JRC:

> the situation may arise again any time . . . perhaps tomorrow in the *New Republic*, in one of the Negro papers, in another Jewish paper, in a Socialist paper. Where will the Club be then? Today when there is a strong left wing in the *New Republic* what are the Club's contacts with it? None. Cowley, Wilson and Josephson today, like the Menorah group yesterday are to be found in the Natl Comm, on the Foster and Ford committee, anywhere but here. What is this club contributing to their radicalisation?

Wilson's name was mentioned several times at the JRC national conference in Chicago in May 1932. Mike Gold, in a discussion of the draft JRC programme, advised the delegates of the need to 'remove the fears of fellow-travellers and the near-fellow-travellers that if they come close to us they will be dominated by petty bureaucrats'.[37] Gold warned that 'Dos Passos, Wilson, Cowley . . . they won't come to the meetings. They sense mechanisation. You believe in proletarian writing, Wilson believes in Proustian . . . I say bring him into the movement, if he is a writer of great influence and great talent.' In a subsequent contribution to the national conference, Joseph Freeman opposed the attempt to dictate to artists and writers. Where differences exist, they must educate and persuade. 'It is our task to help Edmund Wilson to change his mind.'[38] By 1932 Wilson had become an important figure in American literary life. To Hemingway he was 'a serious and honest bird who discovered life late. Naturally he is shocked and would like to do something about it.'[39] On the left Wilson was, after Dreiser and Dos Passos, the most important bourgeois liberal moving left. In their thinking about him all the uncertainties, contradictions and disagreements within the JRC surfaced.

During the summer of 1932 the idea of issuing their own 'Manifesto' was overtaken by the presidential campaign. After the Communist Party nominated William Z. Foster, a former Wobbly whom Wilson and many other New York intellectuals liked, the 'Manifesto' was merged, and submerged, in a pamphlet of endorsement drawn up by the party. *Culture and Crisis: An Open Letter to the Writers, Artists, Teachers, Physicians, Engineers, Scientists and Other Professional Workers of America* appeared in September 1932, with the signatures of dozens of writers, among them Dos Passos, Frank, Sherwood Anderson and Wilson. 'There is', wrote Leonard Kriegel, 'no better barometer of how alienated American intellectuals had become by 1932 than to read this manifesto.'[40] But the problem is, alienated from whom? The analysis of the 'crisis' followed lines familiar to socialists and other radicals; even *New Republic* liberals, thanks to Wilson, would have found many elements in the indictment of American capitalism familiar. Certainly in New York, and among New York intellectuals, such ideas circulated freely. Throughout Europe intellectuals, writers and artists were moving into proximity with such ideas by 1932. The language of *Culture and Crisis* may have been remote from Wilson's and Dos Passos's, but the programme was not. It was as alienated as the intellectuals themselves, no more and perhaps no less.

A better indication of his thinking, and of the careful distance at which he kept Communist propaganda, appeared in Wilson's favourable review of Dreiser's *Tragic America*. Dreiser's book seemed to him an important pioneering attempt to sell the idea of Communism to Americans:

> This means . . . translating the Communist ideology, colored at present so largely by Russia, into terms of American life and substituting for the jargon of the official Communist propaganda in America a language which Americans can understand. The resulting Communism . . . will be a Communism which is less preoccupied with echoing and aping Moscow than American Communism seems to be.[41]

In a letter to V. F. Calverton Wilson called at this time for the 'translation of Communist ideology into American terms'.[42] Wilson based his hopes that Americans would prove receptive to the appeal of Communism on the American legacy of democracy and of the existence of a common tongue. Writing in the *New Republic* in May 1932, he argued that 'we have as perhaps no other people have a culture which is revolutionary in the sense that it is ready to try anything and democratic in the sense that it is ready to speak any language and has already in many important instances left bourgeois schooling behind for the vernacular of ordinary life . . .'[43] Wilson assumed the economic crisis, and devoted little attention to specifically economic measures or policies, but in an article in August 1933, continued to emphasize the superstructural or cultural features which set America apart from orthodox Marxian thought:

> The different social groups in America probably come nearer to speaking the same language than in any other country in the world. The farmer and the banker, the employer and the employee, even when the wedge of the class struggle is driven between them, have no difficulty of communication.[44]

Wilson rebuked the American enthusiasts of proletarian literature by reminding them of their own national heritage:

> the nation which has produced 'Leaves of Grass' and *Huckleberry Finn* has nothing to learn from Russia or from any other country, either in the use of the common language or in the expression of the dignity and importance of the common man.

In such passages one can virtually watch Wilson reconciling himself to American culture. The edge of his criticism of America in the late 1920s was now replaced by a moderately proud willingness to celebrate its vernacular and democratic traditions, something remote indeed from Wilson's interests in the 1920s. Another indication of Wilson's political independence came in March 1934, when he joined the editorial board of Calverton's *Modern Monthly*. As we have seen in Chapter 5, Calverton was one of the worst renegades and misleaders in American political and cultural life in the eyes of the Communists. Yet Wilson tactically opposed turning the *Modern Monthly* into a blatant anti-Stalinist organ. Wilson seems to have wanted to avoid confrontation with the party, though he happily disputed its policies and consorted with its enemies; in part this was because he now planned to make a trip to the Soviet Union.[45]

At the point when he joined the *Modern Monthly*, Wilson announced in a letter to Dean Gauss at Princeton that he was 'engaged on some essays' on the evolution of the idea of history from Vico to Marx. Emerging out of his conversion to Marxism, Wilson began to explore in a series of historical essays the roots of 'the great political-intellectual movement of the times'.[46] *To the Finland Station*, to give the project its final title, has always seemed a central and problematic text in the Wilson *oeuvre*. Disagreements about its importance have mainly reflected critics' attitudes towards Wilson's period as a Marxist.[47] Of all the books on Marxism written in America during the 1930s, it alone remains widely read. In fact, it is hard to think of a better book to introduce the whole subject to a reader versed in neither the philosophy nor the politics of socialism. Had the book been published in 1935, or even as late as 1936, it is unlikely that it would have survived so well. Wilson's hostility to Marxism, and his dissection of the Leninist tradition, gave the book a readership throughout the Cold War. The full complexity of Wilson's political position when he began the project, as we have seen, and when it was published in 1940, has not always been appreciated. It exemplifies the equivocal commitments of Wilson's trajectory through radicalism.

He published the first eight chapters (Michelet to Anatole France) in the summer and autumn of 1934. The chapters on the origins of socialism appeared in the *New Republic* in June and July 1937. Those on Marx appeared in the summer of 1938. From that point only two of the remaining thirteen chapters appeared in the *New Republic*. One chapter and an appendix appeared in the newly relaunched *Partisan Review* in 1938. There were moments when he was forced to drop the project to earn money, and during this period he published several other books, the most important being *Travels in Two Democracies* (1936) and *The Triple Thinkers* (1938). He began the book as a Marxist, and planned to 'disarm the bourgeois liberal reader's objections to the Marxists' in the first section, which showed the 'dying out of the bourgeois revolutionary tradition'.[48] This required him to withhold his 'own Marxist lights'.[49] The resulting sketches vividly presented Michelet as a hero of scholarship, an intellectual who was driven out of his purely historical inquiries by the crisis of contemporary French history, but who triumphantly vindicated the individualism, patriotism and intellectual integrity which gave the bourgeois tradition its attractive energy. But as the fires of revolutionary aspirations cooled, or were stifled, Wilson's portraits of the French nineteenth-century intellectual, personified by Renan and Taine, show a diminution of energy, signs of aestheticism and social fears. They have begun, by the end of this section, to resemble the inhabitants of Axel's castle. The choice of writers embodying Wilson's message is arbitrary. To discuss a decline in the capacity to grasp the social whole imaginatively, while omitting Balzac and Zola, suggests the weakness of the first section of the book. His enthusiasm for Taine, Renan and France was long-standing. In 1921 they provided him with 'higher critical standards' than the 'aesthetic ideals, and vast commercial prosperity' of American life.[50] It is arguable that the real subject of the first section of *To the Finland Station* was the fate of his own rational and liberal optimism, and its collapse after 1929. Taine and France stand for the liberalism of Herbert Croly, who with diminishing persuasiveness upheld a faith in democratic institutions and social change through orderly reforms. Wilson bid farewell to Croly when he published 'An Appeal to Progressives' in 1931, and finally rid himself of the legacy of bourgeois liberalism with his essays in the *New Republic* in 1934.

Wilson's trip to Russia in 1935 was made in relation to the work he had already begun on *To the Finland Station*. The book he published on his return, *Travels in Two Democracies*, contained an expanded version of Wilson's diaries, and reflections of a more general nature on the Soviet system. Like his journalism in *The American Jitters*, Wilson wrote of what he experienced and made few concessions to any larger narrative scheme or comprehensiveness. The whole lacks dramatic interest, and conveys more of the atmosphere of the Westerners in Moscow, whether long-established residents or passing visitors like himself, than of the Russians themselves. His command of the Russian language at that time was too restricted, and inhibitions on contacts with foreigners too great, to expect very much from the venture. Reprinting the Russian material in an expanded version in 1956, Wilson declined to apologize for his evident sympathy with the Russian people and the Communist experiment. Hindsight allowed him certain shadings of emphasis, certain clarifications, but no comprehensive volte-face. He did not go to Russia as an innocent, and he did not leave it a disillusioned man. The things he learned there, I will argue, were part of the subterranean process of reconciliation with America which was taking place throughout his fellow-travelling period. Wilson began by making comparisons which strengthened the similarities he observed between Russia and America. By the time he left Russia the 'absolute value' of republican institutions in America seemed ever more firmly fixed in his mind. Stalinist Russia helped him to understand and appreciate Roosevelt's America.

During the voyage from London to Leningrad he related the Five Year Plans (and Virgin Soil reclamations) to an earlier pioneering stage in American history. None of the other European countries had gone through anything akin to it, and in their break away from European history (a point which Wilson does not develop) a certain common ground between Russians and Americans was to be expected: they 'feel a natural sympathy with one another'.[51] A few weeks' experience of daily life in Leningrad disabused Wilson of this belief. Where Americans valued punctuality, accuracy and dependability, the 'native indisposition' of the Russians to be punctual, accurate and dependable, their 'oriental reluctance' to disappoint, drove Wilson nearly to distraction. The American temperament, like its telephone system, seemed to be of a different order altogether. 'Americans who have decided, as I had done, that Americans and Russians are much alike, discover that in the ordinary technique of life their habits are antipodally different.'[52] The street life of Leningrad and Moscow was more orderly, and less violent, than that in New York; the police seemed to Wilson less menacing. He was also impressed by the behaviour of Muscovites in their parks: 'Here the people in the park do own it, and they are careful of what is theirs. A new kind of public conscience has come to lodge in these crowds.'[53] (In 1938 Wilson admitted that he 'soft-pedalled' signs of 'class-stratification' which were already visible in the streets of Moscow.[54]) But the more he observed of the political life around him, the crude and manipulative propaganda, and the fleeting hints he received of fear and political repression, the deeper grew his sense of the profound differences between Russia and America:

> An American in Russia who has become accustomed to the features which at first aroused his admiration – the natural democratic manners, the throwing-open of everything to the people – is likely, as time goes on, to begin to find himself repelled by what seems to him the cold-blooded manipulation of the people by the governing power. He may have left the United States with a conviction that his countrymen who keep up with the Joneses and believe what they read in the Hearst papers, are a conformist and credulous people; but by the time he has been long enough in Russia to react to the docility and timidity of the Russians, he is likely to come to the conclusion that, compared to them, the citizens of the United States are critical and self-reliant.[55]

This line of thought led him to an even stronger disclaimer that a 'socialist government' in America could or should resemble that which he observed in Russia: 'it is totally unrealistic for either the opponents or the champions of socialism to talk as if socialism would mean for us the *naivetés* of the Stalin regime.'[56] (When the United States granted diplomatic recognition to the Soviet Union in 1933, a *Daily Worker* editorial frankly proclaimed that the 'revolutionary way' out of the world crisis demanded the 'emulation of the Soviet Union and its revolutionary victories'.[57] Foster's major contribution to the political campaign in 1932 was a book entitled *Toward Soviet America*.) Wilson left Russia with increased respect for the moral worth of its endeavour. 'You feel in the Soviet Union', he wrote, 'that you are living at the moral top of the world . . .'[58] But he was even more strongly persuaded

> . . . that American republican institutions, disastrously as they are often abused, have some permanent and absolute value. I do not believe that they are certain to be destroyed in the course of the transformation of society . . . On the contrary, I think it probable that, like it, they will make easier the transformation to socialism.[59]

Things he saw in Russia, and things he read, drew Wilson

irrevocably out of the company of fellow-travellers. Like so many American intellectuals of his generation, Trotsky played an important role in Wilson's break with Stalinism. Although news of his break was not made public until early 1937, Wilson had been having political conversations with James T. Farrell and other dissident anti-Stalinists in the autumn of 1936. Farrell noted in his diary Wilson's comment that 'These last two years, Trotsky has been the conscience of the world.'[60] Wilson's analysis of 'The Literary Left' in the *New Republic* of 20 January 1937 revealed how irritated he had become with Stalinists who pursued literary life under the impression that they were 'operating a bombing-plane'.[61] He saw no need to introduce party politics into literary discussion because in America such concerns could be freely expressed elsewhere. Wilson's dismissal of the literary aspirations of the left was magisterial and comprehensive. His treatment of Stalinism followed, in the main, the indictment of Trotsky and his followers, arguing that the climate of lies, falsehood and suppression of opinion meant that there was 'very little hope that any intellectual health will ever come out of Stalinist Communism': a 'political group which adopts as a policy the suppression of opinion and the falsification of history on the scale and with the unscrupulousness of the Stalinists is hardly a beneficient influence for the production of literature or ideas'. Early in 1937 Wilson joined the Trotsky Defense Committee, and published a searching and critical interpretation of Karl Marx in the newly-revived *Partisan Review*, a journal which was engaged in delicate negotiations with Trotsky [see Appendix III]. Wilson's break with the Stalinists brought praise for his political integrity from Farrell:

> In the early thirties he joined the spiritual and intellectual migration of writers to the left. However, he retained his judgment, perception and independence. When new questions were posed, he investigated them in all seriousness. He did not accept ready-made slogans simply because a radical brand was put on them. The result can be seen in his work. Whatever one thinks of the various of his conclusions, Wilson's literary criticism has been the finest written in the last decade.[62]

Wilson resumed work on *To the Finland Station* in March 1936.[63] His personal reservations about 'Stalinist Communism' were much strengthened by his experience in Russia, and there were signs in the literary world that the momentum was swinging away from the Communist Party. Damage-containing exercises after each of the successive Moscow trials, and attempts to defend Russian policy in Spain, met with some success, but as Delmore Schwartz assured James Laughlin, 'everyone worth speaking to in N.Y. has now seen the moral bankruptcy of Marxism in the Moscow trials'.[64] Eastman's break with the party was ancient history; by 1934 Dos Passos's revulsion at party tactics in America, and the unfolding of events in Russia, confirmed a process of disengagement and withdrawal. The ostensibly Stalinist editors of *Partisan Review*, 'Wallace Phelps' and Philip Rahv, had begun to dissociate themselves from 'leftism' by 1934.[65] It was then that Dos Passos warned Wilson that 'the whole Marxian radical movement is in a moment of intense disintegration'.[66] Wilson was an important and influential addition to the growing weight of anti-Stalinists in American intellectual life.

The next section of *To the Finland Station*, on the origins of socialism and the American utopian communities, appeared in the *New Republic* in the summer of 1937. As Wilson presents them, the early socialist protests against inequality and exploitation had in common the belief that human nature, which was deformed by injustice and oppression, could be altered by institutions, whether humane factories or utopian phalansteries. The repeated failures of these communities were due to many factors, from personality to climate, but his most telling point, which shows that Wilson had not by 1937 wholly abandoned Marxist modes of thought, is that the utopian communities failed because they were conceived in ignorance of the mechanisms of class conflict. He has at last cleared the stage for the arrival of Marx, the principal protagonist of the book. Wilson complained in 1937 of his lack of grounding in German philosophy.[67] When his break with the Stalinists was publically confirmed, he embarked on a comprehensive study of the lives and writings of Marx and Engels.

Among the by-products of this work was an influential discussion of 'Marxism and Literature' in the *Atlantic Monthly* in December 1937. Wilson used Marx and Engels against vulgar Marxist attempts to judge literature solely by political tendency. His account of the literary situation in Russia in *Travels in Two Democracies* was mildly hopeful: RAPP had been summarily dissolved ('a blow against literary intolerance') and Wilson noted 'a more general respect for art and a freer attitude toward technique'.[68] Wilson's account of the post-RAPP atmosphere closely resembles that offered by Louis Fischer, quoted in Chapter 5: they were in frequent contact in Moscow.[69] By the time he wrote 'Marxism and Literature' the situation in Russia had deteriorated. The purges, show-trials and cultural sterility of orthodox Soviet letters suggested to Wilson that imaginative literature could not long endure in a dictatorship, and that Marxism in Russia had 'run itself into a blind alley – or rather, it has been put down a well'. He now believed that the tenets of Marxism were of limited value to a critic trying to explain goodness and badness in art. They could help in understanding the origin and social significance of works of art, but little else. Wilson's sober and knowledgeable treatment of the topic helped to settle the question for more than a generation. But perhaps the most revealing passage in the essay is the argument that 'proletarian literature', novels about industrial conflict which, after praising Dahlberg in 1930, he had steadfastly ignored, 'had come quite naturally out of our literature of the past'.[70] Even this, the fairest flower of the Communist literary movement, was to be denied to the 'comrades' and restored to American literature. Communism was not only to be taken from the Communists but to be chewed over and, by 1937, spat out.

In this mood, Wilson, writing in the December 1937 issue of *Partisan Review* on 'Flaubert's Politics', reflected on the things which *L'education sentimentale* revealed about left-wing politics:

Today we must recognize that Flaubert had observed something of which Marx was not aware. We have had the opportunity to see how even a socialism which has come to power as the result of a proletarian revolution has bred a political police of almost unprecedented ruthlessness and pervasiveness – how the socialism of Marx himself, with its emphasis on dictatorship rather than on democratic processes, has contributed to produce this disaster. Here Flaubert, who believed that the artist should aim to be without social convictions, has been able to judge the tendencies of political doctrines as the greatest doctrinaires could not; and here the role chosen by Flaubert is justified.

The speed with which Wilson turned against Marxism is slightly deceptive, since although he sceptically rejected accusations that Russia was a police state in *Travels in Two Democracies* in 1936, we know how inclined he was then to 'soft-pedal' criticisms of what he saw. He now spoke out warmly not so much against the perversion of the revolution, which was the Trotskyite argument (as in *The Revolution Betrayed*, which appeared in translation in New York in 1937), but against Marx, Marxism and socialism itself. Of Marxism, all that remained of use in his eyes was a tool of analysis.

'Marxism and Literature' and 'Flaubert's Politics' hint at what Wilson's articles on Marx and Engels in the *New Republic* (July–September 1938) make clear: though offering a powerful insight into human society, Wilson declines to treat their theories as holy writ. The biographical approach, what Wilson described as the 'spotlighting method',[71] lent itself to Wilson's strengths as a writer, his feel for the atmosphere of ideas, personal relationships, the rich variety of temperaments. Certainly the portrait of Marx conveys the full passion of Marx's writings, and their mould-breaking power. Wilson also convinces us of the pathos of the man, the tragedies of his personal life, his obsessiveness and vindictive energy. Wilson's explication of 'Marxism', and particularly of dialectical materialism, reflects the full extent to which he now believed that Stalin's regime was a 'despotism' and its central tenet, dialectical materialism, nothing more than a religious myth.[72] Marx's heroism lay in his determination 'to make the historical imagination intervene in human affairs as a direct constructive force'.[73] Marx's contemporaries and opponents – Wilson devoted chapters to Lassalle and Bakunin – seemed to lead lives of inexcusable frivolity or romantic irresponsibility. Marx, in desperate poverty, plagued by boils and domestic tragedy, struggled with *Kapital*: he afforded Wilson an image of the 'power of imagination' in history.

By the time 'Karl Marx: Poet of Commodities' appeared in the *New Republic* on 8 January 1940, Stalin and Hitler were allies, the Russians had joined in to destroy the Polish state, and they were invading Finland. Wilson's discussion of Marxism makes it abundantly clear that it no longer commands his loyalty. Too many inconsistencies are revealed; its psychological basis seems too crude. Marx himself had no experience of modern industry and his writings betray neurotic elements of cruelty, sadism and repression. Marx based his thinking about the historical mission of the proletariat upon false historical analogies. Throughout this barrage, with hits roughly equalling misses, the fact that Marx did not know the United States is, in Wilson's eyes, the most disabling weakness of all: 'Marx was incapable of imagining democracy . . .'[74] The passage is worth quoting at length:

> What Karl Marx had no clue for understanding was that the absence in the United States of the feudal class background of Europe would have the effect not only of facilitating the expansion of capitalism but also of making possible a genuine social democratization; that a community would grow up and endure in which the people engaged in different occupations would probably come nearer to speaking the same language and even to sharing the same criteria than anywhere else in the industrialized world. Here in the United States, our social groupings are mainly based on money, and the money is always changing hands so rapidly that the class lines cannot get cut very deep . . .
>
> . . . in the United States, even where class interests divide us, we have come closer to social equality: our government does not guarantee a hierarchy to the extent that the European systems do. We are more lawless, but we are more homogenous; and our homogeneity consists of common tendencies which Marx would have regarded as bourgeois, but which are actually only partly explicable as the results of capitalist competition. The common man, set free from feudal society, seems to do everywhere much the same sort of thing – which is not what Marx had expected him to do because it was not what Marx liked to do himself . . . things which the Americans have more or less managed to get during those periods when their capitalist economy was booming; and they have managed to get other things too, which other people will learn to want and will get: free movement and a fair amount of free speech.[75]

As Wilson saw the world in 1940, the entire historical project of socialism and Marxism was misconceived. 'Socialism by itself can create neither a political discipline nor a culture.' Progress only comes through 'the organic processes of society'. Nor can the proletariat be imagined any longer as the bearers of the revolution: 'it seems today as if only the man who has already enjoyed a good standard of living and become accustomed to a certain security will really fight for security and comfort'.[76] This remarkable passage suggests the strength of the underlying elements of continuity between Wilson the Marxist in 1933 and Wilson the anti-Stalinist in 1940. In 'Art, the Proletariat and Marx' he reminded Americans of their great fortune more closely 'to speak the same language than in any other country in the world'. In 1940 this perception was expanded to include class, social equality, homogeneity and the aspirations of the common man, all of which have improved and prospered under bourgeois capitalism without socialist or Communist intervention.

The remainder of *To the Finland Station* is devoted to Lenin and Trotsky. Wilson judiciously praises Lenin's character, his austere and iron determination, but finds him devoid of intellectual curiosity. Trotsky, more variously gifted, seemed to Wilson a more rigid, self-important dogmatist than Lenin. The book ends with Lenin's return to Petrograd, in which Stalin has little more than a walk-on role. Wilson's 'Marxism at the End of the Thirties', published in March 1941, refers to the transformation of Lenin's party into a 'tyrannical machine'.[77] In an aside in *To the Finland Station* he referred to Stalin's regime as 'combining the butcheries of the Robespierre Terror with the corruption and reaction of the Directory'. When the book appeared in 1940 it was clear that Wilson no longer had the stomach to give Russia the 'benefit of every doubt'.[78]

At every stage in his political evolution in the 1930s, Wilson went with the tide. He did so on his own terms, with his own reservations. Like John Reed, he was guilty of 'American Exceptionalism', the heretical belief (in party eyes) that unique historical conditions exempted America from the full Marxist scenario of class conflict and revolution. Neither Reed nor Wilson really knew the American working class, but their intuitive sense of the American political system and the character of the American people seems to have, at some inner level, played an important role in shaping their conversions to Communism. In Wilson's case, America was his Ariadne's thread which led him back to a more natural and congenial liberalism. Very little survived of his period as a Marxist, beyond *To the Finland Station* itself, and – no small gain this, in retrospect – a greater sympathy for his own country and his fellow countrymen.

7 Communists and Objectivists

GEORGE OPPEN

The face which radical politics turned towards art, and that which artists showed to politics in the twentieth century, radical or otherwise, may be suggested by two meetings.

'Stieglitz, this is Bill Haywood.' Years later, when Stieglitz wrote his memoirs, he recalled his meeting with the tall, burly leader of the Wobblies. Haywood looked around the 291 Gallery and asked Stieglitz why he was wasting his time in such a 'dinky little place'. 'True workers', he said, 'don't believe the artist will ever win the fight for what we're after' and asked why a big man like Stieglitz did not 'leave this place and join the real fight'. Stieglitz's reply was carefully measured:

> Mr. Haywood, I don't believe you understand. You don't believe that my way is the way. You believe that your way is the only way . . . You believe you have followers, hundreds of thousands, maybe millions. I make no distinction between classes and races and creeds. There is no hatred in me unless it be a hatred of pretense and hypocrisy and maybe a hatred of stupidity. Even my own. When the day arrives and what you are doing proves to be true and what I am attempting to do proves to be equally true we'll be standing shoulder to shoulder wherever we meet.[1]

Until then, however . . . Haywood shook his head. 'Too bad', he said, walking out of the gallery.

Margaret Anderson described an even more disastrous meeting in her autobiography. She had long looked forward to introducing her friend and assistant on the *Little Review*, Jane Heap, to the renowned anarchists Emma Goldman and Alexander Berkman.

She hoped that Goldman and Berkman would find Heap, a stylish and clever lesbian, to be 'an incentive toward their clearer thinking'. When they finally met, Heap teased Goldman and playfully appealed to Berkman for sympathy. This subsequently produced a complaint by Emma Goldman about Heap's aggressiveness. When they met a day later, Anderson recalled that they argued bitterly about art:

> They had tried to maintain that 'The Ballad of Reading Gaol' was better art than 'Salomé.' When I used the black swan in Amy Lowell's 'Malmaison' to illustrate a certain way of pointing emotion there was a general uprising. E. G. was a little beside herself.
>
> The working-man hasn't enough leisure to be interested in black swans she thundered. What's that got to do with revolution? . . . If only a few people understand the art you talk about that's proof that it's not for humanity, said Berkman.[2]

Anderson and Heap, easily the most energetic and assiduous groupies of *avant-garde* art in America, were hardly to be persuaded by the earnest, utilitarian, artistic ideas of the anarchists. An unexpected consequence of this meeting, as it filtered into the pages of the *Little Review*, was a famous exchange between Upton Sinclair and Margaret Anderson, which succinctly captured the spirit of the uneasy relations between radicals and the *avant-garde* in the 1920s. Sinclair wrote, cancelling his subscription: 'I no longer understand anything in it, so it no longer interests me.' Anderson's reply was brusque and unequivocal: 'Please cease sending me your socialist paper. I understand everything in it, therefore it no longer interests me.'[3]

Ties between the small rump of the left in the 1920s, and the artistic *avant-garde*, were few and uneasy. The Russian experiment, and the activities of Mayakovsky, the Futurists and the innovators in theatrical practice, appealed to writers who visited the Soviet Union in the 1920s. Soviet literary ideas also attracted interest, as we have seen, among the literary radicals. Michael Gold was among the first to recognize the importance of the Proletcult, and to advocate the creation of an American proletarian literature. He came back from Russia in 1924 with the example of the Workers' Art Theatre in Moscow very much on his mind, and wrote to Upton Sinclair that he hoped to start a similar theatre in New York in which revolutionary plays might be produced.[4] Em Jo Basshe, John Howard Lawson and John Dos Passos were drawn into the enterprise, eventually called the New Playwright's Theater (NPT).[5] For a brief moment when the NPT was busy with productions of the plays of Dos Passos and Upton Sinclair, and when the *New Masses* was launched, one saw the possibilities of radical literary and theatrical practice and revolutionary politics working in tandem.

Unlike *The Liberator* in its final phase, when it was under the domination of the Communist Party, the *New Masses* was initially edited by figures such as Egmont Arens and John Sloan who had been prominent contributors to the old *Masses* before the war. Of the 56 identified contributors, only two were party members, and only a dozen were known to be sympathetic to Communism. The venture was energized by an openness and optimism. Gold wrote to Sinclair, when the magazine was in the planning stages, that there were 'one or two good leads here toward getting a big bunch of money to start a new free non-partisan revolutionary Masses in New York. The old artists and writers are crazy to be talking out again . . .'[6]

One can get a good sense of the spirit of the *New Masses* from the various contributors, from W. C. Williams to Allen Tate; and an even better indication of the mood of the magazine from poems such as 'Vitagraph' by Carl Rakosi, which appeared in the fourth number in August 1926:

> Out in God's country where men are men,
> the terror of Red Gap used to ride on his
> bulletsodden roan.
> He was called God damn Higgins
> and was said to have faith only in his gun,
> his horse, and Denver Nan.
> It turned out she was in cahoots with Gentleman Joe
> who could shuffle a deck faster than you can count,
> and one day the two of them cleaned the poor sucker
>   out of his last red cent.
> But it was the last time Gentleman Joe
> hung his thumb into the armpit of his vest
> and snickered behind his nibbled tooth pick,
> for a masked stranger showed up in the barroom
> that night, with his hand on his hip pocket.

Years later the Reverend Marcus Whitney
pitched his tent in town,
And Denver Nan had her only chance to go straight,
And made good,
And married Good Deed Higgins,
And three cheers for the star spangled banner.
And how about God damn Higgins?
O he used to be hard all right.
He could draw a gun faster than any man in Arizona.

Rakosi's language, as befits the future author of the 'Americana' sequence, celebrates its own clichés. Each is savoured, but wholly without highbrow contempt.

Within the notoriously humourless party, and on the left generally, there was considerable scepticism about the value of such bourgeois literary productions as 'Vitagraph'. Party members such as Michael Gold and Joseph Freeman were confronted with philistines within the party who dismissed (or had never heard of) Toller, Piscator, Becher, Grosz and Mayakovsky. Literature for such people was basically a waste of time, a pointless indulgence.[7] As younger radicals and intellectuals drew closer to the party on political grounds, in the aftermath of the execution of Sacco and Vanzetti and the Passaic textile strike, they were faced with the need to defend revolutionary politics among their literary acquaintances, and to defend art among party comrades.

Of the whole range of Communist critics, Joseph Freeman was perhaps the most sensitive to the paradoxes of the poet in the workers' movement. When Freeman – of bourgeois background and educated at Columbia – gave lectures and readings to workers at the Rand School in New York, he found that they 'fidgeted in their seats and looked out the windows' when he tried to read Eliot or Pound to them. 'The matter was as painful as it was simple', he wrote in *An American Testament*. 'The creator of Apeneck Sweeney was a barrier between the workers in my class and myself. The barrier must be destroyed.' Freeman absorbed from Eden and Cedar Paul's *Proletcult* the message that the radical man of letters should enter fully into the educational activities of the party. The price he paid for this commitment was a division in his sensibility. Freeman published numerous delicate, romantic poems in *The Liberator*:

Though darkness beat about my heart,
    How can I complain? –
I who have touched the simple grass
And felt the quiet rain . . .
            ('Songs for a Lady', September 1921)

Morning unfolds its light upon the bed
Where close beside me lies my love asleep
Still a meditation; her dear head
Lost in the dark releases of her hair . . .
            ('Love at Dawn', April 1922)

Freeman's basic presumption about poetry was that, as he argued in the 'Introduction' to *Proletarian Literature in the United States* (1935), the poet 'deals with experience rather than theory or action'. But when he tried to use certain kinds of political experiences, the poetic results were deadening:

Beat, drums of the world!
let the workers storm from the factories,
the peasants from the farms;
sweep the earth clean of this nightmare,
build new cities, a new world,
ringing with the clear voices of new men!
            ('Four Poems', *Partisan Review*, February–March 1934)

He was unable to remain content with his earlier romantic and introspective work. But the alternative, with beating drums and waving banners, did nothing to lower the barriers between workers and modern literature. His career as a poet, and the course of the *New Masses*, of which he was a principal editor for substantial periods from its founding in 1926, raises uncomfortable questions about whether it was possible to be a 'modern' poet and a Communist.[8]

The changes in political line, and rapid shifts in the mood of John Reed Club writers, dismayed people like Gold and Freeman who had sought to radicalize the *New Masses* in the late 1920s. By 1931, Gold wrote to Upton Sinclair with annoyance and contempt about the youthful sectarians, and the not-so-youthful ones, who were increasingly dominating the John Reed Club and who were trying to take over the *New Masses*:

You get a bourgeois college boy who's never seen a strike or worked in his life – he gets to be a Communist (not party member however) & in 3 months he is patronizing Lenin & improving on Marx & hunting heresies. It gets boring sometimes – but we mean to keep as commonsense a line as we can against some of this stuff.[9]

Throughout this period Joseph Freeman waged a lonely battle against 'vulgar' Marxist literary criticism (such as an attempt to explain the evolution of literature 'by the simple method of describing the economic conditions under which a book is written'[10]), and in 1932 he unsuccessfully tried to return the *New Masses* to a more serious intellectual level.[11] But there were other sources of opposition to what people like Freeman understood by seriousness. 'By the way', Jack Conroy wrote to V. J. Jerome,

... the last two issues of *New Masses* were a distinct improvement. Those highbrow, Olympian discussions that have cluttered the pages of the magazine the last year or so are all right if taken in small doses, but ... I think *The Communist* should remain the theoretical guide of the movement, and the *New Masses* devote more space to creative work.[12]

Against this climate, the publication in 1929 and 1930 of the Rebel Poets' anthologies was a gesture of political hope; in cultural terms, they were rather anachronistic.[13] The editors, Ralph Cheyney and Jack Conroy, were unable to interest an American publisher in an anthology of radical poetry, and eventually had them published in England. Such books represent the final phase of an older, populist way of thinking about poetry as versified social criticism. The theme, and title, of both anthologies was 'unrest': poems were included which portrayed and satirized bourgeois manners, upper-class pretensions, hedonistic college life. Many poems were on specific events: strikes, politics, racial discrimination, unemployment; many satirized contemporary attitudes. There was nothing Marxist about such poems, which made humane protests against oppression and inhumanity. But in the changing literary climate of the American left, in which younger writers who were drawn to the John Reed Clubs were being encouraged to write in a more overtly political manner, and in which a few were seriously trying to become Marxist poets (among whom Zukofsky was one of the most attentive), the old mix of traditional verse forms and social protest sentiment was no longer viable. Under the pressure of the collapse of the economy in 1929, there was a growing feeling, articulated for liberals by Edmund Wilson, that writers had to take sides. To earn their place within the Communist literary movement after the Kharkov conference of the IURW, a harder, more programmatic opposition to capitalism and imperialism was demanded, as was a more direct concern to put literature at the service of the class struggle.

The most interesting expression of the new mood was *We Gather Strength*, an anthology of poems by Herman Spector, Joseph Kalar, Edwin Rolfe and S. Funaroff, which was published in 1933. The political themes are visible and insistent in Rolfe's 'Kentucky – 1932', Spector's 'Anarchist Nightsong' and Funaroff's 'An American Worker'. The Russian *mythos* was still in 1933 a new element in left-wing poetry (Funaroff's 'Dneiprostroi', a poem about the heroic Five Year Plan showpiece about which Wilson also commented), and with Rolfe's 'Homage to Karl Marx' a new hero steps to stage centre. Langston Hughes's 'Ballad of Lenin' appeared in the *Daily Worker* on 20 January 1934, one of many poems dedicated to revolutionary heroes and martyrs. Americans seemed, on the whole, to have been less likely to celebrate Stalin than other Bolshevik leaders. One also notes in *We Gather Strength* the influence of T. S. Eliot and the modern movement in poetry. Funaroff's 'What the Thunder Said: A Fire Sermon' is a pastiche of Eliotian techniques and imagery. None of the poems in this anthology rhyme, and there are no sonnets; free verse is the order of the day; the imagery is often quite 'modern':

> within these urban angularities
> and geometric patterns of despair,
> the flowing lines of music trace
> emotion in sinuous, vague curves through garbage-air
>
> and a squat guy in a straw hat passing
> flips a stub of cigarette to the street . . .
>   (Spector, 'Saturday Eve, East-Side')

Many of the traditional and clichéd images of social-protest poetry live on, with emphasis on 'rotting structures', the 'sure advance' of the proletariat, and the 'crimson banner / flying in the wind'.

Arguably the flowing crimson banners and the urgent cry of 'Defend the Soviet Union!' were ritualistic gestures, concessions made obligatory by the political moment. Within what is often a mechanical use of left-wing imagery, there is occasionally a frantic and despairing urgency:

> Out of darkness, out of the pits now –
> Foreigners only to the light of day –
> claiming the mountains in the sudden glow
> of battle, welded in a mass array,
> shouting!
>
> This is our land, we planted its first seed!
> These are our mines, our hands dig the coal!
> These roads are ours, the wires across the land
> are ours! THIS IS OUR EARTH!
>
> (Rolfe, 'Kentucky – 1932')

More fastidious literary consciences might indeed be moved by the strike in Harlan County, Kentucky, and want to join Rolfe's cry. But there was a more persuasive master, William Carlos Williams, who urged a different tact in 'Spring and All': 'One by one objects are defined.' The massive acts of appropriation in the Rolfe poem were more immediately satisfying (as was the famous conclusion of Odets's *Waiting for Lefty*, with its dramatic calls for a strike) than the modest suggestion of Williams that 'so much depends' upon the seeing of a red wheelbarrow. But it would take a megaphone-art akin to Mayakovsky's to make it work. As poetry, Rolfe is scarcely using the medium. Williams had much to teach the younger poets, and the history of poetry in the interwar years might be written in terms of his example and influence. What was perhaps most important in the early 1930s was the way he combined powerful social criticism with a spare, disciplined technique. The poets who appeared in *We Gather Strength* were alive to the achievement of modern American poetry, and though there is hardly a poem in the anthology which is not flawed in some important respect, at least the flaws are interesting ones. Michael Gold was convinced the book represented something new within the culture of the American left: in the past, he wrote in the introduction to *We Gather Strength,* 'in our revolutionary movement only doggerel has been esteemed'.

Many of the leading Objectivists were either sympathizers or actively engaged in left-wing politics. That well-known poet, 'Louis Zukonski' [*sic*], was reported in the *Daily Worker* of 2 July 1937 to have been elected by the Middle Atlantic Division of the League of American Writers to an official committee to organize support for striking steelworkers. Reznikoff published a poem dedicated to the martyred socialists of Vienna in *Separate Way* (1936). Yet their literary efforts were rebuffed by the Communist literary establishment, and contemptuously dismissed by roughnecks like Herman Spector. Spector's review of two volumes by Charles Reznikoff in the summer 1934 issue of *Dynamo* was essentially a political argument against Objectivism:

> Charles Reznikoff expresses in his poetry the limited world-view of a 'detached' bystander: that is, of a person whose flashes of perception for the immediate esthetics of the contemporary scene are not co-ordinated in any way with a dialectical comprehension of the life-process . . . The fatal defect of the Objectivist theory is that it identifies life with capitalism, and so assumes that the world is merely a waste land. The logical consequence is a fruitless negativism. . . . Impartiality is a myth which defeatists take with them into oblivion.[14]

'Objectivism' was one of the many failings of which Henri Barbusse's journal, *Monde*, was accused at the Kharkov congress in 1930:

> . . . *Monde* . . . should have regarded all the phenomena of the surrounding bourgeois life from the class point of view, this being the only attitude to take towards the objective world at the present historical stage; from the standpoint, that is, of the proletariat armed scientifically with dialectical materialism. Its objectivism should have been the 'objectivism of the class struggle' (Lenin).[15]

The term 'Objectivist' was, on the left, a damaging confession of neutrality. There are reasons for assuming that Zukofsky was aware of this when the term was first used in the February 1931 number of *Poetry*; his political awareness was even more clearly on display when Zukofsky replied to Schappes's cutting review of *An 'Objectivists' Anthology* (March 1933) in the May issue of *Poetry*.[16] He quoted a passage from Lenin's *Leftwing Communism – An Infantile Disorder* on the need for a 'strictly objective estimate of all the class forces and their interrelation in every political action'. Zukofsky further stated that Lenin's perspective 'is the concern of the editorial presentation and the poetry' of the anthology. There are reasons within the anthology itself to take Zukofsky's point seriously. The poems included by Williams are all particularly 'social' (especially 'The pure products of America . . .'); it would be appropriate to discuss the historical sense revealed in Williams's 'It is living coral . . .' and Reznikoff's 'The English in Virginia'; and Zukofsky's *A* contains passages which, in the Poundian mode, undoubtedly register acute contemporary concerns: strikes, unemployment, trade with the Soviet Union, social conflict:

A country of state roads and automobiles,
But the greatest number idle, shiftless, disguised on streets,
The excuse of the experts
'Production exceeds demand so we curtail employment,'
And the Wobblies hollering reply,
Yeah! but why don't you give us more than a meal
     to increase the consumption!

(p. 117)

Schappes noted Zukofsky's content, but complained that 'there is no coherence, no organization, *no direction* in this long but still incomplete poem', which he linked to a nihilistic protest against the poet's isolation in a capitalistic and materialistic society: 'The intelligent alternative . . . is completely to stride beyond these premises of the bourgeoisie: that is, to ally oneself with the revolutionary proletariat.'

As voters and citizens, as feeling individuals, the Objectivists may have intensely desired to ally themselves with the proletariat, revolutionary or not. Zukofsky and Carl Rakosi appear in *Writers Take Sides* (League of American Writers, 1938) favouring the Loyalist cause in Spain. But as poets, such is the paradox of their dilemma, they had far more to learn from fascists, such as Ezra Pound, and bourgeois democrats like Williams, than from the model suggested by Schappes, the Aragon of 'The Red Front'.

Within the perspectives of the Communist Party, Schappes's comments, and Spector's, were predictable. When Williams reviewed *An 'Objectivists' Anthology* in *The Symposium*, January 1933, he addressed the problem which Spector pointed out in Reznikoff: the absence of a connecting link between the 'flashes of perception' and the meaning of such perceptions within the 'life-process'. Williams saw Objectivism as 'the presentation, simply, of certain new objects without obvious connection with the classics and which he [the Objectivist poet] entitles "poems".' Williams goes on to suggest that paradoxically the perception of the newness of the new affirms the 'continued existence of the old'. With a nice example of Eliot-like legerdemain, the Objectivists can thus have their cake and eat it. At the end of the review Williams suggests another definition of the term 'Objectivist':

. . . they are successfully displayed to hold an objective view of poetry which, in a certain way, clarifies it, showing it to be not a seductive arrangement of scenes, sounds and colors so much as a construction each part of which has a direct bearing on its meaning as a whole, an objectification of significant particulars.

The formalist way of viewing the term was certainly more congenial to the principals in later years, and probably comes close to the central point of the anthology itself, and to the ideas which held the Objectivists together in the 1930s. The 'political' meaning of Objectivism kept the poets and the Communist Party at arms' length.

The criticism Spector makes of the 'detached bystander' aspect of Reznikoff's poetry is not without sense, though for Reznikoff detachment was a complex aesthetic and psychological statement of the man himself. Reznikoff's *Testimony*, in the prose version which appeared in *An 'Objectivists' Anthology* and which Spector reviewed, was not a politically committed work in the obvious sense. It revealed a conception of art as the expression of a subtle and intense humanism; an art, in other words, for which the megaphone and waving crimson banner were less than useless. For a wide variety of reasons it is true that Reznikoff shied away from the provision of meanings in his poems. Spector, and other left-wing critics of the 1930s, were asking whether, in a world threatened by fascism and in which millions were unemployed, it was enough merely to see (however clearly) the

Round
Shiny fixed
Alternatives

(Oppen, '1930's')

as one would see a red wheelbarrow, or 'the senseless /
unarrangement of wild things'[17] but not feel called upon to take a
stand on the larger public concerns. It is hard not to feel that the
left were asking important questions about Objectivism; but that
they scarcely waited for an answer.

George Oppen's first book of poems, *Discrete Series*, was
published by the Objectivist Press in 1934. The proletarian
literary movement was in high gear, with novels that year by
Robert Cantwell, Edward Dahlberg, James T. Farrell, Waldo
Frank, Albert Halper and Josephine Herbst. It was the year of
Kenneth Burke's 'My Approach to Communism' and Philip
Rahv's declaration that he hoped to become 'an intellectual
assistant of the proletariat'.[18] John Strachey's *Literature and
Dialectical Materialism*, and Stanley Burnshaw's 'Notes on
Revolutionary Poetry' were published, and the *Partisan Review* was
founded. The 'Call' went out for the League of American Writers.

Oppen's slender book did not make much of an impression on
bourgeois critics. William Rose Benet thought that Oppen's
writing was like 'listening to a man with an impediment in his
speech'.[19] Williams, who had kept up intermittent relations with
the left in the early 1930s,[20] took the occasion of a review of *Discrete
Series* to make an important statement about art and revolution:

> An imaginable new social order would require a skeleton of
> severe discipline for its realization and maintenance. Thus by a
> sharp restriction to essentials, the seriousness of a new order is
> brought to realization. Poetry might turn this condition to its
> own ends. Only by being an object sharply defined and without
> redundancy will its form project whatever meaning is required
> of it. It could well be, at the same time, first and last a poem
> facing as it must the dialectic necessities of its day. Oppen has
> carried this social necessity, so far as poetry may be concerned,
> to an extreme.[21]

To look at Edwin Rolfe's 'Kentucky – 1932' through Williams's
eyes is to see how little it achieves sharp definition, form without

redundancy. Its effects are achieved at the cost of a blurring of perception, for only thus would we miss the way it is caught up in a web of clichés and unrealized social emotion. *Discrete Series* represents precisely the 'sharp restriction to essentials' which Williams indicates. If anything, those essentials, those images, through which Oppen works are too spare. He describes people in a theatre removing their coats and sitting down as a 'semaphoring chorus'. In another poem, a social portrait (reminiscent of rather wordier things in Pound's *Lustra*) turns upon a single word, 'Pertain', and its elusive connotation:

> Your breasts
> Pertain to lingerie.

Discrete Series is a book which omits the explanations that we have come to expect from poetry. A point which Williams made in his review of *An 'Objectivists' Anthology* provides us with an essential term: 'These pieces, these lines, these words, neither are they fragments but their power is cumulative[,] rather in tension than in story.' By *story* Williams identified what Spector felt was missing from Objectivism: the connections and explanations which would have clarified and asserted the meanings of the things seen. Oppen has never felt the need to thicken the outline of the sharply-defined object. Perhaps he has seldom felt a hunger for the completeness and artifice of the story in his poems.

There is a sense in which the early Oppen was a poet of estrangement. Not, as Williams suggested, because the Objectivist poet presented objects 'without obvious connection' and called them 'poems', but because he was writing in a society in which the connections, explanations and stories had been corrupted, distorted, mystified, turned into ideology. *Discrete Series* embodies a revolutionary art in which the links between objects and meanings can no longer be asserted (as Spector thought) as a matter of 'dialectical comprehension'. In the face of a comprehensive and radical epistemological uncertainty (though there is a danger in exaggerating the extent to which Oppen is a philosophical poet), he sought an art which was free from the smothering cloud of anecdote and story which envelops our culture.

He found no place in the left-wing literary movement of the 1930s, which was an ironic blessing. He had nothing to repent when repentance was in season. Mary Oppen describes the fate of *Discrete Series* in two sentences: 'The Gotham Book Mart bought some of the books; very few were sold, and the rest were stored. Politics were dominant and danger was imminent.'[22]

THE INVENTION OF THE OBJECTIVISTS

The Objectivists were summoned into existence by Louis Zukofsky. He brought Charles Reznikoff, George Oppen and Carl Rakosi together for a brief, fertile moment in the early 1930s. Although in later years there was precious little agreement about what they had collectively sought to do, it is possible to return to contemporary documentation to trace the evolution of the group, and to suggest the place of the Objectivists in American letters.

Reznikoff was the oldest of the four. Born in New York in 1894, his parents were recent immigrants from the Jewish Pale of Settlement in Russsia. By 1918 he was a published poet. Rakosi was born in Berlin in 1903 and taken to America as a child. He grew up in Kenosha, Wisconsin. His poems began to appear in the *New Masses* in 1926, and in other little magazines at the end of the decade. Rakosi worked in the midwest as a psychotherapist, and was the outsider of the group. Other than Zukofsky, he did not meet the other Objectivists until the 1970s. Zukofsky was born in New York in 1904 of recent immigrant stock. Oppen, who was born in New Rochelle, New York, in 1908, came from a prosperous, assimilated, long-established German Jewish family. The Objectivists, then, were urban Jews. They shared with their co-religionists the characteristic pattern of upward social mobility. Reznikoff's parents were uneducated; their eldest son attended Cornell Medical School, and Charles studied at the School of Journalism at Missouri University, and took a law degree at New York University. Zukofsky studied at Columbia University, and taught briefly at the University of Wisconsin at Madison. Oppen attended college in Oregon, but did not take a degree. Rakosi studied English, psychology and social work at a string of universities in Wisconsin, Pennsylvania, Chicago and Texas. With the exception of Rakosi, who had professional training, they remained in social terms marginal men: Reznikoff did not practise law, Zukofsky had various irregular teaching appointments, Oppen became a political organizer among the unemployed in Brooklyn, and then a cabinet-maker. Reznikoff worked for many years in Zionist journalism. The Objectivists were forced to assume that they could not sustain themselves as writers. Poetry had to be squeezed in between the other calls upon their nervous energy. The public response to their work was one of indifference or hostility, and it is hardly surprising that the literary careers of the Objectivists were deformed or broken. For most of his life Reznikoff was forced to print and publish his verse on a small press which he stored in his sister's home in Brooklyn. Rakosi did not publish a volume until he was thirty-seven, the slight *Selected Poems* of 1941. It was followed by another small book, and then silence until *Amulet* in 1967. He had ceased to write, and was believed by his publishers to have died. Oppen, too, ceased to write when he became more directly involved in politics. After *Discrete Series* in 1934, his next book *The Materials* did not appear until 1962: it was long enough to have been forgotten twice over. Zukofsky was the least fortunate in the publication of his work. His poems appeared infrequently in little magazines from the late 1920s, but he was not published in a trade edition until the 1960s. That was rectified in a great burst between 1965 and 1970, but reference books and critical studies of the period can take up to a decade to notice such a rediscovery. The Objectivists appear, individually or collectively, in few of the standard books on American poetry. Recognition of a sort has come, but they remain as writers as marginal to the mainstream of American poetry as they were as Jews marginal to the larger intentions of American life.

The Objectivists had their heroes, godfathers, patrons and masters in Rutherford, New Jersey (William Carlos Williams) and in Rapallo, Italy (Ezra Pound). Never slow to encourage potential protégés, Pound printed a long poem by Zukofsky in the third number of *The Exile* in 1928. He advised Williams of the existence of a promising young poet in New York. Williams invited Zukofsky to visit him in Rutherford, and a fruitful relationship followed.[23] They exchanged manuscripts and commented upon each other's work. Zukofsky became, in the words of Williams's biographer, a 'significant force' in the older poet's life.[24] Pound encouraged Basil Bunting to write to Zukofsky.

Bunting, who was then living in Italy as Pound's amanuensis, sent his manuscript poems to Zukofsky and later recalled that

> Zukofsky . . . went through poems I sent him very meticulously, word by word, making suggestions here, fierce strictures there and sometimes recommending the wastepaper basket. (He would also sometimes express enthusiasm for particular lines or passages.) This he did when, as in the early thirties, I think his admiration for my work was very tepid indeed . . .[25]

In addition, in 1930 Pound suggested Zukofsky to Harriet Monroe, the editress of *Poetry*, as a suitable guest editor of an issue devoted to the younger *tendenz* poets:

> Waal, waal, my deah Harriet, I sho iz glad to let these young scrubs have the show to their selves, an ah does hope they dust out your office. My only fear is that Mr. Zukofsky will be just too Goddam prewdent.[26]

The Objectivists assumed a public identity with the February 1931 issue of *Poetry*, but we need to complete the story of the formation of the group before considering their publications. Zukofsky met George Oppen and his wife Mary, not long after they had returned from France, at a party in New York in the winter of 1928–9.[27] They lived in Columbia Heights; Zukofsky lived nearby, on Willow Street. '. . . I would usually get sleepy and go to bed', Mary Oppen recalled, 'and George and Louis would go on talking, and then Louis would have to go teach the next morning so they'd go home and George would walk him over and they would have coffee, and then Louis would walk George back home and they would go on and on and on.'[28] Zukofsky was writing an essay on Pound, and looking for American material for Pound's magazine, *The Exile*.[29] He wrote to Pound on 6 March 1930 about Oppen's poems; he also showed the typescript, which was published in 1934 as *Discrete Series*, to Charles Reznikoff, and took Oppen to meet Reznikoff near the latter's law office in Brooklyn. 'We met in the neighborhood of the office at a cafeteria', Reznikoff wrote, 'and talked about verse and our respect for what Ezra Pound had written about writing verse . . .'[30] By January 1930 Oppen and Zukofsky were planning some sort of publishing venture. Zukofsky would assume editorial responsibility, from

Madison, Wisconsin, where he went to teach; the Oppens, who
planned to return to France, would find a good, cheap printer and
superintend the actual production of the books. Other
possibilities were also emerging. Zukofsky informed Pound in
1930 that Reznikoff had a small press. 'In any kuntry but
Murka', Pound wrote to Williams, 'this wd. solve a lot of
problems.'[31] The Oppens travelled to Rapallo to meet Pound, but
relations were uneasy; Mary Oppen was unwelcome. Carl Rakosi,
who had also been published by Pound in *Exile*, met Zukofsky at
the University of Wisconsin in 1930–1. (Rakosi was a close friend
of the poet Kenneth Fearing at this time.) Thus the basic
connections were formed. Pound was the patron and instigator;
Zukofsky the fulcrum and *animateur*; Oppen had money; Rakosi
contributed poems; and Reznikoff had a small press, a little
money, and some practical business experience.

Williams provided the Objectivists with a name, and a theory of
the poem. With Oppen and Reznikoff at Zukofsky's apartment in
Brooklyn Heights, Williams elaborated the basic notion of what
the Objectivists were seeking:

But, we argued, the poem, like every other form of art, is an
object, an object that in itself formally presents its case and its
meaning by the form it assumes. Therefore, being an object, it
should be so treated and controlled – but not as in the past. For
past objects have about them past necessities – like the sonnet –
which have conditioned them and from which, as a form itself,
they cannot be freed.

The poem being an object (like a symphony or cubist
painting) it must be the purpose of the poet to make of his words
a new form: to invent, that is, an object consonant with his day.
This was what we wished to imply by Objectivism, an antidote,
in a sense, to the bare image haphazardly presented in loose
verse.[32]

The inadequacy of the 'bare image' and the structural dilemmas
of the Imagist verse of the later phase, described by Pound as
'Amygism', stand for the Objectivists as the point of departure. In
a letter to Zukofsky in 1928 we see Williams already using the
term: 'Poems are inventions richer in thought as image. Your
early poems, even when the thought has enough force or

freshness, have not been *objectivized* in new or fresh observations.'[33]

When Zukofsky explained the Objectivists' programme in *Poetry* in 1931, a subtler totality of effect was suggested. He proposed a poetry which went beyond sincerity to 'a perfect rest, complete appreciation':

> This rested totality may be called objectification – the apprehension satisfied completely as to the appearance of the art form as an object . . . its character may be simply described as the arrangement, into one apprehended unit, of minor units of sincerity . . .[34]

This might profitably be related to the notion of the beautiful in Pater, and to the tendency within Symbolist aesthetics to perceive the art work as a reconciliation of tensions, as an achieved, atemporal stasis. (But what you cannot do is to find any common ground between the Zukofskian aesthetic and the revolutionary or proletarian artistic aspirations in America.) The description offered by Zukofsky intimates that form and arrangement would be the natural by-product of the authenticity of the 'minor units of sincerity'. It was, unfortunately, a rather sophisticated way of whistling optimistically in the dark. Zukofsky's *A*, begun in the 1920s, is the only attempt to write a long poem on Objectivist principles. Without the structural scaffolding which Pound took from Dante and Homer in *The Cantos*, *A* is hermetic and, in parts, an extravagantly 'difficult' poem. Zukofsky has followed the logic of his argument to its conclusion with a dedication which can only seriously be compared to Joyce's labours on *Finnegans Wake*. No matter what else might be said about *A*, it simply cannot be described as an 'apprehended unit', to be 'objectivized' in any meaningful way.

Other Objectivists, we can now see, had a rather more modest understanding of the concept. Reznikoff, who had throughout the 1920s remained faithful to the ideals of Imagism *circa* 1915, regarded the term as describing a writer

> . . . who does not write directly about his feelings but about what he sees and hears; who is restricted almost to the testimony of a witness in a court of law; and who expresses his feelings indirectly by the selection of his subject-matter . . .[35]

Rakosi seems to have been the closest to Reznikoff in temperament. The distance separating their work, with its distinctive bitter ironies and compassion, from the exactitudes of Oppen (in Hugh Kenner's apt phrase, a 'geometer of minima') and the cerebral Zukofsky suggests how limited the group was from the start: the shared ground was smaller than contemporary observers noted, and grew smaller still in the intervening years. Objectivism was Zukofsky, and, to a lesser extent, Oppen; the others had different ambitions and cannot be measured by their congruence with Zukofsky's programme.

This is not to say that there was not such a thing as an Objectivist poem. What Williams described in his autobiography of the meeting with Zukofsky, Oppen and Reznikoff was essentially clear. They agreed in principle that the poem was not to be the vehicle for the expression of subjective or 'personal' emotions; they were all anti-romantic. The insistence on form, on the poem as fully-realized object, was perhaps too generalized to serve as an adequate definition of a school. But it left them with a clear distinction between the kind of poem they wanted to write, which would be spare, definite, minimal, imagistic, and the increasingly subjective and sprawling verse of the 1920s. There was another consideration, however, which was to play an important role in all of their lives: the Depression. The literary consequences of the collapse of the stock market in the autumn of 1929 was felt in various ways. The sales of books fell off, commissions from magazines were competed for more energetically; little magazines like *Pagany*, which had printed many of the Objectivists, found it virtually impossible to pay printers' bills; private patrons suddenly found themselves with dramatically-reduced income from investments. The Objectivists, like so many other writers of their generation, and of their religion, were moved by the spectre of mass unemployment, and feared the likely consequences of fascism at home and abroad. They moved into the orbit of the Communist Party, and were then confronted by the consequences of the politization of literature. In the past, as Michael Gold noted, doggerel and versified social concern had dominated the literary ideals of the left. In 1915 Upton Sinclair edited a massive anthology, *The Cry for Justice*, which brought together any and every brand of literary concern, from bourgeois liberal to Marxian socialist: literature in traditional forms was the vehicle for an appeal to reason–

decency–humanity–legality ar 1 so on. In literary terms, such a collection represented the *bien ensant* progressive spirit; the forms were provided, and remained inexamined. By the 1930s a more sophisticated versification was expected on the left: the impact of Eliot and Pound was beginning to be felt. There was also a strong pressure on writers to *write* as Marxists: not only were poems to be about the class struggle, but poets should try (it was suggested) to incorporate the class struggle through the act of writing itself, which would be dialectical and materialist. In the process of Stalinizing the literary left, clear distinctions were needed to separate proletarian and revolutionary writing from the bourgeois and liberal literary values which dominated American culture. Among the first criteria to be accepted was to govern the relationship between the writer and his readers: an explicit commitment to socialism, or the class struggle, was expected. Any literature which suggested a neutral stance, which was tainted by bourgeois aestheticism (as in Thornton Wilder) or political indifferentism, was harshly condemned. Yet as poets the Objectivists were pursuing goals which assumed the absence of integral ties between the poet and his audience. (There was no audience for the poems they wanted to write.) Comrades within the party identified Objectivism with a lack of explicit political commitment, and rejected their work. In later years the Objectivists tended to describe the idea behind the movement in formal terms. George Oppen wrote: '"Objectivist" meant, not an objective viewpoint, but to objectify the poem, to make the poem an object. Meant form.'[36]

The gap between the verse in the *New Masses, Anvil* and *Dynamo* (and in the many little John Reed Club magazines), and that which Zukofsky collected in *An 'Objectivists' Anthology*, was too great to be meaningfully crossed. The choice facing them was either to write the sort of poems which would be acceptable to the editors of the radical journals, to write for the diminishing number of apolitical *avant-garde* little magazines, or to stop writing altogether. Oppen and Rakosi chose silence. (Of course there were complex psychological dimensions to their silence: politics can only explain an aspect of their dilemma.[37]) Zukofsky chose, in the Russian metaphor, to write for his desk drawer. After a period in the mid-1930s when Reznikoff published several political poems (especially 'Jerusalem the Golden', in which he contrasted the remote God of Spinoza with the humane, secularized Judaism of Karl Marx, upon which hopes of enlightenment and progress might be based), Reznikoff felt more comfortable with Biblical and Zionist material – subjects far removed from the active concerns of the American left. Politics, indeed the 'noise of history', scattered the movement, interrupted their careers, and helped to heighten the differences between them.

The February 1931 issue of *Poetry*, which announced their existence, did little to clarify their intention. Zukofsky included poems by young left-wing writers (Norman Macleod, Harry Roskolenkier, John Wheelwright), contributions from expatriates (Samuel Putnam, Charles Henri Ford), as well as material from writers who had established themselves in the previous decade, such as Williams. There was little common ground between them. When Zukofsky prepared the manuscript of *An 'Objectivists' Anthology*, he increased the number of poems by Williams to over 25 pages. Pound sent in a feeble satire (beginning 'Gentle Jheezus sleek and wild'), which was to some extent atoned for by the inclusion of T. S. Eliot's 'Marina'. Only one poem by Oppen was included, and two by Rakosi. Reznikoff's presence was more substantial and varied: Zukofsky included the text of the verse drama 'Rashi', a selection from the prose version of *Testimony*, and the splendid poem 'The English in Virginia'. By far the most substantial contributions came from Kenneth Rexroth (39 pages) and from Zukofsky (45 pages), who also contributed an introduction entitled ' "Recencies" in Poetry'.

An 'Objectivists' Anthology was published by George Oppen's To Publishers in 1932. It was reviewed with greater or lesser hostility in *Hound & Horn* (October–December 1932) by Yvor Winters, and in *Poetry* (March 1933) by M. U. Schappes. Winters took some pleasure in the absence from the anthology of any of the truly talented writers of his generation. Schappes complained that Zukofsky's *A* reflected 'anarchy and chaos, spiritual and aesthetic'. William Carlos Williams contributed a generally sympathetic review to *The Symposium* (January 1933), but admitted some reservations when he described the Objectivists' method as 'the presentation, simply, of certain new objects without obvious connection with the classics and which he entitles "poems" '. In 1938 Williams's misgivings about Zukofsky emerged in a letter to Norman Holmes Pearson:

I admire Louis but his work is either the end, the collapse or the final justification of the objective method. He is building up a literary argument for Marxism. He is placing sentences, paragraphs, slices of speech in a line – for their flavor and special character – by that to build a monument, a literary creation. It is very difficult to grasp and impossible to follow with a mind of my type. Yet it is very good (in theory) and solid in practice. But is it literature? I dunno. I do not know. It seems an impossible method, without sequence, without 'swing,' without consecutiveness except one have the mind of a mathematician plus the inventiveness of such a poet as never existed in this world. So maybe it is good, if it is good.[38]

The experimental poems by Rexroth and Zukofsky strain to breaking point the Objectivist goal of the poem as 'rested totality'. The effect on contemporary readers less than a decade after the appearance of 'The Waste Land', and before Pound's *A Draft of XXX Cantos* had been published in America, was perhaps predictable. *An 'Objectivists' Anthology* found very few readers; it was not a commercial or a critical success.

Oppen had in the meantime published another book in France: Williams's *A Novelette and Other Prose* (1932). On his return to America the publishing venture was given a new name, the Objectivist Press, and was organized along cooperative lines. The poets would individually pay for their own books to be published. The first title to appear was Williams's *Collected Poems 1921–31*, to which he gave $250 towards the cost of production. Williams's career was at a low ebb in the early 1930s, as he wrote to Pound: 'What shall you say about me? That I have a volume of verse which I have been in the process of making for the past ten years, that it is the best collection of verse in America today and that I can't find a publisher . . .'[39] Pound sympathized, but very much doubted whether the *Collected Poems 1921–31* was 'the best collection of verse in America today': he described it in a letter as 'Bill's worst book . . . But there is some damn good stuff there. After all, the footchoor [future] can leave out the slop. No, he ain't better than pore or ole Possum, and we damn well need 'em *both*.'[40]

Williams's book was followed in 1934 by George Oppen's *Discrete Series*, with a preface by Ezra Pound, and by three titles by Charles Reznikoff: *Jerusalem the Golden*, *Testimony*, with an introduction by Kenneth Burke, and *In Memoriam: 1933*. A volume by Basil Bunting was projected but never realized. Apparently money could not be found for volumes by Rakosi or Zukofsky. Williams's next two titles were issued by the Alcestis Press. Pound's work was being published by Farrar & Rinehart and other commercial publishers. The final book from the Objectivist Press was Reznikoff's *Separate Way* in 1936. Williams covered his expenses, but the others sold poorly. Large quantities were stored in the basement of the Gotham Book Mart, where they remained for decades.

Neither the anthology nor the press succeeded in establishing Oppen or Reznikoff in New York literary life. After *Separate Way*, Reznikoff printed and published his books under his own name. Rakosi's first book was published by James Laughlin's New Directions Press in 1941. Laughlin, a disciple of Pound's, became Williams's and Pound's principal American publisher in the 1940s. It is a pity that he did not attempt to put Zukofsky, Oppen or Reznikoff before the public at that time. What little notice they received was soon forgotten. Their experience was not particularly uncommon. The fate of Henry Roth, author of *Call It Sleep* (1934), was to fall into a similar limbo, and like the Objectivists to be resurrected in the 1960s.

The subsequent careers of the Objectivists belong, more properly, to another chapter in the history of modern American poetry. Oppen and Rakosi emerged from their silence to find appreciative readers. Reznikoff remained the most consistent poet of the four, bringing to accounts of the Nazi death camps the same terrifying objectivity which characterized his poems from the 1920s on urban ghetto life. Zukofsky's lonely, bitter independence brought him admirers in the end, particularly Charles Tomlinson and Robert Creeley, but little public recognition or comprehension of his work.[41] In his last decade Zukofsky's relations with Oppen soured, and he refused to attend Reznikoff's funeral.

They were the heirs of the Imagists, the protégés and logical successors of the line of Pound and Williams. The Objectivists sought to formulate a new and more exacting notion of poetic form than that which had currency in the 1920s. The disruption of their careers, and the artistic isolation which they experienced, have a distinct poignancy. They were all men of the left whose relationship with the left-wing literary movement of the 1930s was disastrous. An interviewer once asked George Oppen how his political friends reacted to the fact that he was a poet. Oppen's reply:

> I didn't tell them. Therefore they didn't react. The situation of the Old Left was the theory of Socialist Realism, etc. It seemed pointless to argue. We stayed carefully away from the people who wrote for the *New Masses*.[42]

It is Oppen's *realism* which is so desolating. 'It seemed pointless to argue' might serve as an epitaph, as much for the social idealisms of the Objectivists as for the left in the 1930s and its relationship to modern literature.

Appendix I: *A Letter on John Reed's 'The Colorado War'*

Boulder, Colorado.
December 5 1915

My dear Mr Sinclair:–

I have your letter of 1st inst.

I do not think the reporter always got me quite right, or as fully as he might have got me.

I did, however, think at the time I testified that Reed's paper in *The Metropolitan* contained some exaggerations. I did not intend to say that he *intentionally* told any untruths, and doubtless he had investigated carefully and could produce witnesses to substantiate what he said. Some things are matters of opinion. Some others are almost incapable of proof. The greater part of Reed's paper is true.

But for example, p. 14 1st column July (1914) *Metropolitan*: 'And orders were that the Ludlow colony must be wiped out. It stood in the way of Mr. Rockefeller's profits.' I believe that a few brutes like Linderfelt probably did *intend* to wipe this colony out, but that *orders* were given to this effect by any responsible person – either civil or military – is incapable of proof.

So the statement that 'only seventeen of them [strikers] had guns', I believe from what Mrs Hollearn [post-mistress] tells me is not quite correct.

On p. 16 Reed says the strikers 'eagerly turned over their guns to be delivered to the militia' – Now it is pretty clear from what happened later that many guns were *retained*: on Dec. 31st I was at Ludlow when some 50 or so rifles – some new, some old – were found under the tents and there were *more* – not found. The boy beaten by Linderfelt (p. 16 – 3rd Column) *could walk* tho he was *badly* beaten.

We could not *find* (see p. 66) '*Hundreds* of strike-breakers [who]

187

escaped at night over the hills in the snow' – tho, during the Congressional Investigation we found *some*.

It is doubtful if Judge McHendrie p. 67 (Column 1.) could properly be called 'an *appointee* of the C.F & I.' – tho he *had been* a partner of Northcutt.

P. 69 'four militiamen . . . slouched up to the men's diamond . . . *leveling their rifles insolently on the crowd* ' – I have tried to verify this and have failed, but may be it was so.

It is almost impossible to show definitely *who fired the first shot* on the morning of April 20th – but he puts it as if it were established that, after the signal bombs were set off, (p. 69), '*suddenly, without warning, both machine guns pounded stab-stab-stab full on the tents.*'

P. 72 (Column 1) 'Children on the sidewalks were mowed down by the bullets' – (This at 7th St. in Walsenburg) – I may be misinformed as to this – but I'm told it was not so.

Nevertheless – there was much more truth than error in Reed's paper, and I ought not to have left the impression that I thought it *untrue as a whole*.

Of course, the *absolute truth* is bad enough – even the facts as admitted by the Operators' friends and by the Militia are enough to damn them in the eyes of civilized men.

What I was trying to express in my testimony at this point was, I suppose, the fact that exaggerated, wild, statements had been made on both sides, but that the operators had been in this [indecipherable] the more guilty. The accounts of '*Ludlow*' prepared by the hired writers of the operators – notably that called '*The Story of Ludlow*' by one Paddock (an editor of this city) – are full of the *grossest lies* – far exceeding anything that I call exaggerations in Reed's paper.

Sincerely Yours,
James H. Brewster

[Sinclair Mss, Lilly Library, Indiana University. Brewster (1856–1920) was a lawyer and later professor of law.]

Appendix II: *Some Versions of the Isadora Duncan Myth*

Duncan was herself an extravagant self-mythologizer.[1] In their turn, her audiences and admirers endowed Duncan's performances with many of their own preoccupations: cultural nationalism, the struggle for sexual freedom, and the urge to unrestrained self-expression are the major themes which appear in responses to her art. It has been less clearly understood that there were political dimensions to the Duncan cult, and that during the First World War, when she utterly committed herself to the Allies' cause, Duncan began to be seen with different eyes by the artists and writers in Greenwich Village who led the enthusiastic discovery of her genius.

In July 1908 Isadora Duncan returned home to America. In the eight years since her departure for Europe she gained fame and notoriety. 'I had created an Art, a School, a Baby', Duncan wrote in her autobiography. 'Not so bad. But, as far as finances went, I was not much richer than before.'[2] Her manager tried to put Duncan in a Broadway theatre with a small orchestra, but the temperature in the city was in the nineties, the critics were hostile, and the booking was an outright failure. Despite her legendary performances in Budapest, Vienna, Munich, Berlin, Paris and London, New Yorkers seemed impervious to the Duncan phenomenon. A tour of smaller American cities was an even more emphatic flop. Without sufficient funds to return to Europe, Duncan took a studio in the Beaux Arts Building in New York, where she danced for select audiences of poets and artists. Greenwich Village warmed to her. Painters and writers, including Robert Henri, George Bellows, Edwin Arlington Robinson, Ridgely Torrence and William Vaughn Moody attended Duncan's evenings. Max Eastman became a devotee, as did Mitchell Kennerley, Percy MacKaye and Arnold Genthe. Word soon reached the New York press that there was a 'Duncan cult' in the Village. Duncan was described in the New York *Sun* as 'a dancing sprite, an amber figurine offering you wine from an uplifted cup, throwing roses at Athene's shrine, swimming on the crest of the purple waves of the Aegean Sea'.[3] When Walter Damrosch persuaded her to perform at the Metropolitan Opera House accompanied by a full orchestra, a successful tour followed which culminated in a triumphant performance before President Roosevelt.

The younger generation of writers and artists saw in her the promise of a new, liberated life devoted to self-expression, high art and progressive social ideals. To William Carlos Williams, when he saw Duncan dance at her studio in October 1908, she seemed an inspiration for the artistic life. He wrote to his brother Edgar that her dance 'doubly strengthened my desire and my determination to accomplish my part in our wonderful future'. He devoted a poem to her:

Isadora when I saw you dance the interrupting years fell back,
It seemed with far intenser leave than lack
Of your deft steps hath e'er conferred no flaw . . .[4]

(This was very early Williams indeed.) The painter Robert Henri saw in Duncan 'one of the prophets who open to our vision the possibility of a life where full natural expression will be the aim of all people'.[5] Leonard D. Abbott, a leading figure in the Ferrer School in New York, saw Duncan as 'a natural-born anarchist'.[6] Despite the classical ambition behind her dance, Americans saw Duncan as the embodiment of the Whitman legacy. The sculptor George Grey Barnard asked her to model the figure of 'America Dancing' for a Whitmanesque sculptural project.[7] To Max Eastman she was a 'winged apostle to the whole world of Walt Whitman's vision of a poised and free-bodied and free-souled humanity'.[8]

Duncan sought to revive the ideals of classical Greek dance, abandoning the traditional flared tulle skirt and tights of classical ballet for a loosely-draped tunic. She danced barefoot, on a stage empty of decoration. Duncan was convinced that she had discovered the true austerity of classical art, a primitive, archaic expressiveness which could be conjured out of twentieth-century consciousness. But according to Lewis Mumford, 'what mattered in Isadora's Hellenic dances and dramatic presentations was not the Greek themes or the gauzy costumes but the uninhibited vitality, the sense of a glorious nakedness about to be affirmed, not only in the rituals of lovers but in every part of life'.[9] Hart Crane admiringly described Duncan, standing before a hostile and incomprehending audience in Cleveland, with right breast and nipple exposed, telling everyone to go home and read Walt Whitman's 'Calamus'. 'Glorious to see her there . . . telling the audience that truth was not pretty . . .'[10]

Duncan made a religion of impulse, and became a symbol of the 'new paganism'.[11] Floyd Dell, who saw Duncan and her young dancers in her loft on lower Fifth Avenue, wrote a poem, 'On Seeing Isadora Duncan's School', which he published in the New York *Tribune* of 4 February 1915:

> It is a poem and a prophecy –
> A glimpse across the forward gulf of time
> To show our dazzled souls what life shall be
> Upon the sunlit heights toward which we climb:
> A flaming challenger to a world benighted
> A lamp of daring in our darkness lighted.

Abraham Walkowitz, a painter in Alfred Stieglitz's circle, saw Duncan dance at Rodin's studio: 'Her body was music. It was a body electric like Walt Whitman.' Walkowitz did more than 5000 drawings of Isadora Duncan in motion.[12]

A profligate life and unashamed sexual liberation made her an outlaw, a renegade, pursued by police, hounded by detectives, condemned by clergymen. There was little tradition or admiration of aristocratic libertinism in America. Duncan came as a breath of fresh air to young writers such as Dell and Randolph Bourne, who had fought their way out of the 'old tyrannies' of small-town life:

> We grow up in the home that society has shaped or coerced our parents into accepting, we adopt the customs and language and utensils that have established themselves for our present through a long process of survival and invention and change. We take the education that is given us, and finally the jobs that are handed out to us by society. As adults, we act in the way that society expects us to act; we submit to whatever regulations and coercions society imposes on us. We live almost entirely a social

life, that is, a life as a constituted unit in Society, rather than a free and personal one.[13]

Louis Fraina, soon to become a founding member of the Communist Party, saw in Duncan's art a realization of 'the natural unity of feeling, thought, and expression which in social life was fragmented and crushed'.[14] To other radicals, Duncan seemed to transcend all ideologies in a vision of beauty. Floyd Dell made the point that she

> has made us despise the frigid artifice of the ballet and taught us that in the natural movements of the body are contained the highest possibilities of choreographic beauty. It has been to many of us one of the finest experiences of our lives to see, for the first time, the marble maidens of the Grecian urn come to life in her, and all the leaf-fringed legends of Arcady before our enamored eyes. She has touched our lives with the magic of immemorial loveliness.[15]

When he reviewed the photographer Arnold Genthe's *The Book of the Dance* in *The Masses* in 1916, Dell returned once again to the first time he saw Duncan:

> It does not console me to remember that through that darkness there flamed such meteors as Nietzsche and Whitman, Darwin and Marx, prophetic of the splendors of millenium. When I think that if I had lived and died in the darkness of that century I should never have seen with these eyes the beauty and terror of the human body, I am glad of the daylight of my own time. It is not enough to throw God from his pedestal, and dream of superman and the co-operative commonwealth: one must have *seen* Isadora Duncan to die happy.
>
> I remember the revelation it was of the full glory of the human body, when I first saw her dance. The beauty of it was terrific and blinding; it re-created the soul anew with its miraculous loveliness, the loveliness of youth and joy. And it still haunts me, that last time, when I saw the tragic poem which was unfolded in her slow and poignant rhythms – the magnificence of grief and pain . . . and then, a future more radiant than any I have ever seen in my Socialist or Nietzschean vision . . .[16]

These sentiments were not soon forgotten in the Village. The changed mood of the 1930s is nicely indicated when Joseph Freeman (to whom Dell dedicated his book on Upton Sinclair in 1927) mockingly quoted from this review: 'Grateful for the daylight of his own time, he [Dell] felt that it was not enough to throw God from his pedestal and dream of supermen and the co-operative commonwealth. To die happy, one must have seen Isadora Duncan.' [17] By the standards of the left in the 1930s, Dell's praise encapsulated the self-indulgent bohemianism which the party's cultural cadres attacked. Duncan stood for a style of radicalism which had largely disappeared from the political landscape a dozen years later.

'Until America entered the war', wrote Freeman, 'the radiant Duncan myth remained intact.' [18] During her American tour in 1915, and 'indignant at the apparent indifference of America to the war', Duncan did an improvisation to the 'Marseillaise' at the Metropolitan Opera House. 'It was a call to the boys of America to rise and protect the highest civilisation of our epoch – that culture which has come to the world through France.' [19] John Sloan's drawing of Duncan in *The Masses* of May 1915 was a less than adulatory response to her new-found martial enthusiasms. His Duncan is overweight, knock-kneed and wears too much eye makeup. The audiences cheered and cheered. In 1917, again at the Met, her performances each night ended with the 'Marseillaise'. 'At that time I believed, as did many others, that the whole world's hope of liberty, regeneration and civilisation depended on the Allies winning the war . . .' [20] Joseph Freeman recalled the dismay her patriotic dances caused among the left-wing intellectuals. 'Floyd Dell heaped more bitter scorn upon her than upon John Dewey and Thorstein Veblen.' [21]

Disillusionment with Duncan was harshly expressed. Margaret Anderson, editor of the *Little Review*, saw Duncan perform at the Met in 1917, but could find nothing behind her work other than the dream of an adolescent mind:

Isadora felt a great deal. She shook her head and arms in such a fury of feeling that she appeared to be strangling; and when there was no way of reaching a further intensification she shook her whole body in a kind of spasm of human inability to bear the grief of the world. And every move was a futile and pitiable one because never once did her body become that mould through which a design is to shape its course and flow into its ultimate form.[22]

Anderson concluded that Duncan was 'a woman of small intelligence, a monument of undirected adolescent vision, an ingrained sentimentalist'. It was more difficult to take Duncan seriously in the 1920s. The black poet Claude McKay noted that by then she had become 'fat and flabby'.[23] Walter Duranty, the New York *Times* correspondent in Moscow, described her as someone who had become 'fat and lazy and drank to excess'.[24] Eunice Tietjens, assistant editor of Harriet Monroe's *Poetry*, saw Duncan dance at the Trocadero in Paris. She primly noted that Duncan's feet and legs were 'heavy and ugly'.[25] Joseph Freeman had tea with Duncan in London: 'Isadora's body was bloated, the skin of her face loose and wrinkled, her eyes bleary and infinitely tired'.[26] Duncan had changed; but so too had those who saw her. Scandal seemed to follow her everywhere. She became so impulsively intimate with Scott Fitzgerald one evening in St Paul-de-Vence that Fitzgerald's wife Zelda, in a typically self-destructive gesture, threw herself down a darkened flight of stone steps.[27] When Mabel Dodge's memoirs of her Greenwich Village years appeared in 1936, yet one more unflattering portrait of the dancer was preserved for posterity. In 1915 Dodge and Walter Lippmann invited the Mayor of New York, John P. Mitchel, to meet Duncan. When she failed in an attempt to bring the mayor on to a large sofa beside her, Duncan angrily lectured the politician over the case of Mrs Sniffen, a New York woman convicted of murdering her children, and about whom Duncan had written two long letters to the New York *Sun*.[28] The death of her own children in an automobile accident in 1913 had undoubtedly changed Duncan's personality. She became more fanatical, nihilistic, boring.

For some of those who saw her in the 1920s, traces of the old magic remained. Claude McKay spent an evening with Duncan at her studio in Nice:

I had never seen her in her great glory and couldn't imagine that she could still be wonderful when she was so fat and flabby. But what she did that night was stupendous. I was the only audience besides the pianist. And she danced from Chopin, Tchaikovsky, Wagner and Beethoven. Her face was a series of different masks. And her self was the embodiment of Greek tragedy, *un être* endowed with divinity.[29]

Eunice Tietjens had much the same experience when Duncan danced:

> When Isadora appeared she was barelegged. I had never seen, nor had anyone else, bare legs on the stage. And Isadora's feet and legs were heavy and ugly; moreover she had fallen, and on one knee was a great sordid scab as big as a dollar. I had been trained to be aesthetic, and I shuddered at the sight.
>
> But she had not been dancing five minutes before such defects ceased to exist and that warm exultation came over me which I have known at rare intervals in the presence of great art. The younger generation, who have from infancy seen scantily clad girls flinging their limbs about in 'aesthetic dancing,' can have no adequate realization of what it meant to see for the first time the human form come alive under their eyes . . .[30]

Max Eastman first met Duncan in 1908, when she was doing studio performances. It was in 1917, when Duncan had her six young girl pupils with her, and worked with a complete and inspired orchestra, that she 'really achieved for a time the whole of her aesthetic dream'.[31] After one performance, Eastman scribbled down a sonnet which he sent to Duncan and subsequently published in *The Liberator*: 'Who is this naked-footed lovely girl', he asked, 'Of summer meadows dancing on the grass?'

> So young and tenderly her footsteps pass,
> So dreamy-limbed and lightly wild and warm –
> The bugles murmur and the banners furl,
> And they are lost and vanished like a storm![32]

Eastman soon found himself taking tea with Duncan. In his memoir he confessed to having mixed feelings about her as a person. 'I was repelled by her conversational and behavioral heroics, her confusion, all through life, of gesticulation with gesture.'[33] After tea she dragged out a Ouija board and insisted that Eastman join her in a consultation. With his rigorous training in pragmatic philosophy at Columbia University, and his reinterpretation of Marxism in the name of modern science, Duncan couldn't have chosen a more comic and ingenuous way to proposition Eastman. The Ouija board's message was that Eastman should father a child by the dancer. He withdrew in consternation, the tables uncomfortably turned on one of the most dedicated womanizers in New York.

To no small extent, the staff of *The Masses* invented the cult of Duncan in America. The enthusiasm of Floyd Dell was sufficient to carry Eastman along. Robert Henri, John Sloan and the artists needed no persuading; nor, later, did Claude McKay. In Duncan, the magazine, and the Village, had its symbol, nowhere better expressed than in a poem by Joel Elias Spingarn, Professor of Comparative Literature at Columbia University:

> In the crowded theater, home of painted faces,
> Came the West Wind, breathing joy and life and freshness,
> Came the Springtime, making winter warm with dreaming –
> Came (to thrill our pulses) Isadora Duncan.
> There we saw you – while our breath took shape in woman –
> Marry human motion to immortal music.[34]

Like so many other aspects of cultural radicalism, Duncan and those who created her cult were never quite the same after the war.[35]

Appendix III: *Trotsky and 'Partisan Review': A Correspondence*

INTRODUCTORY NOTE

The correspondence between Trotsky and the *Partisan Review* began in July 1937 and ended in February 1940. Relations between the magazine and Trotsky were the subject of bitter polemic in the period after the *Partisan Review* was relaunched in 1937 as an independent anti-Stalinist radical journal. The editors were unhappy at the accusations in the *New Masses* and *Daily Worker* that they were 'Trotzkyist Schemers'. 'We do not consider ourselves "Trotskyists" . . .', the editors replied in December 1937. In a retrospective survey of the magazine's achievement in 1946, the editors, Phillips and Rahv, carefully described the magazine's restricted involvement with Trotsky:

> It goes without saying that we were intransigently anti-Stalinist; and though in some quarters – where people took their cue from the Stalinists – we were quickly stamped as Trotskyite, the truth is that of all the editors only Dwight Macdonald was a member of that party, and he but for a short time. Our editorial position could then be said to have been Trotskyite only in the sense that we mainly agreed with Trotsky's criticisms of the Soviet regime and that we admired him as a great exponent of the Marxist doctrine. Beyond that we were not willing to accept many of the specific theories and practices of the Trotskyites, while they, on their part, greeted the first issue of our new publication with a diatribe that demonstrated nothing more than their affinity with the Stalinists – at least so far as their attitude toward the intellectuals was concerned.[1]

Subsequent discussions of the *Partisan Review*, with certain shadings of emphasis, have followed the editors' own account.[2]

The relationship turns out to be more complicated than most commentators have suggested. When Dwight Macdonald wrote to Trotsky on 7 July 1937 his own credentials as a supporter of Trotsky, and his prominent role on the Committee for the Defense of Leon Trotsky, were emphasized. The new journal, he explained, was to be 'independent Marxist', but the emphasis would be on cultural rather than political matters. Macdonald's letter did not come out of the blue. James T. Farrell and James Burnham, close collaborators of the editorial group, had informed Trotsky of the group's break with the Stalinists the month before, and of their plans for a new magazine.

Trotsky was in the middle of a deep and destructive intrigue within the Socialist Party.[3] His supporters in the Clarity Group were advised, in a secret letter in June 1937, that it might be necessary to resume full tactical independence – taking with them the cream of militants in the Young People's Socialist League. He had received visits from Herbert Solow and Eleanor Clark, sympathizers with Trotsky who were close to the *Partisan Review* editors. He was, in fact, busily extending the range of his contacts with anti-Stalinist intellectuals, very few of whom were not a little flattered to receive a letter from Lenin's collaborator and the dynamo of the Red Army. Trotsky began to contribute to *The Nation* in the summer of 1937. His supporters were busy, too. Pioneer Publishers was founded in New York in 1937. A new journal, *Socialist Appeal*, was designed to be the organ of the newly-independent Trotskyists.[4] It was a particularly fraught spring and summer. In Spain, Trotsky's quasi-allies in the POUM were being shot down by Stalinists in the streets of Barcelona. The civil war in Spain, the Moscow trials and the Popular Front strategy of the Communist International, created an explosive situation in which, for a moment, a vast dislocation on the left seemed possible. The letter from Macdonald in July 1937 was a further sign to Trotsky of the decay of Stalinism in American intellectual life. He cautiously welcomed the venture, but wanted to explore a little further the nature of the 'independent' Marxism of the *Partisan Review*. His caution was, in part, caused by the fact that Trotsky had more supporters in America than anywhere else in the world. He had to be careful not to offend their *amour propre* by too quickly welcoming a group of young ex-Stalinists.

Writing to Trotsky on 23 August 1937, Macdonald maintained the 'cultural' rather than 'political' orientation of the journal. They broke from Stalinism, he suggested, because it was having a disastrous influence on radical culture. He knew that they would be attacked as Trotskyists but, despite the fact that most of the editors were to some extent sympathetic to Trotsky's programme, and were not ashamed or apprehensive at such links in the public mind, the journal would not involve itself in immediate political controversies. This seemed 'vague' and 'evasive' to Trotsky, and he declined to take up the invitation to contribute. He awaited the first issues of the *Partisan Review* with interest (Trotsky to Macdonald, 11 September 1937). A month later Trotsky broke off relations with Calverton's *Modern Monthly* over the presence of a Stalinist, Carleton Beals, on the editorial board. He was determined not to compromise with enemies and waverers.

The correspondence was resumed on 15 January 1938, when Macdonald invited Trotsky to contribute to a symposium on Marxism. The possible contributors included Karl Korsch, Boris Souvarine, Harold Laski, Meyer Schapiro, Lewis Corey, Bertram Wolfe, Sidney Hook, Ignazio Silone, August Thalheimer, Edmund Wilson, Victor Serge and Fenner Brockway, a pot pourri of anti-Stalinists which repelled Trotsky. He rejected the idea of the symposium, and the 'political corpses' who had been invited provoked Trotsky to lash out at Macdonald: 'You evidently wish to create a small cultural monastery, guarding itself from the outside world by scepticism, agnosticism and respectability' (Trotsky to Macdonald, 20 January 1938).

After this outburst, the prickly task of dealing with Trotsky was handed over to Philip Rahv, who wrote a letter of condolence on the death of Trotsky's son, Leon Sedov (Rahv to Trotsky, 28 February 1938). After an encouraging acknowledgement of their letter, Rahv wrote again to Trotsky in Coyoacan:

March 1, 1938

Dear Mr. Trotsky

We, of *Partisan Review*, also wish to be frank with you. Far from appearing to be 'sharp, impermissible and sectarian,' your letter raises questions which go to the heart of our editorial problems. We gladly accept your invitation to a further exchange of opinions.

Your letter, as a matter of fact, has helped to crystallize some of the dissatisfaction with the development of the magazine we ourselves had begun to feel. The magazine's uncertain line is to some extent conditioned by the uncertainty of the objective situation. Given the narow social and literary base from which we are operating – the isolation of the magazine from the main body of radical intellectuals, and the unprecedented character of our project in the sense that it is the first anti-Stalinist left literary journal in the world, encumbered with a Stalinist past and subject to the tremendous pressure of the American environment towards disorientation and compromise – given all these adverse conditions it was inevitable that in the first few months of its existence the magazine should grope for direction, feel its way towards possible allies, incline to deal somewhat gingerly and experimentally with issues that ideally require a bold and positive approach, and lastly – that in its recoil from the gross deceptions, the loud, arrogant proclamations and hooligan tactics of Stalinism, it should in some respects have leaned over backward to appear sane, balanced, and (alas) respectable. All these are errors, but they are by no means fatal. They are more errors of tone than errors of ideological faith. It is not at all our intention to write off our weaknesses to the account of 'objective conditions'; nevertheless we must insist that an estimate of the magazine in subjective terms *alone*, that is, in terms of estimating the heroism or profundity of the small group of literary men who edit the magazine, leaves so many factors out of consideration as to produce a distortion of what exists. Your letter shows that you are judging us solely by the contents of the first two issues, and we submit that in basing your judgment of two such small objects on a perspective of world thought and world history, as you seem to do, you are adopting a standpoint that is much too general and historical, a standpoint that is ultimatist insofar as it ignores the determinate situation we find ourselves in, the paucity of the literary forces at our disposal, and the unprepared state of our audience for reacting with some degree of understanding – let alone affirmatively – to an intransigent revolutionary position.

Our problems are further complicated by the literary character of the magazine. It is much easier to designate a clear-cut program for a purely ideological organ. In literature, however, – even under favorable circumstances, when an ascendant and unified revolutionary movement inspires the intellectual with militancy and self-confidence – the problem of finding the precise relation between the political and imaginative, the problem of discovering the kind of editorial modulation that will do damage to neither, is so difficult as to exclude any simple and instantaneous solution. In this sphere, in fact, the most elementary questions are still hotly debated; and a correct political line is altogether insufficient as a reply to the bitter and suspicious queries by means of which the writer challenges the claims of ideological systems of political leaders. Moreover, the experience of totalitarian Communism has only served to lend greater credence to the sceptical and agnostic tendencies that are at present making headway all around us. Such tendencies cannot be excommunicated by jaunty epithets like 'philistine' and 'genteel'. On the contrary, an effort should be made to link whatever element of truth and justification these tendencies contain to the scientific spirit of Marxism, to its genius for empiric observation and experiment.

The magazine, in our opinion, has so far accomplished two things. First, it irrevocably cut loose from Stalinism, and in this sense, it has indeed scandalized quite a few 'men of good will' and 'friends of humanity'; second, it has repulsed all attempts to convert this break with Stalinism into a means of slipping back into the bourgeois fold (a course often followed by disillusioned 'revolutionists' with cultural connections). Such articles as Macdonald's on the *New Yorker*, Abel's on Silone, Gide's on Soviet Russia and Rahv's on the writer's congress (in our third issue) have made these facts clear. But now we have reached a turning point. The three issues we have published have established the magazine's identity – its independence of organizational control and its defiance of the dominant trends in the intellectual life of the country. Whether this was accomplished by laying on 'with a whip' or by the use of less notorious weapons is really immaterial. We realize, however, that these relatively primitive tasks are already behind us. The problem of giving the magazine a firm direction, of filling the notions of independence and freedom with an aggressive radical content still remains to be solved.

Our plan is to re-orient the magazine, to stiffen its political spine. In the April issue we are going to publish a long editorial statement that no one will be able to dismiss on the ground of its being abstract, or gently negative. We intend to call things by their right names. But will-power and courage alone cannot do away with the absence of literary forces, of contributors able to meet exacting standards. Because of the lack of such forces we have been compelled to publish some purely formalist critical pieces and poems. We are prepared to defend such contributions on the basis that they are very good examples of a certain kind of discipline and intelligence – and certainly to be preferred to the pseudo-radical shouting in verse and prose that one finds in other left-wing periodicals. Yet it is obvious that an alliance with 'intelligence' per se opens no prospects to the magazine. And in this connection we must say that your attitude to us has been far from encouraging. You must realize that contributions from you would affect the character of the magazine in a drastic way and lift its morale. Instead – and you have done this in the magazine's most formative and crucial period – you have shrugged your shoulders, content to issue criticisms that expose the weak sides of the enterprise. Such criticisms are helpful; your active participation, however, in solving our problems would be much more to the point.

Now as to the symposium on Marxism. In its very nature a symposium presupposes a tolerance of several points of view on the part of its organizers. Otherwise what excuse is there for publishing a diversity of opinions? Whether or not it is accurate to characterize, as you do, some of the people we have invited to contribute as 'political corpses', your characterization is by no means axiomatic to the majority of our readers. And, in the meantime, these 'corpses' are not entirely bereft of influence over the living. By a dramatic juxtaposition of the militant revolutionary position with the extremely vulnerable attitudes of centrism and reformism we hoped to enable the reader to distinguish between the quick and the dead. Like the united front in large political situations, such a symposium can become, on a small scale, an instrument for eliminating from the reader's mind some of the alternatives to Marxist policy which a revolutionist has long ago learned to scorn but which still have some vogue in a backward political environment.

In your letter you complain that we phrase the questions about Marxism as if we were beginning history from a clean page. Unfortunately, to many people the successive defeats of the working class the world over and the moral abyss revealed by the

Moscow trials are tantamount to a theoretical refutation of the basic principles of Marxism. Surely this melancholy fact will never be abolished by the refusal of Marxists to take it into account. After a defeat, one must often start all over again – though, of course, not on the same level as the first time. We, for example, believe that the 'basic principles' have stood the test of history; but in order to convince others that this is so we cannot approach them with the pride of knowledge. And to re-evaluate the Marxist–Leninist tradition is not necessarily to 'revise' it.

We have tried to answer you with the same honesty as your own letter displayed. And, we too, should welcome a continuance of the discussion.

Sincerely,
Philip Rahv
(for the Editorial
Board)

P. S. One concrete suggestion: may we have your permission to publish in Partisan Review an English translation of one or two chapters from the first volume of your new book on Lenin. It is available here in French.

The Marxism symposium number has been postponed for several months. We hope you will re-consider your decision not to participate in it.

Coyoacan, D. F.
March 21, 1938.

Philip Rahv
Partisan Review
22 East 17th St.,
New York City, N.Y.

Dear Mr. Rahv:

Your letter of March 1st pleased me greatly. For my part I am ready to do everything in order to establish friendly collaboration between us. But I wish also to avoid everything that might lead to a break between us after our collaboration has begun. That is why

I considered and still consider that it is best to prolong the period of preliminary exchange of opinion and mutual approchement in order more certainly to assure a stable base for our future relations. A serious step forward has already been made on this road. I await with interest the April number of *Partisan Review* with the programmatic declaration announced by you. But I wish right now to express several considerations which will probably partly coincide with your intentions and partly perhaps go further.

(1) The complete independence of your publication from the Stalinist bureaucracy is of course a very valuable fact. But *independence* alone is insufficient. A *struggle* against the demoralizing influence of Stalinism on the mental life of the left wing of the intelligentsia is necessary. You have already begun this struggle. However, it seems to me, that you have not given it the necessary scope and have not yet found a corresponding tone for it. Stalinism is not 'sectarianism', as such deferential semi-opponents as the Lovestonites often write. Sectarianism presupposes a definite sum of convictions, though they be narrow and limited, and a fanatical defense of these convictions. The Stalinists have no convictions. They are depersonalized people, well-drilled, at bottom completely demoralized functionaries, lackeys, sycophants. The usurped authority of the revolution plus military discipline plus an unlimited treasury have transformed Stalinism into a most ghastly ulcer upon political and intellectual progress. Certain measures are necessary for the struggle against incorrect theory; other measures for the struggle against epidemic cholera. Stalinism is infinitely nearer to Cholera than to false theory. The struggle must be intense, truculent, merciless. An element of 'fanaticism' in this struggle is not only valid but salutary. We will leave it to the Philistines to ridicule 'fanaticism'. Nothing great has been accomplished in history without fanaticism.

(2) It is necessary to discredit the *New Masses* fully and to the end. It seems to me that your magazine might devote a special number to the *New Masses*. A new current, rather than dissipate itself, must be capable of concentrating its blows. What Herbert Solow did with the *New Masses* in the form of light innuendos (No. 3) is incomprehensible to wide circles and should be presented in the form of a series of articles embracing the phenomenon of the *New Masses* from every angle. It is necessary to empty this filthy pail of Stalinism to the bottom. A serious article should in addition

be accompanied by satire and caricature. It is impossible to progress without a whip!

(3) It is my deep conviction that it is necessary to break the state of neutrality in regard to the *Nation* and the *New Republic*. There was a period when these publications 'reconciled' the American intellectuals and liberal bourgeoisie to the U.S.S.R. It is true that they identified the parasitic and ever more reactionary bureaucracy with the October Revolution and Socialism. It is true that they became reconciled to the U.S.S.R. precisely because they hoped it had become 'respectable'. In any case during that period they had their own 'idea': they worshipped the posterior of the victorious revolution. At the moment they have lost this 'idea.' The Soviet bureaucracy has been discovered to be unrespectable – and not accidentally. The sages of the *Nation* and the *New Republic* have been revealed as understanding absolutely nothing about the evolution of the U.S.S.R., that is to say, about the most important phenomenon of our epoch. A Louis Fischer, cynical literary sycophant, more careful but also more repulsive than even Walter Duranty, simply led them by the nose. At present the *Nation* and the *New Republic* are mainly concerned that their readers should not notice that the priest hiding in the oracle is not very wise. Hence come the waves of diplomacy, ruses, lies, falsehoods, filling up the pages of these publications. It is necessary to destroy their influence on radical thought! The struggle against the *Nation* and the *New Republic* ought to be written openly on the banner of the *Partisan Review*.

(4) By this I do not at all wish to say that the *Partisan Review* needs to be transformed into a purely political journal. One and the same tendencies and methods, in different forms and to different degrees pass through all spheres of culture. What a terrible poison the propaganda of 'proletarian humanism' represented – a propaganda tuned on the pitch-pipe of Stalin-Yagoda – on the eve of the series of Moscow trials! The unfortunate Bukharin travelled to Prague and Paris especially to preach the new gospel of Stalin. Culture, philosophy, ethics, and the politics of Stalinism mingled, undividedly in a disgusting heap. It is necessary to destroy this heap. The bombastic, pretentious and hypocritical authorities of the *Nation* and the *New Republic* stand in the way of every movement forward.

(5) I have no illusions about the number of your friends and partisans and take into consideration the enormous force of

resistance which the circles of left intellectuals cemented by Stalinism or demoralized by 'disillusionment' represent. But the way out of these difficulties in no case lies along the road of adaptation or semi-adaptation to these circles. On the contrary: you can mobilize friends, widen their circle, and inspire the waverers with respect only by means of a clear and bold formulation of the problems and through an aggressive policy.

(6) The older generation of radical intellectuals has been poisoned by Louis Fischerism. Attempting at the present time to cleanse itself of this poison it is becoming hostile to Marxism. (Eugene Lyons and his kind seriously imagine that yesterday they were 'Marxists' and 'Bolsheviks'!) The best elements of this generation will perhaps return to the road of the revolution in the future when Marxism embraces the vanguard of the American workers. But now this whole layer cannot be counted upon. *It is necessary to steer one's course to the youth, to the fresh generation, to those 18 to 20 years old*, to those who in the high schools and the universities are awakening for the first time to political thought under the blows of a new crisis and under the danger of an imminent new war. *The Partisan Review should become the organ of the youth.*

(7) For the time being I am not speaking about the workers. The laws of the working class movement are different, deeper, and more ponderous. One thing can be expected with certainty: a new wave of radicalism in the younger generation of intellectuals under the influence of those deeper processes which are at present occurring in the proletariat. At a certain stage these two processes will meet and the better elements of the intellectuals will fructify the new workers' movement. At present the problem is in a preparatory stage. It is precisely in this preparatory period that the *Partisan Review* can play a very serious role.

(8) You reproach me for having taken a position of 'ultimatism' in relation to the *Partisan Review*. I accept this reproach but wish to reduce it to its valid limits. When a political party adopts the methods of ultimatism in relation to the working class ('accept the program or I will turn my back on you!') then this party dooms itself to isolation and sectarian degeneration. But when it is a question of the formation of a leading staff – of a party or a magazine – then ultimatism is inevitable. A program is that 'ultimatum' which the staff places before its own members. The content of the ultimatum may be different. The methods of adaptation and development of a program may and should be

flexible. But the program from the very beginning should be clear, otherwise a publication cannot answer for its own tomorrow. Such is the content of my 'ultimatism.'

(9) If there is at present in America a young and promising movement in art the *Partisan Review* can, to a certain degree, tie its fate to this movement. It is possible however that there is no such vital movement. One can hope that it will appear as a result of the deep crisis through which the country is passing. But no one has yet been successful in artificially manufacturing such an art current. 'Marxist esthetics' has no recipes and prescriptions for this – and cannot have them. Marxism was the first to show what place technique occupies in the development of mankind; however, this does not mean that a Marxist magazine can substitute for a Patent Bureau in technical inventions. The new generation of poets, artists, and so forth can expect from the *Partisan Review* not a ready-made esthetic recipe but a clearing of the paths for new art forms through a struggle against routine, false authorities, ossified formulas, and first of all against convention and falsehood. In the sphere of esthetic schools and methods the *Partisan Review*, it seems to me, will be constrained to observe in a certain sense a critical 'eclecticism' (yes. . . eclecticism!) It is necessary to give new tendencies an opportunity to appear. Likewise it is impossible to ignore purely formal quests and experiments. Here breadth of approach and pedagogical flexibility upon a stable basic historical conception is very important. I believe that in this respect there are no differences between us.

(10) Since the question of a symposium on Marxism has been postponed we can also postpone the argument about it. Briefly I will say only the following: such a symposium can, *perhaps*, have a positive significance if the authors invited are either individuals who have proved themselves to be seriously concerned about Marxist theory, or if they are prominent individuals in the workers' movement. The majority of the authors named by you are the purest dilettantes in theory and moreover completely unconnected with the working class. Had you invited John Lewis or even William Green to write an article about Marxism for you, I could have understood it, since the theoretical thick-headedness and ignorance of Green represent an important political fact which demands an evaluation. But Souvarine. He has never been a Marxist. His biography of Stalin is the work of a journalist,

mainly valuable because of its quotations (the majority of which are, moreover, borrowed from the *Bulletin of the Russian Opposition* so that the credit for their compilation belongs to a great degree to Leon Sedov.) Souvarine long ago broke with the labor movement. He is absolutely devoid of theoretical capacities. Victor Serge is a talented writer. If he were to write a story for you or a drama from the life of the Russian Opposition, I should be pleased. But he is not at all a theorist. In addition, after a number of years of imprisonment in the U.S.S.R. he is now going through a period of complete confusion. It is true that even confusion can be instruction if it characterizes the mental state of a class, a group, a party. But there is hardly any sense in gathering a collection of examples of individual confusion. Moreover, a Symposium of variegated articles should be supplied with a programmatic article from the editors, exposing the blunderers and establishing a correct viewpoint on Marxism. Has such an article been considered? Who will write it? [. . .]

With sincere greetings
L. D. Trotsky

P. S. The rights to the serial reproduction of *Lenin* belong to the publisher, as a guarantee for advance payment, so that unfortunately I can do nothing in this respect.

Partisan Review
New York, N.Y.

April 10,
1938

Leon Trotsky
Coyoacan, D. F.

Dear Mr. Trotsky:

We wish to thank you for your detailed letter of March 21st. Substantially, I think we can say that we are in agreement with your general analysis of the tasks of the magazine and with your comment on the intellectual situation in this country. Our own experiences during the last six months have convinced us that you were right in claiming that a line of 'adaptation or semi-adaptation' will accomplish very little and that only a firm and aggressive policy can affect the waverers. We were particularly pleased by your paragraph on the necessity of maintaining an attitude of 'critical eclecticism' toward purely literary manifestations and experiments. Hence the Marxist accent of the magazine must emerge all the more sharply in its critical and ideological parts. For this reason we intend to enlarge our scope and to publish more pieces of a general cultural and ideological character than heretofore. We shall continue publishing creative material but only if it really merits acceptance – not merely because we have to meet a certain quota of 'literary content'.

Unfortunately we were unable to get the editorial statement into final shape in time for the April issue. The article on the trials was a partial substitute. At present I am working on an essay (The Sorrows of Ilyitch) whose object is to carry through an attack on the new revisionists, the Kronstadt-wailers, and all the rest of that disillusioned crew who have recently taken to belaboring Lenin and Leninism. The moralizing of these people has become insufferable. It is obvious that they will use anything and anybody, including the theories of Luxemburg and distorted versions of Bolshevik party history, to discredit the October revolution and identify Leninism with Stalinism. We of *Partisan Review* are not political theoreticians, but what we can do is try to translate the political analysis that convinces us into cultural metaphors and psychological perceptions. This type of 'translation' implies, of course, a certain kind of irresponsibility on the political side (if 'irresponsibility' is not to be understood too literally) as well as a fair share of subjectivity, inseparable from literary expression. But I think that this is the only way political ideas can be assimilated into literature. We have no use for the kind of 'politicalization' that Stalinism imposes on its writers (I am speaking about the method); in straight political writing it is indeed necessary to formulate one's thought carefully and with full responsibility to the needs of the organization – but to literary men who have reached the level of politics it is not so much the formulation which is important as the general trend and basic position.

We are planning one or several pieces on the *Nation* and *New Republic*. It seems to us that these organs are the real mainstay of

Stalinism among the intellectuals – much more so than the *New Masses*, which no one reads except devoted party-members and sympathizers utterly emptied of all independent thinking. It is the genteel and hypocritical version of Stalinism within the liberal organs which holds the intelligentsia to the Browders and Fosters. Of course, there are deep class reasons for this attachment; but we do believe that a radical attack on *The Nation* and *The New Republic* would do much to weaken their influence.

Again we want to suggest that you send us an article, or several articles. Would you consider reviewing Ignazio Silone's forthcoming book called *The New Machiavelli* [*The School for Dictators*, 1938], which is a discussion of dictators and dictatorship? We would like something on Russian literature in its current stages during and after the purges – or a general piece on the intellectuals and the Soviet Union – or on Marxism and the attempts, repeatedly unsuccessful and blundering, to integrate it into creative writing and painting – or perhaps some autobiographical material? At all events, do let us know soon about such subjects you may have in mind. I think that at this point collaboration between us is both possible and necessary.

We have decided to drop the symposium on Marxism altogether. Both the reasons you have advanced against it and the contributions that have come in so far have made us feel that our original idea had been badly conceived. If any of the contributions turn out to be worthwhile, we may print one or two as individual pieces . . .

> Sincerely,
> Philip Rahv
> (for the editorial board)

The editors of the *Partisan Review* were in the end able to print only three contributions from Trotsky: 'Art and Revolution' (August 1938), a vivid but thin self-justification of Trotsky's role and policies; the Breton–Rivera 'Manifesto: Towards a Free Revolutionary Art' (Autumn 1938), largely written by Trotsky; and a letter to Breton (Winter 1939) denouncing André Malraux. In March 1938 William Phillips attempted to defend Marxism against the current practices of Marxists.[5] In April Rahv wrote to Trotsky of the 'Marxist accents' of the *Partisan Review*. So fast was the tide turning that in less than a year Rahv signalled the end of all revolutionary hopes: 'The historic process must be conceived on the plane of tragedy.'[6] The memory of their involvement with Trotsky faded in the cruel light of 1939.

[The Trotsky–*Partisan Review* correspondence is held in the Houghton Library, Harvard University, and is reprinted with permission.]

Notes and References

CHAPTER 1

1. Jacob Riis, *How the Other Half Lives*, ed. Donald N. Bigelow (1980; reissued 1957) p. 33.
2. Ibid., pp. 91–2.
3. William Dean Howells, *A Hazard of New Fortunes*. ed. Tony Tanner (1890; reissued 1965) pp. 162–3.
4. Riis, *How the Other Half Lives*, p. 79.
5. Ibid., p. 23.
6. Ibid., p. 226.
7. For a socialist appraisal of Riis see Vida D. Scudder, 'Jacob Riis on Socialism', *New York Evening Call* (8 July 1908).
8. *Letters from Jack London*, ed. King Hendricks and Irving Shepard (1966) p. 165.
9. Andrew Hacker, 'The Lower Depths', *New York Review of Books*, XXIX (12 August 1982) 15–20.
10. Sinclair, *The Jungle*, ch. 7.
11. London, *The People of the Abyss* (1903; reissued 1977 with an Introduction by Jack Lindsay) p. 36.
12. Ibid., p. 75.
13. Earle Labor, *Jack London* (1974) pp. 92–3.
14. London, *Abyss*, p. 88.
15. Ibid., pp. 89–90.
16. Andrew Sinclair, *Jack: A Biography of Jack London* (1978) pp. 88–9.
17. London, *Abyss*, p. 71.
18. Ibid., p. 92.
19. Ibid., p. 122.
20. Kautsky began a review of *Wenn die Natur ruft* (*The Call of the Wild*) in *Die Neue Zeit*, XXVI (1907–8) 376: 'Der name Jack Londons hat unter den amerikanischen Socialisten einen guten Klang.'
21. His 'How I Became a Socialist' was first collected in *War of the Classes* (1905), and is available in many collections of London's writing.
22. Kenneth S. Lynn, *The Dream of Success* (1955) pp. 75–120.
23. London, *The Sea-Wolf*, ed. Matthew J. Bruccoli (1904; reissued 1964) p. 136.
24. Ibid., p. 238.
25. Frederick C. Giffin, 'Leon Trotsky in New York City', *New York History*, XLIX (October 1968) 391–403.
26. Vaillant-Couturier's introduction is reprinted in the Jack London number of *Europe*, nos 561–2 (Janvier–Fevrier 1976) 79–82.

27. Trotsky to Joan London, reprinted in Leon Trotsky, *On Literature and Art*, ed. Paul N. Siegel (1970). There are further letters between Trotsky and Joan London in the Trotsky archive, Houghton Library, Harvard University.

28. Ira Kipnis, *The American Socialist Movement, 1897–1912* (1952) p. 299.

29. London, *The Iron Heel* (1908; reissued 1974) p. 28.

30. London, *Revolution: Stories and Essays*, ed. Robert Barltrop (1979) p. 36.

31. In yet another of the myriad ways that life imitates art, J. Stitt Wilson, a Social Gospeller in Berkeley, California, published a letter to Christian ministers in December 1913, rebuking the 'capitalist profit-orgy' which Christmas has become. Wilson called, like Bishop Morehouse, for a revival of primitive Christianity. There is no record of his subsequent fate. The letter is in the Socialist Party of America Papers, Duke University.

32. London, *The Iron Heel*, p. 174.

33. Ibid., p. 176.

34. Ibid., pp. 193–4.

35. Ibid., p. 190.

36. Ibid., p. 224.

37. Ibid., p. 218.

38. Signs of increasingly sophisticated attention to the role of Avis in *The Iron Heel* are apparent in Labor's *Jack London* (1974) and Joan D. Hedrick, *Solitary Comrade: Jack London and His Work* (1982).

39. *Letters from Jack London*, p. 290. In 1909 Walling sent to London a copy of a letter from Eugene Debs, dated 7 December 1909, in which he indicated agreement with his (and London's) concern at the drift of the Socialist Party to the right: 'I've been watching the situation closely and especially the tendencies to reactionism, to which we are so unalterably opposed. The Socialist Party has already catered far too much to the A.F. of L. and there is no doubt that a halt will soon have to be called. The revolutionary character of our party and our movement must be preserved in all its integrity, *at all costs*, for if that be compromised it had better cease to exist' (Jack London Papers, Huntington Library, San Marino, California, reprinted by permission). The idea that 'revolutionism' might be incompatible with the course of the Socialist Party, as it became ever more strictly a 'political' organization, was strongly argued by Emma Goldman in letters to Jack London in 1911, especially that of 10 August, in the Jack London Papers, Huntington Library. London's resignation was rebuked in 'How You Can Get Socialism', *New York Evening Call* (27 March 1916).

40. Charles N. Watson Jr, 'The Composition of *Martin Eden*', *American Literature*, LIII (November 1981) 397–408.

41. London, *Martin Eden* (1909; reissued 1967) p. 40.

42. Ibid., p. 60.

43. Ibid., p. 74.

44. Ibid, pp. 103–4.

45. Ibid., p. 278.

46. Ibid., p. 273.

47. Ibid., p. 333.

48. See George M. Spangler, 'Suicide and Social Criticism: Durkheim, Dreiser, Wharton, and London', *American Quarterly*, XXXI (Fall 1979) 496–516.

49. *Letters from Jack London*, p. 307.

50. Ibid., p. 367.
51. Ibid., p. 467.

CHAPTER 2

1. Gertrude Atherton, 'Why is American Literature Bourgeois?', *North American Review*, 179 (May 1904) 771–81.
2. James Oppenheim in *The Mystic Warrior* (1921) nicely captures the perspective of the magazine editors:

   > Don't be too gloomy, and don't be sordid,
   > Don't open the stink-pot and the lavatories,
   > Don't offend people's moral scuples and religious creeds,
   > Keep out of politics, and sex, and socialism,
   > Don't be highbrow, don't end up in tragedy –
   > In short, uplift the people . . .

   Quoted by Robert Rosenstone, *Romantic Revolutionary: A Biography of John Reed* (1975) p. 89.
3. See James D. Hart, *The Popular Book: A History of America's Literary Taste* (1950).
4. Sinclair's article was printed as a pamphlet by Charles H. Kerr in The Pocket Library of Socialism, no. 43, in 1904. Sinclair's subsequent friendship with Mrs Atherton is suggested in his *My Lifetime in Letters* (1960) pp. 37–8, 185–92.
5. Biographical details from Leon Harris, *Upton Sinclair: American Rebel* (1975) and Sinclair, *American Outpost: A Book of Reminiscences* (1932), which was expanded and republished as *The Autobiography of Upton Sinclair* (1962).
6. Sinclair, *Autobiography*, p. 34.
7. Ibid., p. 108.
8. Ibid., p. 109.
9. On Herron, see Charles Howard Hopkins, *The Rise of the Social Gospel in American Protestantism, 1865—1915* (1940) pp. 184–200, and Howard H. Quint, *The Forging of American Socialism* (1953) pp. 127–41.
10. From a lecture delivered by Herron in Boston in 1895, reprinted in Paul H. Boase (ed.), *The Rhetoric of Christian Socialism* (1969) pp. 94–104.
11. Kent and Gretchen Kreuter, *An American Dissenter: The Life of Algie M. Simons, 1870–1950* (1969). Simons defended the truthfulness of *The Jungle* in 'Packingtown, *The Jungle* and its Critics', *International Socialist Review*, VI (June 1906) 70–2.
12. John R. Commons, 'Labor Conditions in Slaughtering and Meat Packing', *Quarterly Journal of Economics*, XIX (1904) 1–32; reprinted in Commons (ed.), *Trade Unionism and Labor Problems* (1905) pp. 222–49.
13. Details from Henry Demarest Lloyd, *Wealth Against Commonwealth* (1894), and A. M. Simons, *Packingtown* (1899). Simons makes the interesting point that the packers and related industries, employing between 25 000 and 35 000 at the turn of the century, made up the largest industrial community in the world, far larger than the Krupp works at Essen.

14. The persuasive argument about the packing industry's attitude towards inspection was made by Gabriel Kolko, *The Triumph of Conservatism: A Reinterpretation of American History, 1900–1916* (1963) pp. 101–7.

15. The difference is suggested by documents such as *The God That Failed*, with an Introduction by Richard Crossman (1950), Robert C. Tucker, 'The Deradicalization of Marxist Movements', *The Marxian Revolutionary Idea* (1970), and John P. Diggins, *Up from Communism: Conservative Odysseys in American Intellectual History* (1975). Compare these with the series 'How I Became a Socialist' in *Justice* (19 May 1894–14 September 1895), which includes contributions from H. M. Hyndman, William Morris and Walter Crane. A similar series appeared in *The Comrade* in New York (April 1902–November 1903), with contributions already noted from Jack London, Eugene Debs and others. See also Charles Edward Russell, *Why I Am a Socialist* (1910). There is a trajectory here, a story which has never been fully told.

16. Simons is named as Sinclair's model in the Kreuter's *An American Dissenter*, pp. 78–9.

17. William James, *The Varieties of Religious Experience: A Study in Human Nature* (1902) p. 209. See also James Strachan, 'Conversion', *Encyclopaedia of Religion and Ethics*, vol. IV, ed. James Hastings (1911) pp. 104–10.

18. Jack London in *The Chicago Socialist* (25 November 1905) 2.

19. Debs, *The Appeal to Reason* (21 July 1906) p. 4.

20. Simons, *International Socialist Review*, VI (June 1906) 70.

21. Isaac F. Marcosson, *Adventures in Interviewing* (1919) pp. 280–9.

22. Roosevelt to Sinclair, 15 March 1906, *The Letters of Theodore Roosevelt*, vol. V, ed. Elting E. Morison et al. (1952) pp. 179–80.

23. *The Chicago Socialist* began publication as a daily on 25 October 1906. The first detailed attention to the packing-houses and stockyards ('Manicurists in the Jungle', 22 November 1906) argued that almost all of the improvements and changes were cosmetic, and that conditions were as bad as before the scandal blew up.

24. S. G. H[obson]., review of *The Jungle*, *Fabian News*, XVI (July 1906) 30.

25. The socialist vote in Cook County in the mid-term election in November 1906 was 23 993, a drop of some 17 000 from the Debs vote two years earlier. The mayoral election in April 1907 ended even more disastrously, with a socialist vote down to 13 121 and the elimination of the Democrats from city, county and state power (*Chicago Daily Socialist*, 7 November 1906 and 3 April 1907). The electoral setbacks were analyzed in 'The Chicago Election', *International Socialist Review*, VII (April 1907) 623–5.

26. Sinclair, 'Reminiscences of *The Jungle*', *Wilshire's Magazine*, XIII (May 1909) 20.

27. Sinclair was dissatisfied with the degree of realism in the stage adaptation and arranged for six phonograph recordings of pig squeals to be played each time the doors of the 'pig-sticking parlour' were opened on stage. See 'Real Pig Squeals in Jungle Drama', *Chicago Daily Socialist* (21 November 1906) and Harris, *Upton Sinclair*, p. 150. He defended the shockingly realistic effects thus produced 'on the ground that it is symbolistic of what happens to humans as well as hogs who happen to get caught in the remorseless wheels of our modern industrial system.'

28. Cannon to Sinclair, 20 September 1920, Upton Sinclair Papers, Lilly Library, Indiana University.
29. Sinclair to Cannon, 27 September 1920, Upton Sinclair Papers, Lilly Library, Indiana University. A similar ending was devised by W. G. Henry when London's *The Iron Heel* was 'dramatized' in 1911. The play ended on election eve, 1912, when news of 'immense Socialist gains throughout the country are received in San Francisco', at which point the cast and audience sang the Marseillaise. See Grace V. Silver, 'The *Iron Heel* Dramatized', *International Socialist Review*, xi (June 1911) 752–3.
30. Sinclar, 'A Co-operative Home Colony', *World's Work*, ix (March 1907) 382–7, and Sinclair, 'Helicon Hall', *The New Encyclopedia of Social Reform*, ed. W. D. P. Bliss (1909). Socialists in Chicago regarded the Helicon Hall as an interesting experiment, but one which had little bearing upon socialism as they understood the term. See 'Helicon Hall', *Chicago Daily Socialist* (27 November 1906). Floyd Dell regarded the hall as 'eminently conservative and within its own limitations, entirely successful economic and social experiment': Dell, *Upton Sinclair: A Study in Social Protest* (1927) p. 124.
31. Mark Schorer, *Sinclair Lewis: An American Life* (1961) p. 113.
32. Ira Kipnis, *The American Socialist Movement, 1897–1912* (1952) ch. 4.
33. John Spargo, quoted by Kipnis, ibid., p. 202.
34. Upton Sinclair, 'The Socialist Party', *World's Work*, xi (April 1906) 7431–2.
35. John Chamberlain, *Farewell to Reform* (1932) pp. 184–5.

CHAPTER 3

1. For a brief summary of labour relations in the state see Isaac A. Hourwich, 'Colorado, 1893–1914', *The New Review*, ii (June 1914) 329–32. Eugene O. Porter, 'The Colorado Coal Strike of 1913 – An Interpretation', *The Historian*, xii (Autumn 1949) 3–27, places the blame for the strike squarely upon the shoulders of the operators. The most complete account is George S. McGovern and Leonard Guttridge, *The Great Coalfield War* (1972), based closely upon Senator McGovern's doctoral dissertation, 'The Colorado Coal Strike, 1913–1914' (Northwestern University, 1953), written under the direction of Professor A. S. Link. See Link's *Wilson: The New Freedom* (1956) p. 457 n. 48. Of all the literature on the strike, Zeese Papanikolas' *Buried Unsung: Louis Tikas and the Ludlow Massacre* (1982) is the most original and moving.
2. See 'The Paterson Strike Pageant', *Independent*, lxxiv (19 June 1913) 1406–7, and 'The Pageant as a Form of Propaganda', *Current Opinion*, (July 1913) 32, which summarizes press opinions. On the strike itself, see Steve Golin, 'Defeat Becomes Disaster: The Paterson Strike of 1913 and the Decline of the I.W.W.', *Labor History*, xxiv (Spring 1983) 223ff., and Melvyn Dubofsky, *We Shall Be All: A History of the Industrial Workers of the World* (1969) pp. 268–85.
3. The 'new intellectuals' who were attracted to the Socialist Party after 1911 were more likely to sympathize with the left wing of the party (although the itineraries of Eastman, Lippmann, Walling and LaMonte were sufficiently diverse to make generalization precarious) than to identify with the

aspirations of the somewhat older generation of intellectuals, which included Hunter, Spargo, Simons, Ghent and Hillquit, who were moving towards political accommodation with Victor Berger and the right-wing party bureaucracy. Divergences between the 'new intellectuals' are suggested in Robert Rives LaMonte, 'The New Intellectuals', *The New Review*, II (January (1914) 45–53, which argues against Lippmann's *A Preface to Politics*. See Paul Buhle, 'Intellectuals in the Debsian Socialist Party', *Radical America*, IV (April 1970) 35–58, and William I Gleberzon, ' "Intellectuals" and the American Socialist Party, 1901–1917', *Canadian Journal of History*, XI (April 1976) 43–65.

4. Allen F. Davis, *Spearheads for Reform: The Social Settlements and the Progressive Movement, 1890–1914* (1967).
5. Max Eastman, *Enjoyment of Living* (1948) p. 447.
6. Max Eastman, *Venture* (1927) pp. 224–43. Reed's own account of his initial visit to the strike ('War in Paterson', *The Masses*, June 1913) contains no such scene, but it apparently occurred on a later occasion. See Robert Rosenstone, *Romantic Revolutionary: A Biography of John Reed* (1975) p. 131.
7. Max Eastman, *Enjoyment of Living*, pp. 446–7.
8. W. J. Ghent, *Our Benevolent Feudalism* (1902), pp. 60–1.
9. 'Sociological Departments' were often the sign of progressive and scientific attitudes towards management, and were designed to 'mold working-class social forms to suit the requirements of mechanized production': see Stephen Meyer III, *The Five Dollar Day: Labor Management and Social Control in the Ford Motor Company, 1908–1921* (1981) pp. 96, pp. 123–44.
10. *A Report on Labor Disturbances in the State of Colorado, from 1880 to 1904 . . .* , prepared under the Direction of Carroll D. Wright, Commissioner of Labor (1905) p. 360. Colorado provided some of the most flagrant and deeply-rooted examples for those concerned with the problem of labour disputes: see Rhodri Jeffreys-Jones, 'Theories of American Labour Violence', *Journal of American Studies*, XIII (August 1979) 245–64.
11. John Graham Brooks, *American Syndicalism: The I.W.W.* (1913) p. 20.
12. Ray Stannard Baker, 'The Reign of Lawlessness: Anarchy and Despotism in Colorado', *McClure's Magazine*, XXIII (May 1904) 43–57. Baker returned to Colorado labour problems in his *Woodrow Wilson: Life and Letters*, vol. 4 (*President 1913–1914*) (1931) pp. 385–93.
13. Robert Hunter, *Violence and the Labor Movement* (1914) pp. 302–11.
14. Roosevelt to Costigan, 15 August 1914, *The Letters of Theodore Roosevelt*, vol. 7 (*The Days of Armageddon 1909–14*), ed. Elting Morrison et al. (1954) p. 805.
15. *The Papers of Woodrow Wilson*, vol. 29 (2 December 1913–5 May 1914), ed. A. S. Link et al. (1979) p. 514.
16. *Congressional Record*, 63rd Cong., 2nd sess. (29 April 1914) p. 7441; quoted in Louis Adamic, *Dynamite: The Story of Class Violence in America*, rev. edn (1935) p. 258.
17. George Creel, *Rebel at Large: Recollections of Fifty Crowded Years* (1947) pp. 126–32.
18. See Bohn's 'After Ludlow – Facts and Thoughts', *International Socialist Review*, XV (August 1914) 112–14.
19. George Orwell, *Collected Essays, Journalism and Letters*, vol. 1 (*An Age Like This, 1920–1940*), ed. Sonia Orwell and Ian Angus (1968) p. 269.

20. Eastman, *Enjoyment of Living*, p. 452.
21. Granville Hicks, *John Reed: The Making of a Revolutionary* (1936) pp. 143–4.
22. Eastman, *Enjoyment of Living*, p. 452.
23. Ibid.
24. Michael Gold, 'May Days and Revolutionary Art', *Modern Quarterly*, III (January–April, 1926) p. 161.
25. Eastman, 'A Preface About American Poetry', *Colors of Life* (1918) p. 1.
26. Dell, *The Liberator*, I (December 1918) 44–5, emphasis added.
27. See Dell, 'A Vacation from Sociology', *The Masses*, VI (June 1915) 18, and his *Homecoming: An Autobiography* (1933) pp. 146–7, 346–7.
28. Daniel Aaron's *Writers on the Left* (1961) is less successful generally with the cultural radicalism of the 1920s than with the 1930s. Chapter 5 in the present work traces several aspects of the decade, and its response to Soviet artistic doctrine.
29. See Eastman, *Poems of Five Decades* (1954) *passim*.
30. For Reed in Colorado, and for his activities in the summer of 1914, see Rosenstone, *Romantic Revolutionary*, ch. 11. 'The Colorado War' is reprinted in John Stuart (ed.), *The Education of John Reed: Selected Writings* (1955).
31. For details on Linderfelt (and a photograph), see McGovern and Guttridge, *The Great Coalfield War*, pp. 167–8, and Zeese Papanikolas, *Buried Unsung* (1982) pp. 223–49.
32. McGovern and Guttridge, *The Great Coalfield War*, pp. 229–30.
33. Sinclair's response to the Ludlow massacre and his campaign against the Associated Press are recorded in his *The Brass Check: A Study in American Journalism* (1919) chs 24–5; Leon Harris, *Upton Sinclair: American Rebel* (1975) pp. 144–7; and Floyd Dell, *Upton Sinclair: A Study in Social Protest* (1927) ch. 12. See also John Graham, 'Upton Sinclair and the Ludlow Massacre', *The Colorado Quarterly*, XXI (Summer 1972) 55–67.
34. Mary Heaton Vorse, *A Footnote to Folly: Reminiscences* (1935) p. 76.
35. Elias Milton Ammons to President Woodrow Wilson, 16 May 1914, *The Papers of Woodrow Wilson*, vol. 30 (6 May – 5 September 1914), ed. A.S. Link et al. (1979) p. 38.
36. See Young's 'Madam, you dropped Something!', *The Masses*, VII (February 1916) 17. His version of the feud with the AP is in *Art Young: His Life and Times*, ed. John Nicholas Beffel (1939) pp. 295–301; Eastman's version in *Enjoyment of Living*, pp. 467–73.
37. Philip S. Foner, *History of the Labor Movement in the United States*, vol. 5 (*The AFL in the Progressive Era, 1910–1915*) (1980) p. 200. Sinclair to Jack London, 8 November 1915 (JL 18294), Jack London Papers, Huntington Library, San Marino, California.
38. While preparing *King Coal*, Sinclair was editing *The Cry for Justice* (1915), the most substantial anthology of protest writing in this period. In spirit and ideological perspective this anthology looked backward to an earlier era in American socialism; and it was contradicted by things which he presented in *King Coal*. See also Chapter 7 and note 13.
39. Eastman, *Enjoyment of Living*, p. 498, and William L. O'Neill, *The Last Romantic: A Life of Max Eastman* (1978) pp. 54–5.
40. See Graham Adams Jr, *Age of Industrial Violence, 1910–15: The Activities and*

Findings of the United States Commission on Industrial Relations (1966). Adams also wrote the informative entry on Frank P. Walsh in *Dictionary of American Biography*, vol. xi, Part 2, Supplement 2: To 31 December 1940, ed. Robert Livingstone Schuyler et al. (1958) pp. 690–1. For Creel's role, see *Rebel at Large*, ch. 17.

41. Mackenzie King noted in his diary, 12 January 1915: 'I advised him strongly to nail his colors firmly to the mast at the hearings of the Commission . . . we were living together in a different generation than the one in which his father had lived . . . Today, there was a social spirit abroad, and it was absolutely necessary to take the public into one's confidence, to give publicity to many things, and especially to stand out for certain principles very boldly.' Quoted in R. MacGregor Dawson, *William Lyon Mackenzie King: A Political Biography*, vol. 1 (1874–1923) (1958) p. 237.

42. Lippmann, 'Mr. Rockefeller on the Stand', *New Republic*, i (30 January 1915) 12–13; reprinted in Lippmann, *Early Writings*, ed. Arthur Schlesinger, Jr (1970).

43. Inez Haynes Gilmore, 'At the Industrial Hearings', *The Masses*, vi (March 1915) 8–9.

44. Carl Sandberg, 'The Two Mr. Rockefellers – and Mr. Walsh', *International Socialist Review*, xvi (July 1915) 18–24. James Weinstein in *The Corporate Ideal in the Liberal State: 1900–1918* (1968) pp. 198–9, argued that Wilson was the chief political beneficiary of Walsh's tactics.

45. Quoted by Weinstein, *The Corporate Ideal*, p. 196. John D. Rockefeller brought Bowers into Standard Oil in the 1890s, when the company's interests in mining and steel production were rapidly expanding in the Great Lakes region. When these interests were sold to the United States Steel Company, Bowers went to Colorado where he became the 'vigorous and efficient' managing director of the Colorado Fuel and Iron Company. See John D. Rockefeller, *Random Reminiscences of Men and Events* (1909) pp. 129–30.

46. Quoted by Weinstein, *The Corporate Ideal*, p. 197.

47. Allan Nevins, *John D. Rockefeller: The Heroic Age of American Enterprise*, vol. 1. (1940) p. 670.

48. Rockefeller, quoted by Harris, *Upton Sinclair*, p. 147.

49. MacGregor Dawson, *Mackenzie King*, vol. 1, pp. 239, 245.

50. Lippmann, 'The Rockefeller Plan in Colorado', *New Republic*, ii (9 October 1915); reprinted in Lippmann, *Early Writings*, p. 268.

51. Adams, *Age of Industrial Violence*, p. 175.

52. See the unsigned note in the issue of 14 November 1914.

53. Lippmann: see note 42.

54. It is mildly ironic that in 1930, in discussions between John Dos Passos and Edmund Wilson, Ivy Lee's name was suggested as someone who could 'use American publicity methods to convert the Americans to Communism'. Edmund Wilson to Allen Tate, 26 July 1930, in Edmund Wilson, *Letters on Literature and Politics, 1912–1972*, ed. Elena Wilson (1977) p. 199. In 'An Appeal to Progressives', which appeared in *The New Republic* of 14 January 1931, Wilson again referred to Dos Passos' suggestion in the context of his own witty proposal that liberals in America 'must take Communism away

from the Communists' if they were to regain vigor and confidence again, and address the problems of the nation. Reprinted in Wilson's *The Shores of Light: A Literary Chronicle of the Twenties and Thirties* (1952).

CHAPTER 4

1. Justin Kaplan, *Lincoln Steffens: A Biography* (1974) pp. 183–5.
2. Steffens's obituary of Reed in *The Freeman* (3 November 1920); reprinted in *Lincoln Steffens Speaking* (1936) pp. 311–15.
3. Reed, 'The Foundations of a Skyscraper', *Tamburlane and other Verses* (1917) p. 17. Other published poems are cited from this volume.
4. Ezra Pound, 'Patria-Mia', *The New Age*, xi (19 September 1912) 491–2; reprinted in Pound, *Patria Mia and the Treatise on Harmony* (1962) p. 19.
5. *The Day in Bohemia*. The only usefully available text is the reprint in Mabel Dodge Luhan, *Intimate Memories*, vol. iii: *Movers and Shakers* (1936) pp. 171–85.
6. Reed to Monroe, 11 September 1912, quoted Robert Rosenstone, *Romantic Revolutionary: A Biography of John Reed* (1975) p. 97.
7. William Morris, 'The Lesser Arts' (1877), *On Art and Socialism*, ed. Holbrook Jackson (1947) p. 36.
8. Monroe to John Reed, 28 September 1912. John Reed Papers, Houghton Library, Harvard University.
9. Meynell to Harriet Monroe, December 1912, quoted Monroe, *A Poet's Life* (1938) p. 258.
10. Teasdale to John Reed, 12 March 1913. John Reed Papers, Houghton Library, Harvard University.
11. Reed to Percy MacKaye, 21 December 1912. John Reed Papers, Houghton Library, Harvard University.
12. Rosenstone on 'Sangar', *Romantic Revolutionary*, pp. 88–9, 97. Steffens was still uneasily trying to have the McNamaras, Tom Mooney and other political prisoners released in the 1920s. See Steffens to Allen H. Suggett, 15 June 1927, *The Letters of Lincoln Steffens*, vol. ii, ed. Ella Winter and Granville Hicks (1938) pp. 794–5.
13. 'Eleventh Avenue Racket', John Reed Papers, Houghton Library, Harvard University.
14. Max Eastman, *Enjoyment of Living* (1948) p. 406.
15. Reed, *Adventures of a Young Man: Short Stories from Life* (1975) pp. 138–9.
16. Ibid., p. 63.
17. Ibid., p. 50.
18. Michael Gold, review of Knut Hamsun, *Growth of the Soil*, *The Liberator*, iv (May 1921) 30.
19. Reed to Lippmann, 28 April 1913. Walter Lippmann Papers, Sterling Memorial Library, Yale University.
20. Reed, 'The Colorado War', *Metropolitan Magazine*, xl (July 1914); reprinted in *The Education of John Reed: Selected Writings*, ed. John Stuart (1955).
21. Paul Hollander, 'The Ideological Pilgrim', *Encounter*, xli (November 1973) 3–15; and *Political Pilgrims: Travels of Western Intellectuals to the Soviet Union, China, and Cuba, 1928–1978* (1981).

22. Reed, *Adventures*, p. 141.
23. See Chapter 3, note 2. The Pageant is documented, with contemporary responses, by Brooks McNamara (ed.), 'Paterson Strike Pageant', *TDR/The Drama Review*, xv (Summer 1971) 60–71.
24. John Kenneth Turner, *Barbarous Mexico* (1911) p. 216.
25. Ibid., p. 292.
26. Mark T. Gilderhus, *Diplomacy and Revolution: U.S.–Mexican Relations under Wilson and Carranza* (1977) p. 11.
27. Ronald Atkin, *Revolution! Mexico 1910–1920* (1969) pp. 249–73.
28. Reed, *Insurgent Mexico* (1914; reissued 1969 with an Introduction by Renato Leduc) p. 70.
29. Ibid., p. 98.
30. Ibid., p. 76–7.
31. Ibid., p. 90.
32. Lippmann to Reed, 25 March 1914. John Reed Papers, Houghton Library, Harvard University.
33. Reed, *Insurgent Mexico*, p. 73.
34. Ibid., p. 217.
35. Ibid., p. 166.
36. Ibid., p. 157.
37. Ibid., pp. 180–1.
38. Ibid., pp. 186–7.
39. Ibid., p. 193.
40. Ibid., p. 233.
41. O'Hea, *Reminiscences of the Mexican Revolution* (1981) p. 143.
42. Reed, 'The Worst Thing in Europe', *The Masses*, vi (March 1915) 17–18.
43. Charles Scribner's Sons to Reed, 11 September 1916. John Reed Papers, Houghton Library, Harvard University.
44. 'The New Art of War Reporting', *Current Opinion*, lxi (August 1916) 119.
45. Reed, *Education*, p. 91.
46. George Creel to Reed, 1 September 1916. John Reed Papers, Houghton Library, Harvard University. Creel and Reed had worked together in 1914 to publicize the plight of the striking coal-miners.
47. The context is suggested in Robert K. Murray, *Red Scare: A Study of National Hysteria, 1919–1920* (1955).
48. Horace Liveright to Louise Bryant, 15 March 1920. John Reed Papers, Houghton Library, Harvard University.
49. Transcript of Memorial Meeting in memory of Jacob Schwartz, 25 October 1918. Alexander Berkman Collection, Tamiment Library, New York University. Spelling and punctuation have been corrected.
50. Reed, *Ten Days That Shook The World* (1919; reissued 1977 with an Introduction by A. J. P. Taylor) p. 171.
51. Reed to Boardman Robinson, 16 October 1917. John Reed Papers, Houghton Library, Harvard University.
52. Reed, *Ten Days*, p. 254.
53. Ibid., p. 51.
54. Ibid., p. 147.
55. Ibid., p. 156.

56. Leon Trotsky, *The History of the Russian Revolution*, vol. III, trans. Max Eastman (1932–3; reissued in three vols, 1967) p. 217.

57. Such as Alexander Rabinowitch, who follows Trotsky's emphasis on the role of the MRC in *The Bolsheviks Come to Power: The Revolution of 1917 in Petrograd* (1976).

58. Trotsky, vol. III, p. 198.

59. Ibid., p. 175.

60. See Isaac Deutscher's account of the strike of Trotsky's supporters at the Pechora Gulag in 1930, and of their murder by the GPU, in *The Prophet Outcast: Trotsky 1929–1940* (1963) pp. 416–18.

61. Reed, *Ten Days*, pp. 212–13. F. F. Raskolnikov, a leading Bolshevik in the Kronstadt naval garrison, made a similarly frantic (and fruitless) trip to Gatchina in pursuit of a detachment of cyclist troops. Reed's narrative strongly emphasizes the ironies of the situation. See Raskolnikov's *Kronstadt and Petrograd in 1917*, trans. Brian Pearce (1925; reissued 1982) pp. 293–4.

62. Ibid., p. 216.

63. Ibid., p. 100.

64. Ibid., p. 118.

65. Ibid., p. 125.

66. Ibid., p. 163.

67. Ibid., p. 87.

68. Ibid., p. 187.

69. Ibid., p. 203.

70. Ibid., p. 263.

71. Trotsky, vol. III, p. 163.

72. Lenin, quoted in E. H. Carr, *A History of Soviet Russia: The Bolshevik Revolution, 1917–1923*, vol. I (1950) p. 95.

73. American exceptionalism: see Irving Howe and Lewis Coser, *The American Communist Party: A Critical History (1919–1957)* (1957) pp. 164–5, and E. H. Carr, *A History of Soviet Russia: Foundations of a Planned Economy, 1926–1929*, vol. III (1976) part ii, pp. 610–13. Louis Budenz, in the aftermath of Dimitrov's Seventh Congress speech, which inaugurated the dramatic shift of Comintern policy towards bourgeois democracy, found that none of the comrades he was in touch with knew very much about American traditions *per se*. They greeted Budenz's efforts to draw upon American experience in his propaganda work with 'sullen resentment'. Louis Budenz, *This Is My Story* (1947) pp. 145–6.

74. See the account of the events in Chicago in the summer of 1919 in Theodore Draper, *The Roots of American Communism* (1957) pp. 176–96, and Daniel Bell, *Marxian Socialism in the United States* (1967) pp. 112–16. Memoirs by two allies of Reed that summer emphasize his reluctance to break with the Socialist Party. See Benjamin Gitlow, *I Confess* (1940) pp. 42–58, and Bertram D. Wolfe, *A Life in Two Centuries* (1981) pp. 185–99. Reed's role in Chicago is also portrayed in Max Bedacht, 'The Memoirs of Your Father', and Alexander Bittelman, 'Things I Have Learned: An Autobiography', both in the Tamiment Institute Library, New York University.

75. The debate over Reed's 'disillusionment' with Bolshevism is summarized, and dismissed, in Theodore Draper, *The Roots of American Communism* (1957) pp. 284–93; see also the judicious biographical note on Reed in David C.

Duke, *Distant Obligations: Modern American Writers and Foreign Causes* (1983) pp. 101–36, esp. 130–3. Rosenstone, following Draper, dismisses the idea that Reed seriously planned a decisive break with the Communist International. See *Romantic Revolutionary* (1975) p. 379n.

CHAPTER 5

1. Irwin Granich, 'Towards Proletarian Art', *The Liberator*, iv (February 1921) 20-5. The phenomenon of 'party names' in this period is worth noting. In modest emulation of Stalin (Djugashvili), Trotsky (Bronstein), Lenin (Ulyanov), Radek (Sobelsohn) and Martov (Tsederbaum), we get Philip Rahv (Ivan Greenberg), Wallace Phelps (William Phillips), Obed Brooks (Robert Gorham Davis), V. F. Calverton (George Goetz), Fielding Burke (Olive Tilford Dargan), Robert Forsythe (Kyle Crichton), Robert Evans (Joseph Freeman), Mario Michele and Jay Gerlando (Jerre Mangione), to say nothing of Christopher Caudwell (C.J.S. Sprigge) and George Orwell (Eric Blair). When, as a prominent Ullstein journalist, Arthur Koestler joined the Communist Party, it was decided that his membership would be kept secret and that he would have to chose a cover-name ('Ivan Steinberg'). The process is described in the last chapter, 'What's in a Name', of Koestler's *Arrow in the Blue* (1952).
2. Michael Folsom (ed.), *Mike Gold: A Literary Anthology* (1972) p. 62. There is an excellent description of Gold's taste and aesthetic in Richard H. Pells, *Radical Visions and American Dreams* (1973) pp. 176–7, and, perhaps more sympathetically, in Lawrence H. Schwartz, *Marxism and Culture* (1980) *passim*.
3. Bogdanov's role in the history of Russian Social Democracy, and his work as theoretician of proletarian culture, have come under increasing scrutiny. There is a monograph by Dietrich Grille, *Lenins Rivale: Bogdanov und seine Philosophie* (1966) and a comprehensive bibliography by Avrahm Yassour in *Cahiers du monde russe et soviétique*, x (1969) 546–84. A recent selection of his work has appeared in French as *l'Art, la science et la classe ouvrière*, trans. Blanche Grinbaum (1977), with an introduction by Dominique Lecourt which is reprinted in Lecourt's *Proletarian Science? The Case of Lysenko*, trans. Ben Brewster (1977). A series of Bogdanov's lectures, delivered in 1920, appeared in *Labour Monthly* between May 1923 and September 1924. His *A Short Course of Economic Science*, translated by J. Fineberg, was published by the Communist Party of Great Britain in 1923. From this time Bogdanov disappears from contemporary debate. Two of Bogdanov's pre-revolutionary utopian fantasies, *Red Star* and *Engineer Menni*, have been translated by Charles Rougle and published by the Indiana University Press in 1984.

   Bogdanov's thought is described in Leszek Kołakowski, *Main Currents of Marxism: Its Rise, Growth and Dissolution*, vol. ii, *The Golden Age*, trans. P. S. Falla (1978) pp. 424–7. Of use is S. V. Utechin, 'Philosophy and Society: Alexander Bogdanov', in Leopold Labedz (ed.), *Revisionism: Essays on the History of Marxist Ideas* (1962). Elsewhere, Bogdanov appears mainly as Lenin's opponent in a series of fairly obscure philosophical battles. The most detailed treatment of this topic is James White, 'The Philosophical Background to the Lenin–Bogdanov Dispute', a paper delivered to the conference of the Study Group on the Russian Revolution, Birmingham University, January 1978. I am grateful to my colleague John Biggart for letting me see this paper, and for his helpful insights into the Proletcult.

4. Floyd Dell, 'Art Under the Bolsheviks', *The Liberator*, II (June 1919) 11–12, 14–18, and *Education and Art in Soviet Russia in the Light of Official Decrees and Documents*, with a Foreword by Max Eastman (1919).

5. The organizational structure and practical difficulties faced by the Proletcult were described in a hostile article by Leo Pasvolsky, 'Proletkult: Its Pretensions and Fallacies', *North American Review*, 213 (April 1921) 539–50. Lunacharsky explained his policies in 'La Culture proletarienne et le commissariat de l'instruction publique', *Le Phare*, II, no. 18 (March 1921) 382–8.

6. J. F. and W. H. Horrabin, *Working Class Education* (1924) and Stuart Macintyre, *A Proletarian Science: Marxism in Britain, 1917–1933* (1980).

7. Freeman, who was rather better informed on such matters than Gold, knew of the Paul's book and refers to it in *An American Testament* (1938) p. 289.

8. Lecourt, *Proletarian Science?*, p. 143.

9. J.-P. A. Bernard, *Le parti communiste français et la question littéraire, 1921–1939* (1972) p. 37n. Poliansky, chairman of the Central Committee of the All-Russian Council of Proletcult, gives a figure of over 300 000 as the membership in 'The Banner of the "Proletcult" ', *The Plebs* (January 1921) 4. Membership in the Communist Party only reached 472 000 by 1924. See Hélène Carrère d'Encausse, *A History of the Soviet Union, 1917–1953*, vol. II, trans. Valence Ionescu (1981) pp. 1–2.

10. Quoted by Sheila Fitzpatrick, *The Commissariat of the Enlightenment: Soviet Organization and the Arts Under Lunacharsky* (1970) p. 95. According to Poliansky (see note 9) 'the part played by sympathising but non-proletarian elements must be more than anywhere else *purely technical and auxiliary*'. Kołakowski writes (*Main Currents*, II, p. 443): 'The culture of the proletarian [in Bogdanov's thought] must borrow nothing from the tradition of the privileged classes but must make a Promethean effort to create *ex nihilo*, paying attention to its own needs and to nothing else whatever.'

11. On the Proletcult International, see A. Dodonova, 'Souvenirs sur le Proletkult', *Action Poètique*, no. 59 (September 1974) 143–7; Annie Sabatier, 'Le Proletkult International', *Action Poètique*, no. 59 (September 1974) 295–300. Benjamin Goriely discusses the impact of Proletcult on poetry in *Les Poètes dans la revolution russe* (1934) pp. 122–4. The failure of the Proletcult International left the various Communist parties without guidance or an agreed interpretation of how a proletarian culture was to be created. In France, as Bernard shows (*Le p.c.f. et la question littéraire*, pp. 52–3), the critics of *l'Humanité* displayed 'du bon goût littéraire et du beau style' but took an essentially apolitical stance on literary questions. A similar attitude is evident in Eastman's and Dell's *Liberator*. Lenin's draft resolution to the Proletcult Congress of 8 October 1920 is reprinted in V. I. Lenin, *On Literature and Art* (1967) pp. 154–5. Lenin's attitude towards art and towards Soviet cultural policy is surveyed in Jean-Michel Palmier, *Lénine, l'art et la revolution*, vol. I (1975). Carmen Claudin-Urondo, *Lenin and the Cultural*

Revolution, trans. Brian Pearce (1977), is particularly good on Lenin's rejection of the Proletcult.

12. Ernest J. Simmons, 'The Origins of Literary Control', *Survey*, no. 36 (April–June 1961) 78–84, and no. 37 (July–September 1961) 60–7. There is an extended discussion of this article in Palmier, *Lénine*, 96ff., and in Vyacheslav Polonsky, 'Lenin's View of Art', trans. Max Eastman, *Modern Monthly*, vii (January 1934) 738–43.

13. Quoted in Ernst Fischer, *Art Against Ideology*, trans. Anna Bostock (1969) p. 177.

14. See Irving Howe, with Kenneth Libo, *World of Our Fathers* (1976) esp. part 3, 'The Culture of Yiddish'. Gold's *Jews Without Money* (1930), a striking bestseller when it was first published, is of obvious importance. Like Henry Roth's masterpiece, *Call It Sleep* (1934), Gold's book was criticized in the party press for a lack of explicit political content, as well as a certain 'nationalistic vehemence' (review by Joshua Kunitz in *New Masses*, March 1930). See on Gold, Chapter 7, note 9, and Kenneth William Payne, 'Michael Gold to *Jews Without Money*' (unpub. PhD diss., University of Sussex, 1975).

15. See Irving Howe and Lewis Coser, *The American Communist Party: A Critical History (1919–1957)* (1957); and, from a different political perspective, Gabriel Kolko, 'The Decline of American Radicalism in the Twentieth Century', *Studies on the Left*, vi (September–October 1966).

16. V. F. Calverton, *The Newer Spirit: A Sociological Criticism of Literature* (1925) pp. 147–9.

17. See *Daily Worker Special Magazine Supplement* (21, 28 August; 4 September 1926); *The Communist* (June 1927; March, April, June 1928). At this time Calverton's party connections were quite good. 'Yesterday', he wrote to Joseph Freeman on 15 May 1927, 'Bill (Wm.Z.) Foster of the Workers' Party stopped in to see [me] before leaving for Russia himself. He was kind enough to give me a number of letters of introduction to Lunacharsky, Bukharin, Clara Setkin, and so forth.' Joseph Freeman Papers, Box 148, Hoover Institution, Stanford University.

18. Alfred Kazin, *Starting Out in the Thirties* (1966) p. 65. Certain elements within the party resented Calverton's access to the party press, others attacked his failings as a critic. See William Dunne in the *Daily Worker* (16 June 1926); Joseph Freeman's witty satire, 'Bulgarian Literature: Or, The Perfect Critical Method', *New Masses*, iii (August 1927) 9–10; and H. M. Wicks, *Daily Worker* (7 February 1928). These attacks increased in tempo and righteous indignation as the party moved into the Third Period, and may be traced in the Calverton Papers in the New York Public Library, and in articles by A. B. Magil, *The Communist* (May 1929), and A. Landy, *The Communist* (October 1931). The party *summa* on Calverton was delivered by David Ramsey and Alan Calmer in the *New Masses* (January 1933). Attempts were made to silence Calverton's defenders by pressing the charge of plagiarism: see the letter from Nathan Adler, Edwin Rolfe and Sol Funaroff to Max Eastman, 2 June 1933, a carbon copy of which is in Box 152 of the Joseph Freeman Papers, Hoover Institution. Calverton's response to this scurrilous campaign is suggested in a letter to Robert Gorham Davis (NYPL, copy kindly sent to me by Professor Davis) of 28 January 1933: 'What is . . . amusing is the fact that it was I that lent all the books from

which I am supposed to have plagiarized to the authors of the same-said attack upon me, namely David Ramsey and Alan Calmer, who, when they were my former pupils, were Hyman Rosen and Abe Klein. And then the stuff about my defending the petty-bourgeoisie instead of the proletariat – well I presume there are greater absurdities and greater distortions, but I cannot recall any in recent days that have been worse.' Mike Gold joined in on the attack on Calverton in the *Daily Worker* (6 November 1933) and the 'correctness' of this line was confirmed by A. Stork in *International Literature*, no. 3 (1934).

19. V. F. Calverton, 'Can We Have a Proletarian Literature?', *Modern Quarterly*, VI (Autumn 1932), and 'Proletarianitis', *Saturday Review of Literature* (9 January 1937). Calverton's career is described in Aaron, *Writers on the Left*, ch. 13, and there are contrasting appraisals of his 'case' by Haim Genizi, 'Disillusionment of a Communist: The Case of V. F. Calverton', *Canadian Journal of History*, IX (April 1984) pp. 69–82, and Michael Nash, 'Schism on the Left: The Anti-Communism of V. F. Calverton and his *Modern Quarterly*', *Science and Society*, XLV (Winter 1981–2) pp. 437–52.

20. Lelevitch [L. G. Kalmanson], 'Proletarian Literature in Soviet Russia', *Daily Worker*, Special Magazine Supplement (21 March 1925), and, in the same periodical, Robin E. Dunbar, 'Mammonart and Communist Art' (23 May 1925).

21. Joseph Freeman, *An American Testament: A Narrative of Rebels and Romantics* (1938) pp. 539–42.

22. *New Masses* (July 1928).

23. Quoted from VOKS, by Harriet Borland, *Soviet Literary Theory and Practice During the First Five-Year Plan, 1928–32* (1950) p. 38. See also Edward J. Brown, *The Proletarian Episode in Russian Literature, 1928–1932* (1953); Herman Ermolaev, *Soviet Literary Theories, 1917–1934: The Genesis of Socialist Realism* (1963), and Karl Eimermacher, *Dokumente zur sowjetischen Literatur politik, 1917–1932* (1972).

24. See Theodore Draper, 'The Ghost of Social Fascism', *Commentary*, XLVII (February 1969) 29–42. Draper's analysis of the Third Period in the American CP appears in his *American Communism and Soviet Russia: The Formative Period* (1960) pp. 300–14.

25. See Robert A. Maguire, *Red Virgin Soil: Soviet Literature in the 1920s* (1968), and Hugh McLean Jr, 'Voronskij and VAPP', *American Slavic and Eastern European Review*, VIII (October 1949) 185–200.

26. See Stephen F. Cohen, *Bukharin and the Bolshevik Revolution* (1973) pp. 205, 272 and 355–6. Trotsky's address to the Press Division debate is reprinted in Leon Trotsky, *On Literature and Art*, ed. Paul N. Siegel (1970). The full text of the resolution of 18 June 1925 is reprinted in C. Vaughan James, *Soviet Socialist Realism* (1973) pp. 116–19.

27. This is the cogently argued view of Brown in *The Proletarian Episode in Russian Literature* (1953).

28. The text of the decree of 23 April 1932 is in Vaughan James, *Soviet Socialist Realism*, p. 120. Sheila Fitzpatrick makes the interesting point that the RAPP campaign from 1928 against the 'rightist danger' was not under effective Central Committee control, and suggests a number of ways in which Averbakh was insubordinate. Not the least of which was his unwillingness,

as editor of the RAPP journal, to print or even discuss the April decree. See Fitzpatrick's 'Cultural Revolution as Class War' in *Cultural Revolution in Russia, 1928–1931*, ed. Sheila Fitzpatrick (1978) pp. 8–40 and p. 259 n 61. There is a vivid description of Averbakh in Nadezhda Mandelstam, *Hope Against Hope: A Memoir*, trans. Max Hayward (1971) pp. 164–5, 233.

29. Louis Fischer, 'A Revolution in Revolutionary History', *New York Herald Tribune Books*, section X (27 November 1932) p. 10. See also *The Times* (London), 27 April 1932. News reached Calverton of the 'fall' of RAPP in a letter from Jack Conroy, 30 June 1932. V. F. Calverton Papers, New York Public Library.

30. H. H. Lewis wrote to Calverton on 2 May 1930: '. . . I am poor as a church mouse always. Just milk cows for my room and board here on my father's farm, and earn no money at that. I have made but $130 dollars at writing – sold a story to Mencken 18 months ago.' V. F. Calverton Papers, New York Public Library.

31. The account of the John Reed Clubs which follows is based upon archival sources, the most important being the Joseph Freeman Papers in the Hoover Institution, Stanford University. There are smaller collections of papers and documents in the V. J. Jerome collection at Yale, the Upton Sinclair Papers at Indiana University, and the Dreiser Papers at the University of Pennsylvania. Tangential correspondence will also be found in the V. F. Calverton collection, New York Public Library. The Tamiment Institute, New York University, has a small file of documents, pamphlets and other ephemera. Published accounts of the JRCs, which must be taken with caution, appeared in the *New York Times*, the *New Masses*, *Daily Worker* and in the various JRC periodicals. (See note 35 for a list.) The Soviet journal *International Literature* is an indispensable source of information on left-wing literary activity. Memoirs of the period, especially those written decades later, rarely provide sufficient detail to be of interest. Joseph Freeman's autobiography stopped at 1927; Gold left no memoir; figures on the periphery of the JRCs, such as Horace Gregory, Matthew Josephson, Malcolm Cowley and Granville Hicks have all written of JRC meetings, though none so vividly as Albert Halper's account of Diego Rivera's talk to a packed hall, bursting with hostility (*Good-bye, Union Square* [1970] pp. 89–97). There has been little direct academic attention to the JRCs. The account which appears in Daniel Aaron's *Writers on the Left*, which closely follows Freeman's archive, if not Freeman's interpretation, has held up remarkably well. It remains particularly useful on the national JRC conventions. I have emphasized the role of the clubs rather more than Aaron, and, in relating them to the debate over the Proletcult and the whole question of Kharkov and the IURW, have sought to place them in a different context. The clubs are mentioned more briefly in Walter B. Rideout's *The Radical Novel in the United States, 1900–1954* (1956) and James Burkhart Gilbert's *Writers and Partisans* (1968). Lawrence H. Schwartz sheds considerable light on some of the aesthetic issues which were debated within the JRCs in *Marxism and Culture* (1980). Worthy of particular attention is Philip Rahv's 'Proletarian Literature: A Political Autopsy', *Southern Review*, IV (Winter 1939) 616–28. Rahv's own role in the JRC, and his various achievements as a young Stalinist sectarian, are submerged in his attack

upon the Communist Party's activities in the cultural front. It is altogether a powerful but only partially honest polemic. Rahv's activities in the 1930s, and his role in the *Partisan Review*, merit more serious attention than has been the case so far. There is a doctoral thesis on Rahv by Andrew James Dvosin. See also Appendix III.

32. Interview with Ella Winter, 21 March 1979; and Steffens to Mrs C. J. Reed, 25 May 1932, *Letters of Lincoln Steffens*, vol. II, ed. Ella Winter and Granville Hicks (1938) pp. 921–2. See also Ella Winter to Joseph Freeman, 3 June 1932, Box 149, Joseph Freeman Papers, Hoover Institution, Stanford University.

33. Constance Webb, *Richard Wright: A Biography* (1968) pp. 128ff. Webb's account of the Chicago JRC closely follows Wright's contribution to *The God That Failed*, ed. R. H. S. Crossman (1950), but has the advantage of filling in the names which Wright omitted. Wright's *Black Boy* (1945), as originally written, continued his story to his experiences in Chicago. This material, which contains a detailed account of the Chicago JRC, and the internal political life of the Communist Party, was published as *American Hunger*, with an Afterword by Michel Fabre (1977) pp. 60ff. Wright's account of the party attitude towards the Chicago JRC significantly differentiates it from the more relaxed relationship then prevalent in New York. He quotes a comment he heard at the 1934 JRC conference: 'A Chicago Communist is a walking terror' (p. 91).

34. *Daily Worker* (3 June 1932) p. 3.

35. Some JRC periodicals, published 1931–5: *The Red* (Cleveland), *Proletcult* (Seattle and Portland), *The New Force* (Detroit), *The Cauldron* (Grand Rapids, Mich.), *The Hammer* (Hertford, Conn.), *Midland Left* (Indianapolis, Ind.), *The Partisan* (Hollywood and Carmel, California), *Left Front* (Chicago), *Left Review*, formerly *Red Pen* (Philadelphia), *Leftward* (Boston), *Folio* (Los Angeles), *Revolt* (Paterson, N. J.), *War* (Milwaukee), *John Reed Review* (Washington, D.C.) and *Partisan Review* (New York). The JRC periodicals were similar in literary ambition to the various politically unaffiliated left-wing literary magazines of this period, such as *Anvil* (Moberly, Missouri), *Dynamo* (New York), *Left* (Davenport, Iowa), *Left Writer* (New York), *Morada* (Albuquerque, N.M.), *Revolt* (New York), *1933* (Philadelphia) and *Rebel Poet* (Holt, Minnesota). This kind of literary activity was far less common in England in the early 1930s, but there was an impressive range of proletarian writing which certainly compares with the American output.

36. Steffens to Jo Davidson, *Letters of Lincoln Steffens*, vol. II, p. 923, and interview with Ella Winter in London, 21 March 1979. The actual nature of the JRC in Carmel is suggested by Winter in a letter to Joseph Freeman, 3 June 1932: 'Martin Flavin is back from Hollywood. He wants to tell about his experiences there, and they're as strong an indictment against movies produced under capitalism as any communist could make. Is it all right for the John Reed club to sponsor such a meeting, if we get up afterwards and tell them exactly what communism offers? You see we've never received any kind of rules or regulations or constitution telling what the JR clubs are meant to do, and so are rather in the dark. We don't even know what people must subscribe to be allowed to join, and so at present are keeping everybody

out who isn't a communist in feeling.' Box 149, Joseph Papers, Hoover
Institution, Stanford University.

37. Philip Jaffe attended the lecture. See his 'Agnes Smedley: A Reminiscence',
Survey, xx (Autumn 1974) 178. Lawson's talk: *Daily Worker* (21 April 1934) p.
7. Garlin's lecture: *Daily Worker* (5 May 1934) p. 7. Siquieros's talk: *Daily
Worker* (30 May 1934) p. 5. The *New York Times* carried a steady stream of
brief reports of JRC activities, mainly political protests, from 1930.

38. Calmer's report on the Writers Group in 'Report of Regional Conference of
the J.R.C. of the East held on Saturday, July 29, 1933', in Box 153, Joseph
Freeman Papers, Hoover Institution, Stanford University. Compare
Calmer's 'What's Doing in the John Reed Clubs of the U.S.', *Daily Worker*
(18 April 1934) p. 5. The Writers Group discussion of Hicks's essay is
mentioned in a letter from 'Wallace Phelps' to Hicks, n.d. [1934] in the
possession of Mr Robert Gorham Davis.

39. 'Phila. John Reed Club Is Raided', *Daily Worker* (26 May 1932) p. 2; Steven
Lafer, 'Towards a Biography of David Alfaro Siqueiros: His Life, Art and
Politics' (unpub. PhD diss., University of California, Irvine, 1977) p. 105.
Letter to author from Dr Lafer, 3 January 1979.

40. *International Literature*, no. 6 (1934) 146.

41. Bernard, *Le p.c.f. et la question littéraire*, pp. 61–6. See also Henri Barbusse,
'Literature of Tomorrow', *The New Freeman*, ii (5 November 1930) 182–3.
Barbusse, who did not attend the Kharkov congress, played an equivocal
role afterwards. He was unhappy with the sectarianism of Kharkov, and
used his immense influence within the PCF to prevent the Kharkov
programme from being implemented in France. See Wolfgang Klein,
'Barbusse et le mouvement littéraire communiste autour de la conference de
Kharkov (1930)', *Europe*, nos 575–6 (Mars–Avril 1977) 187–93, and Frank
Field, *Three French Writers and the Great War* (1975) pp. 69–70. The Bureau of
the IURW was constantly plagued by backsliders (like Barbusse and
Istrati), and by the need to root out deviations. In the case of the United
States there was a need to deal with leftism and, in the eyes of Moscow, a
persistently low level of theoretical work. There was no American equivalent
to the debate over modernism between Brecht and Lukacs within the
League of Revolutionary Proletarian Writers in Germany, and the chilly
reception afforded Kenneth Burke's 'Revolutionary Symbolism in
America', delivered to the first League of American Writers congress in
April 1935, suggests the limits of the American discussion of these issues.
The implications of Burke's address are nicely analysed in Frank
Lentricchia, *Criticism and Social Change* (1984) pp. 23–38.

42. The account of the Kharkov congress which follows is based on the reports,
resolutions and debates published as a special number of the IURW journal.
See also Johannes R. Becher, 'Vor dem II. Weltkongress der Revolutionären
Literatur Anfang Oktober 1930 in Charkow', *Die Linkskurve*, ii (Oktober
1930) 12–14. Eugene Lyons, for whom 'the proceedings of the congress read
like a much madder Mad Hatter's party', briefly describes the congress in his
Assignment in Utopia (1938) pp. 332–3. Harry Alan Potamkin's role at
Kharkov, and his involvement in the JRC, is described in William
Alexander, *Film on the Left* (1981) pp. 22–3.

43. Freeman, *An American Testament*, pp. 539–42. In 1936 Freeman wrote to Gold

recalling that when Arens and James Rorty kicked Gold out of the magazine for inefficiency, what was really involved was the intense dislike of the petty bourgoisie for revolutionary writers. 'I also pointed out that you would stay with the Revolutionary movement to the end of your life while these people would hang around only so long as it was profitable for them. My prediction was fulfilled. Arens became a highly paid business man who joined the Technocrats, while Rorty became a highly paid advertising man who joined the Trotskyites.' Freeman to Gold, 8 August 1936, Freeman Papers, Box 152, Hoover Institution, Stanford University.

44. Max Eastman, *Artists in Uniform* (1934) pp. 8–9. Eastman's account of Kharkov first appeared in Calverton's *Modern Monthly* (August 1933). The reception of *Artists in Uniform* is described in William L. O'Neill, *The Last Romantic: A Life of Max Eastman* (1978) pp. 153–63. The most extended attack on Eastman's version of events at Kharkov, which was overlooked by O'Neill, is Joseph Freeman's 'What a World!' column in the *Daily Worker* (22 November–2 December 1933). Eastman's summary of the Kharkov programme was reprinted and given wider currency in Stephen Spender's *The Destructive Element* (1935).

45. Fred Ellis, Michael Gold, William Gropper, Joshua Kunitz, A. B. Magil, Harry Alan Potamkin, 'The Charkov Conference of Revolutionary Writers', *New Masses*, vii (February 1931) 6–8. There is a tantalizingly brief memoir by Josephine Herbst, who attended the conference in an unofficial capacity, 'Yesterday's Road', *New American Review*, no. 3 (1968) 84–104. Elinor Langer adds nothing to this account in her *Josephine Herbst* (1984). Herbst and John Herrmann were among those 'who seem to be turning more our way as they go along', as Walt Carman wrote to Joshua Kunitz, 3 October 1930, Kunitz Papers, Columbia University Library.

46. A. B. Magil, in a letter to *New Masses* (16 January 1934).

47. In 'Notes from, Kharkov', *New Masses*, vi (March 1931), Gold alluded to the fact that 'our leftists' had not accepted the Kharkov resolutions in their entirety. He then quoted several *Russian* critics of the policy of tolerating fellow travellers, implying that similar arguments had been heard from some of the American delegates. Howe and Coser fail to note the struggle within the American delegation, and thus oversimplify Gold's role. See *The American Communist Party*, p. 278.

48. Magil, as IURW representative in America, 'was in fairly frequent contact with the comrades of the IURW'. He subsequently 'began to realize' that the attitude of the majority of the delegation at Kharkov had been 'schematic and inflexible', which would in turn lead to the alienation of fellow-travellers and the isolation of party intellectuals (*New Masses* (16 January 1934)). In a letter to the author of 14 February 1979, Mr Magil explained in greater detail the background of the split in the delegation: 'He [Gold] held himself rather aloof from the club and rarely attended meetings. He was regarded as individualistic, undisciplined and only nominally a party member. In our dogmatic, ultra-left fashion we even criticized *Jews Without Money* as petty-bourgeois and anarchistic. Mike, however, had great prestige among the rank and file of the party and its sympathizers, as well as in the Soviet Union. He was *the* American proletarian writer.' There is a photograph of Magil, and a biographical note, in *New Masses* (September 1930). Whittaker

Chambers remembered Magil's 'humorless ponderosity' in *Witness* (1952) p. 241.

49. Philip Rahv, 'The Literary Class War', *New Masses*, VIII (August 1932) 7, and A. B. Magil, 'Pity and Terror', *New Masses*, VIII (December 1932) 16–19.

50. John Howard Lawson to Dos Passos, n.d., quoted in John P. Diggins, *Up from Communism* (1975) pp. 85–6. On their relationship, see Townsend Ludington, 'Friendship Won't Stand That: John Howard Lawson and John Dos Passos's Struggle for an Ideological Ground to Stand On' in Ralph F. Bogardus and Fred Hobson (eds), *Literature at the Barricades* (1982) pp. 46–66.

51. Gold's review of Wilder appeared in the *New Republic* of 22 October 1930, though it must have been written before Gold left for Kharkov. The review of MacLeish was in the same periodical on 26 July 1933. The idea that MacLeish's work revealed a 'fascist unconscious' rapidly became one of the commonplaces of left-wing criticism. It was repeated by Strachey in *Literature and Dialectical Materialism* (1934), and, *inter alia*, by Obed Brooks [Robert Gorham Davis] in *Partisan Review*, I (February–March 1934). In England, however, MacLeish was not so easily identified with the class enemy. See Edgell Rickword's review of MacLeish's *Public Speech* in the *Daily Worker* [London] (4 November 1936).

52. *International Literature*, no. 1 (1932) 107–14.

53. Rufus W. Mathewson Jr, 'Soviet–American Literary Relations, 1929–1935' (unpub. Master's Thesis, Columbia University, 1948).

54. See the review of Jay Du Von's periodical, *Left*, in *International Literature*, nos 2–3 (1932) 145–52.

55. Joseph Freeman, 'Ivory Towers–White and Red', *New Masses*, XII (September 1934) 20–4. This view of Freeman is supported by Daniel Aaron's *Writers on the Left*, and is confirmed by an interview with Ella Winter (21 March 1979), and Horace Gregory's *The House on Jefferson Street* (1971) pp. 182–4.

56. 'American exceptionalism': see Chapter 4, note 73, and Theodore Draper, *American Communism and Soviet Russia*, pp. 163–73. Lovestone was identified with a Bukharinite view that in the late 1920s American capitalism was 'on the upgrade'. The consequence for party policy was a lowering of revolutionary expectations, and an increasing 'Americanization' of the party. After the fall of Trotsky in 1927, Stalin rapidly moved to the 'left' and emphasized that 'we are on the threshold of new revolutionary events' (Draper, p. 279). Bukharin's cautious realism about America was attacked within the Comintern. His increasingly precarious position jeopardized the standing of his supporters, such as Lovestone.

57. Aaron gives a definitive account of the 1934 JRC convention in *Writers on the Left*. For contemporary acounts, see the *Daily Worker* (11 October 1934); Orrick Johns, 'The John Reeds Clubs Meet', *New Masses*, XIII (30 October 1934) 25; *Partisan Review*, I (November–December 1934) 60–1; and Alan Calmer, 'A New Period of American Leftwing Literature', *International Literature*, no. 7 (1935) 75. See also Webb, *Richard Wright*, pp. 131–3.

58. Pells, for example, in the course of an extensive discussion of 'Literary Theory and the Role of the Intellectual' in *Radical Visions*, pp. 151–93,

seriously underestimates the Russian influence on American left-wing literary activity in this period.

CHAPTER 6

1. Edmund Wilson, *Axel's Castle: A Study in the Imaginative Literature of 1870 to 1930* (1931) p. 292.
2. Wilson, *The Twenties: From Notebooks and Diaries of the Period*, ed. Leon Edel (1975) p. 535.
3. Wilson, *The Thirties: From Notebooks and Diaries of the Period*, ed. Leon Edel (1980) p. 174.
4. Wilson to Dell, 19 September 1917, in Wilson, *Letters on Literature and Politics, 1912–1972*, ed. Elena Wilson (1977) p. 31. The differences between the temperaments of Wilson and Dos Passos are nicely suggested by a passage in a letter to Rumsey Marvin of 28 September 1916: 'There are people – you and I and Swinburne – who analyse, who observe, who think, and then there are people who merely follow the bandwagon – The people who are free, who are in revolt, and the people who are shackled by all convention – But the illuminati are not to be found in any one class of society – Lower than the stupidity of the uneducated is the stupidity of the educated . . . – See what I mean? – It is so hard to get away from the lingo, from the little habits of speech and action, from the petty snobberies of ones own class that it takes a distinct effort to see real "illumination" and appreciate it, regardless of garlic or lavender water.' *The Fourteenth Chronicle: Letters and Diaries of John Dos Passos*, ed. Townsend Ludington (1973) p. 48.
5. *The Thirties*, p. 316.
6. Ibid., pp. 401–2.
7. Wilson, *Memoirs of Hecate County* (1946) pp. 274–5.
8. Wilson, 'Dos Passos and the Social Revolution', *New Republic*, LVIII (17 April 1929) 256–7, reprinted in Wilson, *The Shores of Light: A Literary Chronicle of the Twenties and Thirties* (1952) pp. 429–35.
9. Wilson, 'Dahlberg, Dos Passos and Wilder', *New Republic*, LXII (26 March 1930) 56–8; *The Shores of Light*, pp. 442–50. For Dahlberg's view of Wilson see *The Confessions of Edward Dahlberg* (1971) pp. 245–56.
10. *Axel's Castle*, p. 292.
11. John Dos Passos, *U.S.A.* (1966) p. 1083. The reference to Pilate alludes to the role played by Governor Fuller of Massachusetts, who washed his hands of the case by asking A. Lawrence Lowell, President of Harvard University, to examine the transcripts to see if the death verdicts were sound. Heywood Broun compared Governor Fuller to Pilate (' . . . after all Pilate was only a sort of Governor . . . '), but the editor of the New York *World* suppressed the column. Broun's attack on Fuller finally appeared in the issue of 17 August 1927. See James Boylan (ed.), *The 'World' and the 20's: The Golden Years of New York's Legendary Newspaper* (1973) pp. 256–68.
12. Wilson to Scott Fitzgerald, 5 July 1921, *Letters*, p. 64. Wilson was replying to a letter from Fitzgerald of May 1921 which expressed a first flush of disillusionment with Europe. See *The Letters of F. Scott Fitzgerald*, ed. Andrew Turnbull (1963) pp. 326–7.

13. *The Shores of Light*, p. 433.
14. Among the many signs of *rapprochement* between intellectuals and American life, Lincoln Steffens's letter to the sculptor Jo Davidson, 18 February 1929, stands out: 'The artists are the real tories, not the capitalists. Big business in America is producing what the Socialists held up as their goal; food, shelter and clothing for all. You will see it during the Hoover administration, which proposes to deal with the problem of unemployment, profitably; the employed have been taking care of, as consumers, as the market, which, therefore, booms . . . It is a great country, this; as great as Rome. What it needs is a bit of Greece, and the artist won't give us that.' *Letters of Lincoln Steffens*, vol. II, ed. Ella Winter and Granville Hicks (1938) p. 830. Wilson's 'The Literary Consequences of the Crash', *The Shores of Light*, pp. 492–9, traces the breakdown of liberal confidence in the late 1920s. Ironically, by 1940 Wilson's view of America returned towards Steffens's in 1929.
15. Wilson to Allen Tate, 20 May 1929, *Letters*, p. 196.
16. Wilson to Allen Tate, 26 July 1930, *Letters*, p. 199.
17. Dos Passos to Wilson, January 1931, *The Fourteenth Chronicle*, p. 398.
18. Wilson, 'An Appeal to Progressives', *New Republic*, LXV (14 January 1931) 234–8; *The Shores of Light*, pp. 518–33. Wilson's tone was restrained and dignified. Other young writers found it harder to achieve his poise: 'There is only one way to accept America and that is in hate; one must be close to one's land, passionately close in some way or other, and the only way to be close to America is to hate it; it is the only way to love America.' Lionel Trilling, 'The Promise of Realism', *Menorah Journal*, XVIII (May 1930) 482. See also note 36.
19. Wilson to Waldo Frank, 10 August 1932, *Letters*, p. 224. Steffens wrote to Charles Erskine Scott Wood on 3 February 1931 in a similar vein, noting the 'violent and universal' detestation being freely expressed towards President Hoover. *Letters of Lincoln Steffens*, vol. II, p. 888.
20. Wilson reading Marx: *Letters*, p. 211. Wilson, 'What Do Liberals Hope For?', *New Republic*, LXIX (10 February 1932) 345–8. For the impact of Wilson's criticism of *New Republic* liberalism, see Frank A. Warren III, *Liberals and Communism* (1966) pp. 25–7.
21. Wilson, *Travels in Two Democracies* (1936). Although this book has never been reprinted, Wilson expanded his account of his trip to Russia for use in *Red, Black, Blond and Olive: Studies in Four Civilizations: Zuñi, Haiti, Soviet Russia, Israel* (1956). The passage quoted appears on pp. 197–8 of this edition. Further references will be to *Red, Black*. Wilson's *The Thirties* contains his rough notes and diaries written while in Russia.
22. Wilson to Dos Passos, 29 February 1932, *Letters*, p. 222. On the Harlan County struggles, see Daniel Aaron, *Writers on the Left* (1961) ch. VI, and Lawrence Grauman Jr, ' "That Little Running Sore": Some Observations on the participation of American Writers in the Investigations of Conditions in the Harlan and Bell County, Kentucky, Coal Fields in 1931–32', *Filson Club History Quarterly*, XXXVI (October 1962) 340–54.
23. Wilson, *The American Jitters: A Year of the Slump* (1932) pp. 310–11.
24. The 'Manifesto' is printed in Wilson's *Letters*, pp. 222–3.
25. Dos Passos to Wilson, May 1932, *The Fourteenth Chronicle*, p. 409.
26. Ibid.
27. Dos Passos, *U.S.A.*, p. 1162.

28. Ibid., p. 1084.
29. Wilson to Waldo Frank, 17 June 1932, *Letters*, pp. 223–4.
30. Hemingway to Scott Fitzgerald, 12 April 1932, in Ernest Hemingway, *Selected Letters, 1917–1961*, ed. Carlos Baker (1981) p. 339.
31. Fitzgerald to Wilson, March 1933, *The Letters of F. Scott Fitzgerald*, ed., Andrew Turnbull (1963) p. 345.
32. Fitzgerald to Maxwell Perkins, 19 January 1933, *Letters*, p. 230. Perkins had lunch with Wilson after the latter's return from Russia, and wrote to Fitzgerald on 26 October 1935, as though answering Fitzgerald's letter of 1933: 'I had lunch with Bunny Wilson, who seems better and happier than in years, and very enthusiastic about Russia as a country, and a people. I got the impression that his views on Communism were somewhat sobered and more philosophical, and that he thought better of his own country. I suspect he now feels that whatever form of society Russians and Americans are revolving toward is a long slow process.' *Dear Scott/Dear Max: The Fitzgerald-Perkins Correspondence*, ed. John Kuehl and Jackson R. Bryer (1973) p. 226.
33. MacLeish to John Peale Bishop, April 1933, *Letters of Archibald MacLeish, 1907 to 1982* (1983) p. 257. Pound's *ABC of Economics* was published in April 1933.
34. Wilson, 'The Literary Class War: II', *New Republic*, LXX (11 May 1932) 347–9. The first part of this essay appears in *The Shores of Light*, pp. 534–9.
35. Hemingway to Dos Passos, 30 May 1932, *Selected Letters*, p. 360.
36. Material from February and March 1932 in Herbert Solow Papers, Box 8 (John Reed Club file), Hoover Institution, Stanford University. See also Elliot Cohen to Isidor Schneider, 27 November 1929, and Schneider's reply 28 November 1929, in Isidor Schneider Papers, Butler Library, Columbia University. Alan Wald in 'The Menorah Group Moves Left', *Jewish Social Studies*, XXXVIII (Summer–Fall 1976) 289–320, gives a slightly rosier account of relations with the JRC than the Solow Papers suggest. See also Mark Krupnick, 'The Menorah Journal Group and the Origins of Modern Jewish-American Radicalism', *Modern Jewish Social Studies* (1980) 56–67.
37. 'The First National Conference of the John Reed Clubs, held at the Lincoln Center, Chicago, on Sunday, May 29, 1932', transcript, Joseph Freeman Papers, Box 153, Hoover Institution, Stanford University.
38. Ibid.
39. Hemingway to Paul Romaine, 6 July 1932, *Selected Letters*, p. 363.
40. Leonard Kriegel, *Edmund Wilson* (1971) p. 43.
41. Wilson, 'Equity for Americans', *New Republic*, LXX (30 March 1932) 185–6.
42. Quoted from the V. F. Calverton Papers, NYPL, by Haim Genizi, 'Edmund Wilson and the *Modern Monthly*, 1934–1935: A Phase in Wilson's Radicalism', *Journal of American Studies*, VII (December 1973) 301–9.
43. Wilson, 'The Literary Class War: II', pp. 347–9.
44. Wilson, 'Art, the Proletariat and Marx', *New Republic*, LXXIII (23 August 1933) 41–5.
45. See Genizi, note 42.
46. Wilson, 'Marxist History', *New Republic*, LXXII (12 October 1932) 226–8.
47. See Kriegel, *Edmund Wilson* (1971) p. 55 ('Wilson's finest book') and George

H. Douglas, *Edmund Wilson's America* (1983) p. 103 ('a work of minor importance for Wilson').

48. Wilson to Christian Gauss, 21 October 1934, *Letters*, p. 249.
49. Wilson to Malcolm Cowley, 19 October 1934, *Letters*, p. 249.
50. Wilson to Fitzgerald, 5 June 1921, *Letters*, pp. 63–4.
51. *Red, Black*, pp. 164–5.
52. Ibid., p. 175.
53. Ibid., p. 216.
54. Wilson to Muriel Draper, 14 November 1938, *Letters*, p. 311. Draper was in Moscow with Wilson in 1935.
55. *Red, Black*, p. 242.
56. Ibid., p. 245.
57. *Daily Worker* (20 November 1933) quoted in Robert Paul Browder, *The Origins of Soviet–American Diplomacy* (1953) p. 174.
58. *Red, Black*, p. 375.
59. Ibid.
60. Alan Wald, *James T. Farrell: The Revolutionary Socialist Years* (1978) p. 61. Farrell's diary is quoted p. 155, n. 20. See also Wald's 'Memories of the John Dewey Commission Forty Years Later', *Antioch Review*, xxxv (Fall 1977) 438–51.
61. Wilson, 'The Literary Left', *New Republic*, LXXXIX (20 January 1937) 345–8; *The Shores of Light*, pp. 640–50, as 'Communist Criticism'.
62. Farrell in *American Mercury* (December 1939), quoted Wald, *James T. Farrell*, p. 82. The counter-attack against *To the Finland Station* was led by V. J. Jerome, 'Edmund Wilson: To the Munich Station', *New Masses*, xxxi (4 April 1939) 23–6; but Wilson was ignored in Michael Gold's attack on literary renegades, *The Hollow Men* (1941).
63. Wilson to Phelps Putnam, 24 March 1936, *Letters*, p. 276.
64. Schwartz to James Laughlin, 22 January 1938, in James Atlas, *Delmore Schwartz: The Life of an American Poet* (1977) p. 110. See also on this period Irving Howe and Lewis Coser, with the assistance of Julius Jacobson, *The American Communist Party* (1957) ch. VIII, and John P. Diggins, *Up from Communism* (1975).
65. See their 'Problems and Perspectives in Revolutionary Literature', *Partisan Review*, I (June–July 1934) 3–10.
66. Dos Passos to Wilson, 23 March 1934, *The Fourteenth Chronicle*, p. 435.
67. Wilson to Gauss, 2 June 1937, *Letters*, p. 293.
68. *Red, Black*, pp. 226–7.
69. See Chapter 5, note 29, and Wilson, *The Thirties*, pp. 551, 561–2. Wilson, writing to Cowley in April 1937 (*Letters*, p. 287), deplored Fischer's tendency towards 'snobbery' and scorn for 'the masses' in Russia.
70. Wilson, 'Marxism and Literature', *Atlantic Monthly*, 160 (December 1937) 741–50; reprinted in Wilson's *The Triple Thinkers* (1938).
71. Wilson, *To the Finland Station* (1940) p. 141.
72. Ibid., pp. 196, 194.
73. Ibid., p. 162.
74. Ibid., p. 324.
75. Ibid., pp. 321–3.
76. Ibid., p. 323. See the present writer's *The Art of the Real* (1977) pp. 33–5 for

the change of political climate in which Wilson was writing in 1940–1.
77. Wilson, 'Marxism at the End of the Thirties', *Call: Official Weekly Publication of the Socialist Party* (22 February; 1, 8 March 1941). Collected in *The Shores of Light* in 1952, Wilson substituted it for the Appendices to *In the Finland Station* for the Anchor Books edition in 1953.
78. Wilson to Draper, 14 November 1938, *Letters*, p. 311. See also Wilson, *The Thirties*, p. 538. The full sentence reads 'One's feeling toward the Soviets protective – strange effect of abolition of bourgeoisie – still true that it's not possible to be neutral. Proletariat on the signs of classless society.' This was apparently a very typical feeling on the part of visiting intellectuals. The scientist J. D. Bernal and Margaret Gardiner were in Moscow in 1934 when Kirov was assassinated. Gardiner heard talk that Stalin was implicated in the murder, but Bernal dismissed it as 'malicious gossip'; he also rejected any idea that there was 'a heavy pall of suspicion and fear' in Moscow. He simply felt nothing was amiss. His biographer, Maurice Goldsmith, continues: 'But many years later, when deeply disturbed by the happenings in Hungary, he said to me [Margaret Gardiner], "You know, you were right that time in Moscow, only I didn't want to admit it. I wanted to give them the benefit of the doubt."' See Goldsmith, *Sage: A Life of J. D. Bernal* (1980) p. 65.

CHAPTER 7

1. Alfred Stieglitz, 'Ten Stories', *Twice-a-Year*, nos 5–6 (1940–1) 136–7.
2. Margaret Anderson, *My Thirty Years' War: An Autobiography* (1930) pp. 119, 125–7.
3. Ibid., p. 128.
4. Michael Gold to Upton Sinclair, 7 January 1924. Lilly Library, Indiana University.
5. Michael Gold, 'White Hope of American Drama', *The New Magazine* section of the *Daily Worker* (26 February 1927) p. 8.
6. Gold to Sinclair, n.d. [1925]. Lilly Library, Indiana University.
7. Joseph Freeman, *An American Testament* (1938) p. 355.
8. For Freeman at the Rand School, see ibid., p. 210. There has been no history of the *New Masses*. For a generally sympathetic survey, see David Peck, ' "The Tradition of American Revolutionary Literature": The Monthly *New Masses*, 1926–1933', *Science and Society*, XLII (Winter 1978–9) 385–409. Rather more hostile accounts are Aaron, *Writers on the Left* (1961) and Richard Pells, *Radical Visions and American Dreams* (1973). There is an index to contributions, 1929–33, by Estelle Gershgoren Novak in the *Bulletin of Bibliography*, XXVIII (July–September 1971) 89–108. The Joseph Freeman Papers at the Hoover Institution, Stanford, California, contain extensive, detailed and very candid material on the *New Masses*. On Freeman's role, see Daniel Aaron's, *Writers on the Left* (1961), and Kent M. Beck, 'The Odyssey of Joseph Freeman', *The Historian*, XXXVII (November 1974) 101–20.
9. Gold to Sinclair, n.d. [1931]. Lilly Library, Indiana University. Gold was referring to Melvin P. Levy, whose review of *Jews Without Money* appeared in the *New Republic* (26 March 1930). It greatly displeased Gold and a

controversy developed. Edmund Wilson used this as an example in his 'The Literary Class War' in the *New Republic* (4 May 1932); reprinted in *The Shores of Light*, pp. 534–9. Philip Rahv and A. B. Magil, like Levy, were shock troops of the cultural revolution. Less visible publically, but a mighty force within the John Reed Clubs, Conrad Komorowski was a model Red Guard in cultural skirmishes. See Chapter 5, note 48.

10. Joseph Freeman, 'Literary Patterns', *New Masses*, v (June 1929) 14.
11. Freeman, 'Ivory Towers – White and Red', *New Masses*, xii (11 September 1934) 20–4.
12. Jack Conroy to V. J. Jerome, 2 August 1933. V. J. Jerome Papers, Sterling Memorial Library, Yale University.
13. *Unrest: The Rebel Poets Anthology*, edited by Jack Conroy and Ralph Cheyney, 1929 and 1930. A similar volume, edited by Marcus Graham, was *An Anthology of Revolutionary Poetry* (1929). It was privately published and aided financially by a small committee which included William Rose Benet, Alice Stone Blackwell, Percy MacKaye and A. D. Ficke. A selection of *New Masses* verse, translated by N. Guterman and P. Morhange, was published by Les Revues in Paris as *Poèmes D'Ouvriers Américains* (1930). It is perhaps worth recalling here that *May Days: An Anthology of Verse from 'Masses' — 'Liberator'*, edited by Genevieve Taggard, appeared in 1925.
14. Reprinted in *Bastard in the Ragged Suit: Writings of, with drawings by, Herman Spector*, ed. Bud Johns and Judith S. Clancy (1977) pp. 104–5.
15. 'Resolution on *Monde*', *Literature of the World Revolution*, Special Number 1931 (Reports, Resolutions, Debates of the Second International Conference of Revolutionary Writers) p. 105.
16. There is a letter from Zukofsky to Kenneth Burke, Isidor Schneider and Edwin Berry Burgum, 1 March 1936, in the Schneider Papers, Butler Library, Columbia University, which graphically demonstrates the extent to which he was steeped in Marxist culture.
17. Williams, 'This Florida: 1924', *An 'Objectivists' Anthology*, ed. Louis Zukofsky (1932) p. 103.
18. 'For Whom Do You Write? Replies from Forty American Writers', *The New Quarterly*, i (Summer 1934) 12.
19. William Rose Benet, 'The Phoenix Nest', *Saturday Review of Literature*, x (24 March 1934) 580.
20. See Dickran Tashjian, *William Carlos Williams and the American Scene, 1920–1940* (1978); Mike Weaver, *William Carlos Williams: The American Background* (1971); and Robert von Hallberg, 'The Politics of Description: W. C. Williams in the Thirties', *ELH*, xlv (Sring 1978) 131–51. Despite his settled distaste for socialism and Marxism, the left maintained a generally friendly attitude towards Williams in the 1930s: see Michael Gold in the *Daily Worker* (12 October 1933); Milton Howard's review of Williams's *Collected Poems* in *Daily Worker* (10 February 1934); and Edwin Seaver's review of *White Mule* in *Daily Worker* (28 July 1937).
21. Williams, 'The New Poetical Economy', *Poetry*, xliv (July 1934) 223–4.
22. Mary Oppen, *Meaning a Life: An Autobiography* (1978) p. 146.
23. Williams to Louis Zukofsky, 23 March 1928, *The Selected Letters of William Carlos Williams*, ed. John C. Thirlwall (1957) p. 93.
24. Reed Whittemore, *William Carlos Williams: Poet from Jersey* (1975) pp. 239–40.

25. Basil Bunting, 'Pound and "Zuk" ', *Paideuma*, vii (Winter 1978) 373–4. There are eighty-eight letters from Bunting to Zukofsky, dating from July 1930 to December 1964, in the Humanities Research Center, University of Texas at Austin.

26. Pound to Harriet Monroe, 24 October 1930, *The Letters of Ezra Pound, 1907–1941*, ed. D. D. Paige (1951) p. 307.

27. Mary Oppen, *Meaning a Life*, p. 85.

28. Burton Hatlen and Tom Mandel, 'Poetry and Politics: A Conversation with George and Mary Oppen', *George Oppen: Man and Poet*, ed. Burton Hatlen (1981) p. 43.

29. Pound's isolation from the American literary scene at this time is emphasized in a letter from Archibald MacLeish to Harriet Monroe, 29 November 1930: 'Ezra is so completely out of touch with America that he recently wrote one of the boys he supposed he would be lynched if he set foot in New York. Poor devil, not more than ten people would know who he was.' *Letters of Archibald MacLeish, 1907 to 1982*, ed. R. H. Winnick (1983) p. 236. Zukofsky's essay on Pound appeared as 'Les Cantos d'Ezra Pound' in *Échanges*, no. 3 (June 1930), and as 'The Cantos of Ezra Pound' in *The Criterion*, x (April 1931). It has been reprinted in *Prepositions: The Collected Critical Essays of Louis Zukofsky* (1967) pp. 61–77. Zukofsky published an essay, 'Beginning Again with William Carlos Williams', in *Hound & Horn*, iv (January–March 1931) 261–4; *Prepositions*, pp. 45–7. One of the other Objectivists, Carl Rakosi, published an essay on Williams in *The Symposium*, iv (October 1933) 439–47.

30. Charles Reznikoff, 'A Memoir', *Ironwood*, no. 5 (1975) 29.

31. Pound to Williams, 16 January 1930, *Letters*, p. 305. See also Pound to H. B. Lathrop, 16 December 1931, *Letters*, p. 317.

32. *The Autobiography of William Carlos Williams* (1951) pp. 264–5.

33. Williams to Zukofsky, 5 July 1928, *Selected Letters*, p. 101, emphasis added.

34. Louis Zukofsky, 'Sincerity and Objectification, with Special Reference to the Works of Charles Reznikoff', *Poetry*, xxxvii (February 1931) 274. The relevant passage was reprinted in *An 'Objectivists' Anthology*, pp. 204–5.

35. See the interview with Reznikoff in *Contemporary Literature*, x (1969).

36. George Oppen to Mary Ellen Solt, 18 February 1961, quoted Mike Weaver, *William Carlos Williams: The American Background* (1971) p. 55.

37. Tillie Olsen has discussed this phenomenon in *Silences* (1978), but it deserves to be given more organized, and more sophisticated, psychological and historical treatment.

38. Williams to Norman Holmes Pearson, 7 November 1938, *Selected Letters*, p. 175.

39. Williams to Pound, 15 March 1933, *Selected Letters*, p. 138.

40. Pound to T. C. Wilson, 1934, *Letters*, p. 338.

41. There are numerous memoirs in the Zukofsky number of *Paideuma*, vii (Winter 1978), the most substantial of which are included in *Louis Zukofsky: Man and Poet*, ed. C. F. Terrell (1979).

42. Charles Amhanian and David Gitin, 'A Conversation with George Oppen', *Ironwood*, no. 5 (1975) 23. In an interview with L. S. Dembo, Oppen put this in a slightly different light: 'In a way I gave up poetry because of the

pressures of what for the moment I'll call conscience.' *Contemporary Literature,* x (1969) 174.

APPENDIX II

1. See Isadora Duncan, *My Life* (1928).
2. Ibid., p. 230.
3. Quoted from the New York *Sun* (15 November 1908) in *My Life*, p. 236. This is the context in which Duncan appears in Leslie Fishbein, *Rebels in Bohemia: The Radicals of 'The Masses', 1911–1917* (1982) pp. 44–5.
4. W. C. Williams to Edgar Williams, 21 October 1908, quoted in Reed Whittemore, *William Carlos Williams: Poet from Jersey* (1975) p. 52. See also Paul Mariani, *William Carlos Williams: A New World Naked* (1981) p. 67, who quotes from the same letter.
5. Henri, quoted in 'Isadora Duncan and the Libertarian Spirit', *The Modern School*, ii (April 1915) 37. Henri linked Duncan to the artist-heroes like Whitman, Rousseau, Dostoievsky, Zola, Ibsen and de Maupassant in his talks to art students. See William Innes Homer, with Violet Organ, *Robert Henri and His Circle* (1969) p. 159, and Henry F. May, *The End of American Innocence: A Study of the First Years of Our Own Time, 1912–1917* (1960) p. 287.
6. Abbott to Joseph Ishill, 23 February 1928. Ishill Papers (bMsAm 1914), Houghton Library, Harvard University.
7. Duncan, *My Life*, pp. 231–2.
8. Max Eastman, *Heroes I Have Known* (1942) p. 86.
9. Lewis Mumford, *My Works and Days: A Personal Chronicle* (1979) p. 21.
10. John Unterecker, *Voyager: A Life of Hart Crane* (1970) p. 264.
11. See Arthur Frank Wertheim, *The New York Little Renaissance: Iconoclasm, Modernism and Nationalism in American Culture, 1908–1917* (1976), and Leslie Fishbein, *Rebels in Bohemia*, ch. 3.
12. Floyd Dell, *Homecoming: An Autobiography* (1933) pp. 274–5. On Walkowitz's obsession with Duncan, see William Innes Homer, *Alfred Stieglitz and the American Avant-Garde* (1977) pp. 140–1. In addition to Stieglitz, Arnold Genthe and other *avant-garde* photographers were also fascinated by Duncan. See Charles H. Caffin, 'Henri Matisse and Isadora Duncan', *Camera Work*, no. 25 (January 1909) 17–20.
13. Randolph Bourne, 'Old Tyrannies', *Untimely Papers*, ed. James Oppenheim (1919), reprinted in Bourne's *The Radical Will: Selected Writings 1911–1918*, ed. Olaf Hansen (1977) p. 171.
14. Fraina, quoted in Lee Baxandall, 'The Marxist Aesthetic of Louis C. Fraina', in *Proletarian Writers of the Thirties*, ed. David Madden (1968) p. 204.
15. Floyd Dell, *Women as World Builders: Studies in Modern Feminism* (1913) p. 43.
16. Dell, '"Who Said that Beauty Passes like a Dream?"', *The Masses*, vii (October 1916) 27. See also Dell's 'The Russian Ballet', *New Review*, iv (March 1916) 81–2.
17. Joseph Freeman, *An American Testament: A Narrative of Rebels and Romantics* (1938) pp. 101–2. See also Granville Hicks, 'A Retired Literary Radical: Floyd Dell's Autobiography', *Daily Worker* (11 October 1933) p. 5, and

Michael Gold, 'Floyd Dell Resigns', *New Masses*, v (July 1929) 10–11. In a letter to Upton Sinclair of 29 March 1930 (Upton Sinclair Papers, Lilly Library, Indiana University) Dell refuted Gold's criticisms. The relation between Dell and Gold, who began writing for *The Masses* under Eastman's and Dell's patronage, is a good example of the changes in literary life between 1920 and 1930.

18. Freeman, *An American Testament*, p. 102.
19. Duncan, *My Life*, p. 332.
20. Ibid., p.351.
21. Freeman, *An American Testament*, p. 102. The mood of Village intellectuals after the United States entered the war is powerfully revealed in Randolph Bourne's attack on Dewey, 'The War and the Intellectuals', *The Seven Arts*, III (June 1917) 133–46.
22. Margaret C. Anderson, 'Isadora Duncan's Misfortune', *Little Review*, II (April 1917) 5–7.
23. Claude McKay, *A Long Way from Home* (1937) p. 212.
24. Walter Duranty, *'I Write as I Please'* (1935) p. 223.
25. Eunice Tietjens, *The World at my Shoulders* (1938) pp. 12–13.
26. Freeman, *An American Testament*, pp. 193–4.
27. Matthew J. Bruccoli, *Some Sort of Epic Grandeur: The Life of F. Scott Fitzgerald* (1981) p. 254. This story is told, with varying details, in most of the dozen or so biographies of Fitzgerald.
28. Mabel Dodge Luhan, *Intimate Memories*, vol. III, *Movers and Shakers* (1936) pp. 319–31.
29. McKay, *A Long Way from Home*, p. 212.
30. Tietjens, *The World at My Shoulders*, pp. 12–13.
31. Eastman, *Heroes I Have Known*, p. 73.
32. Eastman, 'Isadora Duncan', *The Liberator*, I (March 1918) 21.
33. Eastman, *Heroes I Have Known*, p. 77.
34. J. E. Spingarn, 'To Isadora Duncan, Dancing', *Poems* (1924) pp.12–14.
35. Duncan's subsequent enthusiasm for the Bolshevik Revolution did not have a comparable impact upon the younger writers and intellectuals in America. Some note was paid to her, as in Eugene Lyons, 'An Interview with Isadora Duncan', *The Worker* (10 February 1923) p. 4, but the frame of artistic values had firmly altered.

APPENDIX III

1. William Phillips and Philip Rahv, 'In Retrospect: Ten Years of *Partisan Review*', *The Partisan Reader: Ten Years of 'Partisan Review' 1934–1944*, ed. William Philips and Philip Rahv, with an Introduction by Lionel Trilling (1946) p. 683. See also Dwight Macdonald, *Politics Past: Essays in Political Criticism* (1970) pp. 12–13.
2. See James Burkhart Gilbert, *Writers and Partisans: A History of Literary Radicalism in America* (1968); Richard H. Pells, *Radical Visions and American Dreams* (1973); and Alan Wald, 'Revolutionary Intellectuals: *Partisan Review* in the 1930s', *Occident*, n.s. VIII (Spring 1974) 118–33.

3. M. S. Venkataramani, 'Leon Trotsky's Adventure in American Radical Politics 1935–7', *International Review of Social History*, IX (1964) 1–46.
4. Leon Trotsky, 'A Militant, Revolutionary and Critical Marxist Review is Needed', *Writings of Leon Trotsky [1936–7]*, 2nd edn, Naomi Allen and George Breitman (1978) p. 312.
5. William Phillips, 'The Esthetic of the Founding Fathers', *Partisan Review*, IV (March 1938) 11–21.
6. Philip Rahv, 'Trials of the Mind', *Partisan Review*, IV (April 1938) 3–11; see also Andrew James Dvosin, 'Literature in a Political World: The Career and Writings of Philip Rahv' (Unpub. PhD diss., New York University, 1977).

Bibliography

I. BIBLIOGRAPHIES

Lee Baxandall, compiler, *Marxism and Aesthetics: A Selected Annotated Bibliography* (New York: Humanities Press, 1968).

Donald Drew Egbert and Stow Persons (eds), *Socialism and American Life*, vol. 2, Bibliography, Descriptive, and Critical (Princeton University Press, 1952).

Walter Goldwater, 'Radical Periodicals in America, 1890–1950', *Yale University Library Gazette*, xxxvii (April 1963) 133–77.

Charles A. Gulick, Roy A. Ockert, Raymond J. Wallace, compilers, *History and Theory of Working-class Movements: A Select Bibliography* (Berkeley, California: Bureau of Business and Economic Research, and the Institute of Industrial Relations, University of California, Berkeley, 1955).

Estelle Gershgoren Novak, '"New Masses": Five Yearly Indexes of Poetry, Fiction, Criticism, Drama, and Reviews for the Years 1929 through 1933', *Bulletin of Bibliography*, xxviii (July–September 1971) 89–108.

David Peck, *American Marxist Literary Criticism 1926–1941: A Bibliography* (New York: American Institute of Marxist Studies, 1975).

Virginia Prestridge, compiler, *The Worker in American Fiction: An Annotated Bibliography* (Champaign, Illinois: Institute of Labor and Industrial Relations, 1954).

Walter B. Rideout, *The Radical Novel in the United States 1900–1954* (Cambridge, Massachusetts: Harvard University Press, 1956; reissued New York: Hill and Wang, 1966). Contains appendix listing socialist and proletarian novels pp. 292–300.

II. UNPUBLISHED SOURCES

Theses

William A. Bloodworth Jr, 'The Early Years of Upton Sinclair: A Study of the Development of a Progressive Christian Socialist' (PhD, University of Texas, 1972).

Andrew James Dvosin, 'Literature in a Political World: The Career of Philip Rahv' (PhD, New York University, 1977).

Steven Lafer, 'Toward a Bibliography of David Alfaro Siqueiros: His Life, Art, and Politics' (PhD, University of California, Irvine, 1977).

Rufus W. Mathewson Jr, 'Soviet–American Literary Relations 1929–1935' (MA, Columbia University, 1948).

Kenneth William Payne, 'Michael Gold to *Jews Without Money*' (PhD, University of Sussex, 1975).

Manuscript and Archival Material

Max Bedacht	Tamiment Institute Library, New York University.
Alexander Berkman	Tamiment Institute Library, New York University.
Alexander Bittelman	Tamiment Institute Library, New York University.
Basil Bunting	Humanities Research Center, University of Texas, Austin.
V. F. Calverton	New York Public Library.
John Dos Passos	Alderman Library, University of Virginia, Charlottesville.
Theodore Dreiser	Van Pelt Library, University of Pennsylvania.
Max Eastman	Lilly Library, Indiana University, Bloomington.
Emma Goldman	Huntington Library, San Marino, California.
Joseph Freeman	Hoover Institution, Stanford University.
V. J. Jerome	Sterling Memorial Library, Yale University.
Joshua Kunitz	Butler Library, Columbia University.
Walter Lippmann	Sterling Memorial Library, Yale University.
Jack London	Huntington Library, San Marino, California.
Robert Minor	Butler Library, Columbia University.
John Reed	Houghton Library, Harvard University.
Isidor Schneider	Butler Library, Columbia University.
Upton Sinclair	Lilly Library, Indiana University, Bloomington.
Herbert Solow	Hoover Institution, Stanford University.
Lincoln Steffens	Butler Library, Columbia University.
Leon Trotsky	Houghton Library, Harvard University.
William English Walling	Huntington Library, San Marino, California.

III. PUBLISHED SOURCES

A Report on Labor Disturbances in the State of Colorado, from 1880 to 1904 . . ., prepared under the Direction of Carroll D. Wright, Commissioner of Labor (Washington, D.C.: United States Government Printing Office, 1905).

Daniel Aaron, 'Edmund Wilson's Political Decade' in *Literature at the Barricades: The American Writer in the 1930s*, eds Ralph F. Bogardus and Fred Hobson (Tuscaloosa: University of Alabama Press, 1982).

——, *Writers on the Left: Episodes in American Literary Communism* (New York: Harcourt, Brace & World, 1961; reissued New York: Avon-Discus, 1965).

Louis Adamic, *Dynamite: The Story of Class Violence in America* (New York: Viking, 1931; rev. edn 1935).

Graham Adams Jr, *Age of Industrial Violence 1910–15: The Activists and Findings of the United States Commission on Industrial Relations* (New York: Columbia University Press, 1966).

William Alexander, *Film on the Left: American Documentary Film from 1931 to 1942* (Princeton University Press, 1981).

Charles Amirkhanian and David Gitin, 'A Conversation with George Oppen', *Ironwood*, no. 5 (1975) 21–4.

Margaret C. Anderson, 'Isadora Duncan's Misfortune', *Little Review*, III (April 1917) 5–7.

——, *My Thirty Years' War: An Autobiography* (London: Alfred A. Knopf, 1930).

Gertrude Atherton, 'Why is American Literature Bourgeois?', *North American Review*, 179 (May 1904) 771–81.

Ronald Atkin, *Revolution! Mexico 1910–1920* (London: Macmillan, 1969).

James Atlas, *Delmore Schwartz: The Life of an American Poet* (New York: Farrar, Straus & Giroux, 1977).

Ray Stannard Baker, 'The Reign of Lawlessness: Anarchy and Despotism in Colorado', *McClure's Magazine*, XXIII (May 1904) 43–57.

——, *Woodrow Wilson: Life and Letters*, vol. 4, *President: 1913–1914* (Garden City, New York: Doubleday, Doran, 1931).

Henri Barbusse, 'Literature of Tomorrow', *The New Freeman*, II (5 November 1930) 182–3.

Johannes R. Becher, 'Vor dem II. Weltkongress der Revolutionären Literatur Anfang Oktober 1930 in Charkow', *Die Linkskurve*, II (October 1930) 12–14.

Kent M. Beck, 'The Odyssey of Joseph Freeman', *The Historian*, XXXVII (November 1974) 101–20.

Daniel Bell, *Marxian Socialism in the United States* (Princeton University Press, 1967).

William Rose Benet, 'The Phoenix Nest', *Saturday Review of Literature*, X (24 March 1934) 580.

Jean-Pierre A. Bernard, *Le parti communiste français et la question littéraire, 1921–1939* (Grenoble: Presses Universitaires, 1972).

Paul H. Boase (ed.), *The Rhetoric of Christian Socialism* (New York: Random House, 1969).

A. Bogdanoff, *A Short Course of Economic Science*, trans. Joseph Fineberg (London: Communist Party of Great Britain, 1923).

Alexander Bogdanov, *L'Art, la science et la classe ouvrière*, trans. Blanche Grinbaum (Paris: Maspero, 1977).

Frank Bohn, 'After Ludlow – Facts and Thoughts', *International Socialist Review*, XV (August 1914) 112–14.

Harriet Borland, *Soviet Literary Theory and Practice During the First Five-Year Plan, 1928–1932* (New York: King's Crown Press, Columbia University Press, 1950).

Randolph Bourne, 'The War and the Intellectuals', *The Seven Arts*, II (June 1917) 133–46.

——, *The Radical Will: Selected Writings 1911–1918*, ed. Olaf Hansen (New York: Urizen Books, 1977).

James Boylan (ed.), *The 'World' and the 20's: The Golden Years of New York's Legendary Newspaper* (New York: The Dial Press, 1973).

John Graham Brooks, *American Syndicalism: The I.W.W.* (New York: The Macmillan Company, 1913).

'Obed Brooks' (Robert Gorham Davis), 'Archibald Macleish', *Partisan Review*, I (February–March 1934) 52–6.

Robert Paul Browder, *The Origins of Soviet—American Diplomacy* (Princeton University Press, 1953).

Deming Brown, 'Soviet Criticism of American Proletarian Literature of the 1930s', *American Contributions to the Fourth International Congress of Slavicists. Moscow, September 1958* (The Hague: Mouton, 1958).

Edward J. Brown, *The Proletarian Episode in Russian Literature 1928–1932* (New York: Columbia University Press, 1953).

Louis Francis Budenz, *This Is My Story* (New York: McGraw–Hill, 1947).

Mari Jo Buhle, *Women and American Socialism, 1870–1920* (Urbana, Illinois: University of Illinois Press, 1981).

Paul Buhle, 'Intellectuals in the Debsian Socialist Party', *Radical America*, IV (April 1970) 35–58.

Basil Bunting, 'Pound and "Zuk"', *Paideuma*, VII (Winter 1978) 373–4.

Charles H. Caffin, 'Henri Matisse and Isadora Duncan', *Camera Work*, no. 25 (January 1909) 17–20.

Alan Calmer, 'What's Doing in the John Reed Clubs of the U.S.', *Daily Worker* (18 April 1934) p. 5.

——, 'A New Period of American Leftwing Literature', *International Literature*, no. 7 (1935) 73–8.

V. F. Calverton, *The Newer Spirit: A Sociological Criticism of Literature*, with an Introduction by Ernest Boyd (New York: Boni & Liveright, 1925).

——, 'Labor and Literature: The Worker in American Literature; Railroad in Fiction; Religion in Literature', *Daily Worker Special Magazine Supplement* (21, 28 August; 4 September 1926).

——, 'Literature and Economics: Introduction; Bourgeois Literature; The Proletarian Trend; Later Developments of the Proletarian Trend', *The Communist*, VI (June 1927) 225–31; VII (March 1928) 181ff.; VII (April 1928) 247–51; VII (June 1928) 378–81.

——, 'Can We Have a Proletarian Literature?', *Modern Quarterly*, VI (Autumn 1932) 39–50.

——, 'Proletarianitis', *Saturday Review of Literature*, XV (9 January 1937) 3–4, 14–15.

E. H. Carr, *A History of Soviet Russia*, 14 vols (London: Macmillan, 1950– 1978).

David Caute, *The Fellow-Travellers: A Postscript to the Enlightenment* (London: Weidenfeld & Nicolson, 1973).

John Chamberlain, *Farewell to Reform: Being a History of the Rise, Life, and Decay of the Progressive Mind in America* (New York: Liveright, 1932; reissued Chicago: Quadrangle Books, 1965).

Whittaker Chambers, *Witness* (New York: Random House, 1952).

Carmen Claudin–Urondo, *Lenin and the Cultural Revolution*, trans. Brian Pearce (Lewes: Harvester Press, 1977).

Stephen F. Cohen, *Bukharin and the Bolshevik Revolution: A Political Biography, 1888–1938* (London: Wildwood House, 1973).

John R. Commons, 'Labor Conditions in Slaughtering and Meat Packing', *Quarterly Journal of Economics*, XIX (1904) 1–32; reprinted in Commons (ed.), *Trade Unionism and Labor Problems* (New York: Ginn, 1905) pp. 222–49.

Jack Conroy and Ralph Cheyney (eds), *Unrest: The Rebel Poets Anthology for 1929* (London: Arthur Stockwell, 1929).

Malcolm Cowley, *The Dream of the Golden Mountains: Remembering the 1930s* (New York: Viking Press, 1980).

George Creel, *Rebel at Large: Recollections of Fifty Crowded Years* (New York: G. P. Putnam's Sons, 1947).

R. H. S. Crossman (ed.), *The God That Failed: Six Studies in Communism* (London: Hamish Hamilton, 1950).

Allen F. Davis, *Spearheads for Reform: The Social Settlements and the Progressive Movement* (New York: Oxford University Press, 1967).

Robert MacGregor Dawson, *William Lyon Mackenzie King: A Political Biography*, 2 vols (London: Methuen, 1958–63).

Eugene V. Debs, 'Debs' Opinion of *The Jungle*', *The Appeal to Reason*, no. 555 (21 July 1906) 4.

——, 'Homestead and Ludlow', *International Socialist Review*, xv (August 1914) 105–7.

Floyd Dell, *Women as World Builders: Studies in Modern Feminism* (Chicago: Forbes & Co., 1913).

——, 'A Vacation from Sociology', *The Masses*, vi (June 1915) 18.

——, 'The Russian Ballet', *The New Review*, iv (March 1916) 81–2.

——, ' "Who Said That Beauty Passes Like a Dream" ', *The Masses*, vii (October 1916) 27.

——, Review of Max Eastman, *Colors of Life*, *The Liberator*, i (December 1918) 44–5.

——, Review of *Ten Days That Shook the World* by John Reed, *The Liberator*, ii (May 1919) 44–5.

——, 'Art Under the Bolsheviks', *The Liberator*, ii (June 1919) 11–12, 14–18.

——, 'John Reed: Revolutionist', *New York Call* (31 October 1920).

——, *Intellectual Vagabondage: An Apology for the Intelligentsia* (New York: George H. Doran, 1926).

——, *Upton Sinclair: A Study in Social Protest* (New York: George H. Doran, 1927).

——, *Homecoming: An Autobiography* (New York: Farrar, Rinehart, 1933).

L. S. Dembo, 'Interview with George Oppen', *Contemporary Literature*, x (Spring 1969) 159–77.

Hélène Carrère d'Encausse, *A History of the Soviet Union, 1917–1953*, trans. Valence Ionescu, 2 vols (London: Longman, 1981).

Isaac Deutscher, *The Prophet Outcast: Trotsky 1929–1940* (London: Oxford University Press, 1963).

John P. Diggins, *Up from Communism: Conservative Odysseys in American Intellectual History* (New York: Harper & Row, 1975).

A. Dodonova, 'Souvenirs sur le Proletkult', *Action Poètique*, no. 59 (September 1974) 143–7.

John Dos Passos, *The Fourteenth Chronicle: Letters and Diaries of John Dos Passos*, ed. Townsend Ludington (Boston: Gambit, 1973).

George H. Douglas, *Edmund Wilson's America* (Lexington: University Press of Kentucky, 1983).

Theodore Draper, *The Roots of American Communism* (New York: Viking, 1957).

——, *American Communism and Soviet Russia: The Formative Period* (New York: Viking, 1960).

——, 'The Ghost of Social Facism', *Commentary*, xlvii (February 1969) 29–42.

Melvyn Dubofsky, *We Shall be All: A History of the Industrial Workers of the World* (Chicago: Quadrangle Books, 1969).

David C. Duke, *Distant Obligations: Modern American Writers and Foreign Causes* (New York: Oxford University Press, 1983).

Robin E. Dunbar, 'Mammonart and Communist Art', *Daily Worker Supplement* (23 May 1925) p. 3.

Isadora Duncan, *My Life* (London: Victor Gollancz, 1928).

William F. Dunne, 'The Confused Mr. Calverton', *Daily Worker* (16 June 1926).

Walter Duranty, *'I Write as I Please'* (London: Hamish Hamilton, 1935).

Max Eastman, *Enjoyment of Poetry* (London: Elkin Mathews, 1913).

——, 'Class War in Colorado', *The Masses*, v (June 1914) 5–8.

——, *Understanding Germany: The Only Way to End War and Other Essays* (New York: Mitchell Kennerley, 1916).

——, *Journalism versus Art* (New York: Alfred A. Knopf, 1916).

——, 'Isadora Duncan', *The Liberator*, i (March 1918) 21.

——, *Colors of Life* (New York: Alfred A. Knopf, 1918).

——, *Education and Art in Soviet Russia in the Light of Official Decrees and Documents*, with a Foreword by Max Eastman (New York: *The Liberator*, 1919).

——, *Venture* (New York: Albert & Charles Boni, 1927).

——, 'Artists in Uniform', *Modern Quarterly*, vii (August 1933) 397–404.

——, *Artists in Uniform: A Study of Literature and Bureaucratism* (New York: Alfred A. Knopf, 1934).

——, 'John Reed and the Old Masses', *Modern Monthly*, x (October 1936) 19–22, 31.

——, 'John Reed and the Russian Revolution', *Modern Monthly*, x (December 1936) 14–21.

——, *Heroes I Have Known: Twelve Who Lived Great Lives* (New York: Simon & Schuster, 1942).

——, *Enjoyment of Living* (New York: Harper & Brothers, 1948).

——, *Poems of Five Decades* (New York: Harper & Brothers, 1954).

——, *Love and Revolution: My Journey through an Epoch* (New York: Random House, 1964).

Karl Eimermacher (ed.), *Dokumente zur sowjetischen Literatur politik 1917–1932* (Stuttgart: Verlag W. Kohlhammer, 1972).

Fred Ellis, Michael Gold, William Gropper, Joshua Kunitz, A. B. Magil, Harry Alan Potamkin, 'The Charkov Conference of Revolutionary Writers', *New Masses*, vii (February 1931) 6–8.

Herman Ermolaev, *Soviet Literary Theories, 1917–1934: The Genesis of Socialist Realism* (Berkeley: University of California Press, 1963).

Frank Field, *Three French Writers and the Great War: Studies in the Rise of Communism and Fascism* (Cambridge University Press, 1975).

Ernst Fischer, *Art Against Ideology*, trans. Anna Bostock (London: Allen Lane, 1969).

Louis Fischer, 'A Revolution in Revolutionary History', *New York Herald Tribune Books*, section x (27 November 1932) p. 10.

——, *Men and Politics: Europe Between the Two World Wars* (New York: Duell, Sloan and Pearce, 1941; reissued New York: Harper–Colophon, 1966).

Leslie Fishbein, *Rebels in Bohemia: The Radicals of 'The Masses', 1911–1917* (Chapel Hill, North Carolina: The University of North Carolina Press, 1982).

F. Scott Fitzgerald, *The Letters of F. Scott Fitzgerald*, ed. Andrew Turnbull (New York: Charles Scribner's Sons, 1963).

Richard Fitzgerald, *Art and Politics: Cartoonists of the 'Masses' and 'Liberator'* (Westport, Connecticut: Greenwood Press, 1973).

Sheila Fitzpatrick, *The Commissariat of the Enlightenment: Soviet Organization of the Arts Under Lunacharsky* (Cambridge University Press, 1970).

——, (ed.), *Cultural Revolution in Russia, 1928–1931* (Bloomington: Indiana University Press, 1978).

Michael Folsom (ed.), *Mike Gold: A Literary Anthology* (New York: International Publishers, 1972).

Philip S. Foner, *History of the Labor Movement in the United States*, vol. 5, *The AFL in the Progressive Era, 1910–1915* (New York: International Publishers, 1980).

'For Whom Do You Write? Replies from Forty American Writers', *The New Quarterly*, I (Summer 1934) 3–13).

William Z. Foster, 'Calverton's Fascism', *The Communist*, x (February 1931) 107–11.

Joseph Freeman, 'Bulgarian Literature: Or, The Perfect Critical Method', *New Masses*, III (August 1927) 9–10.

——, 'Literary Patterns', *New Masses*, v (June 1929) 14.

——, 'What a World! The Struggle Against Max Eastman and V. F. Calverton', *Daily Worker* (22 November–2 December 1933).

——, 'Ivory Towers – White and Red', *New Masses*, XII (11 September 1934) 20–4.

——, *An American Testament: A Narrative of Rebels and Romantics* (New York: Farrar, Rinehart, 1936; abridged edition, London: Victor Gollancz, 1938).

Virginia Gardner, *'Friend and Lover': The Life of Louise Bryant* (New York: Horizon Press, 1983).

Haim Genizi, 'Disillusionment of a Communist: The Case of V. F. Calverton', *Canadian Journal of History*, IX (April 1974) 70–82.

——, 'Edmund Wilson and the *Modern Monthly*, 1934–1935: A Phase in Wilson's Radicalism', *Journal of American Studies*, VII (December 1973) 301–9.

——, 'The *Modern Quarterly*: 1923–1940: An Independent Radical Magazine', *Labor History*, XV (Spring 1974) 199–215.

Arnold Genthe, *The Book of the Dance* (New York: Mitchell Kennerley, 1916).

W. J. Ghent, 'The Next Step: A Benevolent Feudalism', *Independent* (3 April 1902) 781–8.

——, *Our Benevolent Feudalism* (New York: Macmillan, 1902).

Frederick C. Giffin, 'Leon Trotsky in New York City', *New York History*, XLIX (October 1968) 391–403.

James Burkhart Gilbert, *Writers and Partisans: A History of Literary Radicalism in America* (New York: John Wiley, 1968).

Mark T. Gilderhus, *Diplomacy and Revolution: US–Mexican Relations under Wilson and Carranza* (Tucson, Arizona: University of Arizona Press, 1977).

Inez Hayes Gilmore, 'At the Industrial Hearings', *The Masses*, VI (March 1915) 8–9.

Benjamin Gitlow, *I Confess: The Truth About American Communism*, with an Introduction by Max Eastman (New York: E. P. Dutton, 1940).

Susan Glaspell, *The Road to the Temple* (New York: Frederick A. Stokes, 1927).

William I. Gleberzon, '"Intellectuals" and the American Socialist Party, 1901–1917', *Canadian Journal of History*, XI (April 1976) 43–67.

Irwin Granich [later Michael Gold], 'Max Eastman – A Portrait', *New York Call* (9 February 1918) pp. 6, 16.

——, 'Towards Proletarian Art', *The Liberator*, IV (February 1921) 20–5.

Michael Gold, [Review of Hamsun, *Growth of the Soil*], *The Liberator*, IV (May 1921) 30.

——, 'May Days and Revolutionary Art', *Modern Quarterly*, III (January–April 1926) 160–4.

——, 'White Hope of American Drama', *The New Magazine* section of *Daily Worker* (26 February 1927) p. 8.

——, 'John Reed and The Real Thing', *New Masses*, III (November 1927) 7–8.

——, 'Floyd Dell Resigns', *New Masses*, V (July 1929) 10–11.

——, *Jews Without Money* (New York, Liveright, 1930).

——, 'Notes from Kharkov', *New Masses*, VI (March 1931) 4–6.

——, 'Out of the Fascist Unconscious', *New Republic*, LXXV (26 July 1933) 295–6.

——, 'What a World! William Carlos Williams: Pioneer of Proletarian Literature', *Daily Worker* (12 October 1933) p. 5.

——, 'No More Bohemianism', *Daily Worker* (28 February 1934) p. 7.

——, *The Hollow Men* (New York: International Publishers, 1941).

Michael Gold and Joseph North, 'The *Masses* Tradition', *Masses & Mainstream*, IV (August 1951) 45–55; (September 1951) 34–41.

Lawrence Goldman, 'W. J. Ghent and the Left', *Studies on the Left*, III (Summer 1963) 21–40.

Maurice Goldsmith, *Sage: A Life of J. D. Bernal* (London: Hutchinson, 1980).

Steve Golin, 'Defeat Becomes Disaster: The Paterson Strike of 1913 and the Decline of the I.W.W.', *Labor History*, XXIV (Spring 1983) 223ff.

Benjamin Goriely, *Les Poètes dans la revolution russe* (Paris: Gallimard, 1934).

John Graham, 'Upton Sinclair and the Ludlow Massacre', *The Colorado Quarterly*, XXI (Summer 1972) 55–67.

Marcus Graham (ed.), *An Anthology of Revolutionary Poetry*, with an Introduction by Ralph Cheyney and Lucia Trent (New York: Marcus Graham, 1929).

Lawrence Grauman Jr, ' "That Little Running Sore": Some Observations on the Participation of American Writers in the Investigations of Conditions in the Harlan and Bell County, Kentucky, Coal Fields in 1931–32', *Filson Club History Quarterly*, XXXVI (October 1962) 340–54.

Horace Gregory, *The House on Jefferson Street: A Cycle of Memories* (New York: Rinehart & Winston 1971).

Dietrich Grille, *Lenins Rivale. Bogdanov und seine Philosphie.* (Cologne: Verlag Wissenschaft u. Politik, 1966).

N. Guterman and P. Morhange, trans., *Poèmes D'Ouvriers Américains* (Paris: Les Revues, 1930).

Andrew Hacker, 'The Lower Depths', *New York Review of Books*, XXIX (12 August 1982) 15–20.

Albert Halper, *Good-bye, Union Square: A Writer's Memoirs of the Thirties* (Chicago: Quadrangle Books, 1970).

Leon Harris, *Upton Sinclair: American Rebel* (New York: Crowell, 1975).

James D. Hart, *The Popular Book: A History of America's Literary Taste* (Berkeley and Los Angeles: University of California Press, 1950).

Burton Hatlen, 'Art and / as Labor: Some Dialectical Patterns in "A"–1 through "A"–10', *Contemporary Literature*, XXV (Summer 1984) 205–34.

Burton Hatlen and Tom Mandel, 'Poetry and Politics: A Conversation with George and Mary Oppen', in *George Oppen: Man and Poet*, ed. Burton Hatlen (Orono, Maine: National Poetry Foundation, 1981).

Hippolyte Havel, 'Martin Eden', *Mother Earth*, v (June 1910) 140–3.

——, 'The Civil War in Colorado', *Mother Earth*, ix (May 1914) 71–7.

Joan D. Hedrick, *Solitary Comrade: Jack London and His Work* (Chapel Hill, North Carolina: University of North Carolina Press, 1982).

'Helicon Hall', *Chicago Daily Socialist* (27 November 1906).

Ernest Hemingway, *Selected Letters, 1917–1961*, ed. Carlos Baker (London: Granada, 1981).

Josephine Herbst, 'Yesterday's Road', *New American Review*, iii (1968) 84–104.

Granville Hicks, 'John Reed', *New Masses*, viii (December 1932) 24.

——, 'A Retired Literary Radical: Floyd Dell's Autobiography', *Daily Worker* (11 October 1933) p. 5.

——, *John Reed: The Making of a Revolutionary* (New York: Macmillan, 1936).

S. G. H[obson]., Review of *The Jungle* by Upton Sinclair, *Fabian News*, xvi (July 1906) 30.

Paul Hollander, 'The Ideological Pilgrim', *Encounter*, xli (November 1973) 3–15.

——, *Political Pilgrims: Travels of Western Intellectuals to the Soviet Union, China, and Cuba, 1928–1978* (New York: Oxford University Press, 1981).

Eric Homberger, *The Art of the Real: Poetry in England and America since 1939* (London: Dent, 1977).

William Innes Homer, *Alfred Stieglitz and the American Avant-Garde* (Boston: New York Graphic Society, 1977).

William Innes Homer, with Violet Organ, *Robert Henri and His Circle* (Ithaca: Cornell University Press, 1969).

Charles Howard Hopkins, *The Rise of the Social Gospel in American Protestantism, 1865–1915* (New Haven: Yale University Press, 1940).

James Francis Horrabin and Winifred Horrabin, *Working Class Education* (London: Labour Publishing Co., 1924).

Isaac A. Hourwich, 'Colorado, 1893–1914', *The New Review*, ii (June 1914) 329–32.

Milton Howard, 'A Poet Who Writes With His Eye on Slight "Objects"', *Daily Worker* (10 February 1934) p. 9.

Irving Howe and Lewis Coser, with the assistance of Julius Jacobson, *The American Communist Party: A Critical History (1919–1957)* (Boston: Beacon Press, 1957).

Irving Howe, with Kenneth Libo, *World of Our Fathers* (New York: Harcourt Brace, 1976).

William Dean Howells, *A Hazard of New Fortunes*, ed. with an Introduction by Tony Tanner (London: Oxford University Press, 1965; first published 1890).

Robert E. Humphrey, *Children of Fantasy: The First Rebels of Greenwich Village* (New York: John Wiley, 1978).

Robert Hunter, *Violence and the Labor Movement* (New York: Macmillan, 1914).

[Anon.], 'Isadora Duncan and the Libertarian Spirit', *The Modern School*, ii (April 1915) 37–8.

Philip J. Jaffe, 'Agnes Smedley: A Reminiscence', *Survey*, xx (Autumn 1974) 172–9.

C. Vaughan James, *Soviet Socialist Realism: Origins and Theory* (London: Macmillan, 1973).

William James, *The Varieties of Religious Experience: A Study in Human Nature* (London: Longmans, Green, 1902).

Rhodri Jeffreys-Jones, 'Theories of American Labour Violence', *Journal of American Studies*, XIII (August 1979) 245–64.

V. J. Jerome, 'Edmund Wilson: To the Munich Station', *New Masses*, XXXI (4 April 1939) 23–6.

Bud Johns and Judith S. Clancy (eds), *Bastard in the Ragged Suit: Writings of, with drawings by, Herman Spector* (San Francisco: Synergistic Press, 1977).

Orrick Johns, 'The John Reed Clubs Meet', *New Masses*, XIII (30 October 1934) 25.

Justin Kaplan, *Lincoln Steffens: A Bibliography* (New York: Simon & Schuster, 1974).

K[arl] K[autsky], Review of *Wenn die Natur ruft* by Jack London, *Die Neue Zeit*, XXVI (1907–8) 376–7.

Alfred Kazin, *Starting Out in the Thirties* (London: Secker & Warburg, 1966).

Ira Kipnis, *The American Socialist Movement, 1897–1912* (New York: Columbia University Press, 1952).

Wolfgang Klein, 'Barbusse et le mouvement littéraire communiste autour de la conference de Kharkov (1930)', *Europe*, nos 575–6 (Mars–Avril 1977) 187–93.

Arthur Koestler, *Arrow in the Blue: An Autobiography*, (London: Collins with Hamish Hamilton, 1952).

Leszek Kołakowski, *Main Currents in Marxism: Its Rise, Growth, and Dissolution*, trans. P. S. Falla, 3 vols (Oxford: Clarendon Press, 1978).

Gabriel Kolko, *The Triumph of Conservatism: A Reinterpretation of American History, 1900–1916* (Glencoe, Illinois: Free Press, 1963; reissued, Chicago: Quadrangle Books, 1967).

——, 'The Decline of American Radicalism in the Twentieth Century', *Studies on the Left*, VI (September–October 1966).

Kent Kreuter and Gretchen Kreuter, *An American Dissenter: The Life of Algie M. Simons, 1870–1950* (Lexington: University of Kentucky Press, 1969).

Leonard Kriegel, *Edmund Wilson* (Carbondale and Edwardsville: Southern Illinois University Press, 1981).

Mark Krupnick, 'The Menorah Journal Group and the Origins of Modern Jewish–American Radicalism', *Modern Jewish Social Studies* (1980) 56–67.

Earle Labor, *Jack London* (New York: Twayne, 1974).

Robert Rives la Monte, 'The New Intellectuals', *The New Review*, II (January 1914) 45–53.

A. Landy, 'Cultural Compulsives or Calverton's New Caricature of Marxism', *The Communist*, x (October 1931) 851–64.

Elinor Langer, *Josephine Herbst* (Boston: Little, Brown, 1984).

Dominique Lecourt, *Proletarian Science? The Case of Lysenko*, trans. Ben Brewster (London: New Left Books, 1977).

G. Lelevitch, 'Proletarian Literature in Soviet Russia: Report on the 1st All Russian Conference of Proletarian Writers, Moscow, January 6–12, 1925', *Daily Worker Supplement* (21 March 1925).

V. I. Lenin, *On Literature and Art* (Moscow: Progress Publishers, 1967).

Frank Lentricchia, *Criticism and Social Change* (University of Chicago Press, 1984).

A. S. Link et al. (eds), *The Papers of Woodrow Wilson*, 48 vols to date (Princeton University Press, 1966–).

Walter Lippmann, 'Legendary John Reed', *New Republic*, i (26 December 1914) 15–16.

——, 'Mr Rockefeller on the Stand', *New Republic*, i (30 January 1915) 12–13.

[——], 'The Rockefeller Plan in Colorado', *New Republic*, ii (9 October 1915) 249–50.

——, *Early Writings*, ed. Arthur Schlesinger Jr (New York: Liveright, 1970).

——, *Public Persons*, ed. Gilbert Harrison (New York: Liveright, 1976).

Henry Demarest Lloyd, *Wealth Against Commonwealth* (New York: Harper & Brothers, 1894).

Jack London, *The People of the Abyss* (New York: Macmillan, 1903; reissued with an Introduction by Jack Lindsay, London: Journeyman Press, 1977).

——, 'How I Became a Socialist', *The Comrade* (March 1903); collected in *London's Essays of Revolt*, ed. Leonard D. Abbott (New York: Vanguard Press, 1926).

——, *The Sea-Wolf* (New York: Macmillan, 1904; ed. with an Introduction by Matthew J. Bruccoli, Boston: Houghton Mifflin, 1964).

——, 'What Jack London says of *The Jungle*', *The Chicago Socialist* (25 November 1905) p. 2.

——, 'Jack London Reviews *The Jungle*', New York *Evening Journal* (8 August 1906).

——, *The Iron Heel* (New York: Macmillan, 1908; reissued, London: Journeyman Press, 1974).

——, *Martin Eden* (New York: Macmillan, 1909; reissued, Harmondsworth: Penguin Books, 1967).

Jack London, American Rebel, ed. Philip S. Foner (Berlin: Seven Seas, 1958; first published 1947).

Letters from Jack London, ed. King Hendricks and Irving Shepard (London: MacGibbon & Kee, 1966).

——, *Revolution: Stories and Essays*, ed. Robert Barltrop (London: Journeyman Press, 1979).

——, *No Mentor But Myself: A Collection of Articles, Essays, Reviews, and Letters on Writers and Writing*, ed. Dale L. Walker (Port Washington, New York: Kennikat Press, 1979).

Lee Elihu Lowenfish, 'The American Testament of a Revolutionary', [on Joseph Freeman], *Columbia Library Columns*, xxvii (1978) 3–13.

Townsend Ludington, 'Friendship Won't Stand That: John Howard Lawson and John Dos Passos's Struggle for an Ideological Ground to Stand On', in *Literature at the Barricades: The American Writer in the 1930s*, eds Ralph F. Bogardus and Fred Hobson (Tuscaloosa: University of Alabama Press, 1982).

Mabel Dodge Luhan, *Intimate Memories*, 4 vols (New York: Harcourt Brace, 1933–6); vol. 3: *Movers and Shakers*.

A. Lounatcharski, 'La culture proletarienne et le commissariat de l'instruction publique', *Le Phare*, ii, no. 18 (March 1921) 382–8.

A. V. Lunacharski, 'Lenin and Literature', *International Literature*, no. 1 (1935) 55–83.

A. V. Lunacharsky, 'The Role of the Proletarian State in the Development of Proletarian Literature', *International Literature*, no. 4 (1934) 111–17.

Kenneth S. Lynn, 'Jack London: The Brain Merchant', in *The Dream of Success: A Study of the Modern American Imagination* (Boston: Little, Brown, 1955) pp. 75–120.

——, 'The Rebels of Greenwich Village', in *Perspectives in American History*, VIII (1974) 335–77.

Eugene Lyons, 'An Interview with Isadora Duncan', *The Worker* (10 February 1923) 4.

——, *Assignment in Utopia* (London: Harrap, 1938).

Dwight Macdonald, *Politics Past: Essays in Political Criticism* (New York: Viking Press, 1970). First published 1957 as *Memoirs of a Revolutionist*.

George McGovern and Leonard Guttridge, *The Great Coalfield War* (Boston: Beacon Press, 1972).

Stuart Macintyre, *A Proletarian Science: Marxism in Britain, 1917–1933* (Cambridge University Press, 1980).

Claude McKay, *A Long Way from Home* (New York: Lee Furman, 1937).

Hugh McLean Jr, 'Voronskij and VAPP', *American Slavic and East European Review*, VIII (1949) 185–200.

Archibald MacLeish, *Letters of Archibald MacLeish 1907 to 1982*, ed. R. H. Winnick (Boston: Houghton Mifflin, 1983).

Brooks McNamara (ed.), 'Paterson Strike Pageant', *TDR/The Drama Review*, XV (Summer 1971) 60–71.

David Madden (ed.), *Proletarian Writers of the Thirties* (Carbondale: Southern Illinois University Press, 1968).

Charles A. Madison, *Critics and Crusaders* (New York: Henry Holt and Co., 1948).

A. B. Magil, 'The "Marxism" of V. F. Calverton', *The Communist*, VIII (May 1929) 282–5.

——, 'Pity and Terror', *New Masses*, VIII (December 1932) 16–19.

Robert A. Maguire, *Red Virgin Soil: Soviet Literature in the 1920s* (Princeton University Press, 1968).

Nadezhda Mandelstam, *Hope Against Hope: A Memoir*, trans. Max Hayward (London: Collins-Harvill, 1971).

Jerre Mangione, *An Ethnic at Large: A Memoir of America in the Thirties and Forties* (New York: Putnam, 1978).

Isaac Frederick Marcosson, *Adventures in Interviewing* (New York: Dodd, 1919).

Paul Mariani, *William Carlos Williams: A New World Naked* (New York: McGraw-Hill, 1981).

Stephen Meyer III, *The Five Dollar Day: Labor Management and Social Control in the Ford Motor Company, 1908–1921* (Albany: State University of New York Press, 1981).

Harriet Monroe, *A Poet's Life: Seventy Years in a Changing World* (New York: Macmillan, 1938).

Elting Morison et al. (eds), *The Letters of Theodore Roosevelt*, vol. 7: *The Days of Armageddon 1909–14* (Cambridge, Mass.: Harvard University Press, 1954).

William Morris, *On Art and Socialism: Essays and Lectures*, ed. Holbrook Jackson (London: John Lehmann, 1947).

Lewis Mumford, *My Works and Days: A Personal Chronicle* (New York: Harcourt Brace Jovanovich, 1979).

Robert K. Murray, *Red Scare: A Study of National Hysteria, 1919–1920* (Minneapolis: University of Minnesota Press, 1955).

Michael Nash, 'Schism on the Left: The Anti-Communism of V. F. Calverton and his *Modern Monthly*', *Science and Society*, XLV (Winter 1981–2) 437–52.

'National John Reed Club Conference', *Partisan Review*, I (November–December 1934) 60–1.

Scott Nearing and Joseph Freeman, *Dollar Diplomacy: A Study in American Imperialism* (New York: B. W. Huebsch and the Viking Press, 1925).

Allan Nevins, *John D. Rockefeller: The Heroic Age of American Enterprise*, 2 vols (New York: Charles Scribner's Sons, 1940).

Patrick O'Hea, *Reminiscences of the Mexican Revolution* (London: Sphere Books, 1981).

Tillie Olsen, *Silences* (New York: Delacorte Press/Seymour Lawrence, 1978).

William L. O'Neill (ed.), *Echoes of Revolt: The Masses 1911–1917*, with an Introduction by Irving Howe and an Afterword by Max Eastman (Chicago: Quadrangle Books, 1966).

——, *The Last Romantic: A Life of Max Eastman* (New York: Oxford University Press, 1978).

Mary Oppen, *Meaning a Life: An Autobiography* (Santa Barbara: Black Sparrow Press, 1978).

James Oppenheim, *The Mystic Warrior* (New York: Alfred A. Knopf, 1921).

George Orwell, *Collected Essays, Journalism and Letters*, vol. 1: *An Age Like This, 1920–1940*, ed. Sonia Orwell and Ian Angus (London: Secker & Warburg, 1968).

'The Pageant as a Form of Propaganda', *Current Opinion*, LV (July 1913) 32.

Jean-Michel Palmier, *Lénine, l'art et la revolution*, vol. 1 (Paris: Payot, 1975).

Zeese Papanikolas, *Buried Unsung: Louis Tikas and the Ludlow Massacre* (Salt Lake City: University of Utah Press, 1982).

Leo Pasvolsky, 'Proletkult: Its Pretensions and Fallacies', *North American Review*, 213 (April 1921) 539–50.

'The Paterson Strike Pageant', *The Independent*, LXXIV (19 June 1913) 1406–7.

Sherman Paul, *Edmund Wilson: A Study of Literary Vocation in Our Time* (Urbana, Illinois: University of Illinois Press, 1965).

David Peck, '"The Tradition of American Revolutionary Literature": The Monthly *New Masses* 1926–1933', *Science and Society*, XLII (Winter 1978–9) 385–409.

Richard Pells, *Radical Visions and American Dreams: Culture and Social Thought in the Depression Years* (New York: Harper & Row, 1973).

'Wallace Phelps' [William Phillips] and Philip Rahv, 'Problems and Perspectives in Revolutionary Literature', *Partisan Review*, I (June–July 1934) 3–10.

'Phila. John Reed Club Is Raided', *Daily Worker* (26 May 1932) p. 2.

William Phillips and Philip Rahv (eds), *The Partisan Reader: Ten Years of 'Partisan Review' 1934–1944* (New York: The Dial Press, 1946).

V. Poliansky, 'The Banner of the "Proletcult"', *The Plebs* (January 1921) 3–7.

Vyacheslav Polonsky, 'Lenin's View of Art', trans. Max Eastman, *The Modern Monthly*, VII (January 1934) 738–43.

Alessandro Portelli, 'Jack London's Missing Revolution: Notes on *The Iron Heel*', *Science-Fiction Studies*, IX (1982) 180–94.

Eugene O. Porter, 'The Colorado Coal Strike of 1913 – An Interpretation', *The Historian*, XII (Autumn 1949) 3–27.

Ezra Pound, 'Patria-Mia', *The New Age*, XI (19 September 1912) 491–2.

——, *The Letters of Ezra Pound, 1907–1941*, ed. D. D. Paige (London: Faber & Faber, 1951).

——, *Patria Mia and the Treatise on Harmony* (London: Peter Owen, 1962).

Howard H. Quint, *The Forging of American Socialism: Origins of the Modern Movement* (New York: Columbia University Press, 1953).

Alexander Rabinowitch, *The Bolsheviks Come to Power: The Revolution of 1917 in Petrograd* (New York: W. W. Norton, 1976).

Karl Radek, 'Sinclair: "A Hercules Trying to Clean The Augean Stables With a Toothbrush"', *Daily Worker* (26 October 1934) p. 7.

Philip Rahv, 'The Literary Class War', *New Masses*, VIII (August 1932) 7–10.

——, 'Trials of the Mind', *Partisan Review*, IV (April 1938) 3–11.

——, 'Proletarian Literature: A Political Autopsy', *Southern Review*, IV (Winter 1939) 616–28.

Carl Rakosi, 'William Carlos Williams', *The Symposium*, IV (October 1933) 439–47.

David Ramsey and Alan Calmer, 'The Marxism of V. F. Calverton', *New Masses*, VIII (January 1933) 9–15, 18–20, 22–7.

F. F. Raskolnikov, *Kronstadt and Petrograd in 1917*, trans. Brian Pearce (London: New Park Publications, 1982; first published 1925, in Russian).

'Real Pig Squeals in Jungle Drama', *Chicago Daily Socialist* (21 November 1906).

Madeleine Reberioux, 'Critique littéraire et socialisme au tournant de siècle', *Le Movement Social*, LIX (1967) 3–28.

John Reed, 'The Colorado War', *Metropolitan Magazine*, XL (July 1914); reissued, in *The Education of John Reed*, ed. John Stuart, pp. 106–45.

——, *Insurgent Mexico* (New York: D. Appleton and Company, 1914; reissued, with an Introduction by Renato Leduc, New York: International Publishers, 1969).

——, 'The Worst Thing in Europe', *The Masses*, VI (March 1915) 17–18.

——, *The War in Eastern Europe* (New York: Charles Scribner's Sons, 1916).

——, *Tamburlane and Other Verses* (Riverside, Connecticut: Frederick C. Bursch, 1917).

——, *Ten Days That Shook the World* (New York: Boni & Liveright, 1919; reissued, with an Introduction by A. J. P. Taylor, Harmondsworth: Penguin Books, 1977).

——, *The Education of John Reed: Selected Writings*, ed. John Stuart (New York: International Publishers, 1955).

——, *Adventures of a Young Man: Short Stories from Life* (San Francisco: City Lights Books, 1975).

Heinz Rentmeister, 'Les rapports de Jack London avec la classe ouvrière', *Europe*, nos 561–2 (Janvier–Fevrier 1976) 22–30.

Charles Reznikoff, 'A Memoir', *Ironwood*, no. 5 (1975) 29.

Edgell Rickword, 'Where Brotherhood Grows', *Daily Worker* [London] (4 November 1936) p. 7.

Walter B. Rideout, *The Radical Novel in the United States, 1900–1954: Some Interrelations of Literature and Society* (Cambridge, Mass.: Harvard University Press, 1956; reissued New York: Hill & Wang, 1966).

Jacob Riis, *How the Other Half Lives: Studies among the Tenements of New York*, with an Introduction by Donald N. Bigelow (New York: Sycamore Press, 1957; first published 1890).

John D. Rockefeller, *Random Reminiscences of Men and Events* (New York: Doubleday, Page, 1909).

Robert A. Rosenstone, *Romantic Revolutionary: A Biography of John Reed* (New York: Alfred A. Knopf, 1975).

Charles Edward Russell, *Why I Am a Socialist* (New York: Doran, 1910).

Annie Sabatier, 'Le Proletkult International', *Action Poètique*, no. 59 (September 1974) 295–300.

Carl Sandburg, 'The Two Mr. Rockefellers – and Mr. Walsh', *International Socialist Review*, xvi (July 1915) 18–24.

——, 'The Walsh Report', *International Socialist Review*, xvi (October 1915) 198–201.

David J. Saposs, *Communism in American Politics* (Washington D. C.: Public Affairs Press, 1960).

Morris U. Schappes, 'Historic and Contemporary Particulars', *Poetry*, xli (March 1933) 340–3.

Mark Schorer, *Sinclair Lewis: An American Life* (New York: McGraw-Hill, 1961).

Lawrence H. Schwartz, *Marxism and Culture: the CPUSA and Aesthetics in the 1930s* (Port Washington, New York: Kennikat Press, 1980).

Vida D. Scudder, 'Jacob Riis on Socialism', *New York Evening Call* (8 July 1908).

Edwin Seaver, 'Books of the Day', *Daily Worker* (28 July 1937) p. 9 (review of Williams's *White Mule*).

David E. Shi, *Matthew Josephson, Bourgeois Bohemian* (New Haven: Yale University Press, 1981).

Grace V. Silver, 'The *Iron Heel* Dramatized', *International Socialist Review*, xi (June 1911) 752–3.

Ernest J. Simmons, 'The Origins of Literary Control', *Survey*, no. 36 (April–June 1961) 78–84; no. 37 (July–September 1961) 60–7.

A. M. Simons, *Packingtown*, Pocket Library of Socialism no. 4 (Chicago: C. H. Kerr & Co., 1899).

——, 'Packingtown, *The Jungle* and its Critics', *International Socialist Review*, vi (June 1906) 70–2.

——, 'The Chicago Elections', *International Socialist Review*, vii (1 April 1907) 623–5.

Andrew Sinclair, *Jack: A Biography of Jack London* (London: Weidenfeld & Nicolson, 1978).

Upton Sinclair, *Our Bourgeois Literature: The Reason and the Remedy*, Pocket Library of Socialism no. 43 (Chicago: C. H. Kerr & Co., 1904; first published *Collier's Weekly*, 8 October 1904).

——, 'The Socialist Party', *World's Work*, xi (April 1906) 7431–2.

——, 'A Co-operative Home Colony', *World's Work*, ix (March 1907) 382–7.

Upton Sinclair, 'Helicon Hall', in *The New Encyclopaedia of Social Reform*, ed. W. D. P. Bliss (New York: Funk & Wagnalls, 1909).

——, 'Reminiscences of *The Jungle*', *Wilshire's Magazine*, XIII (May 1909) 20.

——, 'Colorado', *International Socialist Review*, XV (July 1914) 44–7. [Text of Sinclair's comments on his trip to Denver and Ludlow.]

—— (ed.), *The City for Justice: An Anthology of the Literature of Social Protest*, with an Introduction by Jack London (New York: John C. Winston Co., 1915; reissued Pasadena: Upton Sinclair, 1925).

——, *King Coal: A Novel*, with an Introduction by Dr Georg Brandes (New York: Macmillan, 1917).

——, *The Brass Check: A Study in American Journalism* (Pasadena: Upton Sinclair, 1919).

——, *American Outpost: A Book of Reminiscences* (New York: Farrar, Rinehart, 1932).

——, *My Lifetime in Letters* (Columbia, Missouri: University of Missouri Press, 1960).

——, *The Autobiography of Upton Sinclair* (London: W. H. Allen, 1962).

George M. Spangler, 'Suicide and Social Criticism: Durkheim, Dreiser, Wharton, and London', *American Quarterly*, XXXI (Fall 1979) 496–516.

John Spargo, Review of *The Iron Heel*, by Jack London, *International Socialist Review*, VIII (April 1908) 628–9.

——, *The Spiritual Significance of Modern Socialism* (New York: B. W. Huebsch, 1908; London: Arthur F. Bird, 1909).

Herman Spector, Joseph Kalar, Edwin Rolfe and S. Funaroff, *We Gather Strength*, with an Introduction by Michael Gold (New York: Liberal Press, 1933).

Stephen Spender, *The Destructive Element* (London: Jonathan Cape, 1935).

J. E. Spingarn, *Poems* (New York: Harcourt, Brace, 1924).

Harold R. Stearns (ed.), *Civilization in the United States: An Inquiry by Thirty Americans* (New York: Harcourt Brace, 1922).

Ronald Steel, *Walter Lippmann and the American Century* (London: Bodley Head, 1981).

Lincoln Steffens, *Lincoln Steffens Speaking* (New York: Harcourt Brace, 1936).

——, *The Letters of Lincoln Steffens*, 2 vols, ed. Ella Winter and Granville Hicks (New York: Harcourt Brace, 1938).

Paul Stein, 'Jack London's *The Iron Heel*: Art as Manifesto', *Studies in American Fiction*, VI (1978) 77–92.

Frederick Boyd Stevenson, 'Sinclair, the Beef Trust Griller', *Wilshire's Magazine*, X (August 1906) 12.

Alfred Stieglitz, 'Ten Stories', *Twice-a-Year*, nos. 5–6 (1940–1) 136–7.

A. Stork, 'Mr. Calverton and His Friends', *International Literature*, no. 3 (1934) 97–124.

James Strachan, 'Conversion', *Encyclopaedia of Religion and Ethics*, ed. James Hastings (New York: Charles Scribner's Sons, 1911).

John Strachey, *Literature and Dialectical Materialism* (New York: Covici Friede, 1934).

Genevieve Taggard (ed.), *May Days: An Anthology of Verse from 'Masses'– 'Liberator'* (New York: Boni & Liveright, 1925).

Dickran Tashjian, *William Carlos Williams and the American Scene, 1920–1940* (New

York: Whitney Museum of American Art, with University of California Press, Berkeley, 1978). 'Proletarian Portraits', pp. 115–36.

C. F. Terrell (ed.), *Louis Zukofsky: Man and Poet* (Orono, Maine: National Poetry Foundation, 1979).

Eunice Tietjens, *The World at my Shoulders* (New York: Macmillan, 1938).

Lionel Trilling, 'The Promise of Realism', *Menorah Journal*, xviii (May 1930) 480–4.

Leon Trotsky, *The History of the Russian Revolution*, 3 vols, trans. Max Eastman (London: Victor Gollancz, 1932–3: reissued London: Sphere Books, 1967).

——, *On Literature and Art*, ed. Paul N. Siegel (New York: Pathfinder Press, 1970).

——, *Writings of Leon Trotsky [1936—7]*, 2nd edn, ed. Naomi Allen and George Breitman (New York: Pathfinder Press, 1978).

Robert C. Tucker, *The Marxian Revolutionary Idea* (London: George Allen & Unwin, 1970).

John Kenneth Turner, *Barbarous Mexico: An Indictment of a Cruel and Corrupt System* (London and New York: Cassell, 1911).

John Unterecker, *Voyager: A Life of Hart Crane* (London: Anthony Blond, 1970).

S. V. Utechin, 'Philosophy and Society: Alexander Bogdanov', in *Revisionism: Essays on the History of Marxist Ideas*, ed. Leopold Labedz (London: George Allen & Unwin, 1962).

Paul Vaillant-Couturier, '*Le Talon de Fer*: Introduction (1932)', *Europe*, nos 561–2 (Janvier–Fevrier 1976) 79–82.

Robert von Hallberg, 'The Politics of Description: W. C. Williams in the Thirties', *ELH*, xlv (Spring 1978) 131–51.

Mary Heaton Vorse, *A Footnote to Folly: Reminiscences* (New York: Farrar, Rinehart, 1935).

Alan Wald, 'Revolutionary Intellectuals: *Partisan Review* in the 1930s', *Occident*, n.s. viii (Spring 1974) 118–33.

——, 'The Menorah Group Moves Left', *Jewish Social Studies*, xxxviii (Summer–Fall 1976) 289–320.

——, 'Memories of the John Dewey Commission Forty Years Later', *Antioch Review*, xxxv (Fall 1977) 438–51.

——, *James T. Farrell: The Revolutionary Socialist Years* (New York University Press, 1978).

Frank A. Warren, III, *Liberals and Communism: The 'Red Decade' Revisited* (Bloomington and London: Indiana University Press, 1966).

Charles N. Watson Jr, 'The Composition of *Martin Eden*', *American Literature*, liii (November 1981) 397–408.

Mike Weaver, *William Carlos Williams: The American Background* (Cambridge University Press, 1971).

Constance Webb, *Richard Wright: A Biography* (New York: G. P. Putnam's Sons, 1968).

James Weinstein, *The Corporate Ideal in the Liberal State: 1900–1918* (Boston: Beacon Press, 1968).

Arthur Frank Wertheim, *The New York Little Renaissance: Iconoclasm, Modernism and Nationalism in American Culture, 1908–1917* (New York University Press, 1976).

Reed Whittemore, *William Carlos Williams: Poet from Jersey* (Boston: Houghton Mifflin, 1975).

William Carlos Williams, 'The New Poetical Economy', *Poetry*, xliv (July 1934) 220–6.

——, *The Autobiography of William Carlos Williams* (New York: Random House, 1951; reissued New York: New Directions, 1967).

——, *Selected Letters of William Carlos Williams*, ed. John C. Thirlwall (New York: McDowell, Obolensky, 1957).

Edmund Wilson, *Axel's Castle: A Study in the Imaginative Literature of 1870 to 1930* (New York: Charles Scribner's Sons, 1931).

——, *The American Jitters: A Year of the Slump* (New York: Charles Scribner's Sons, 1932).

——, 'What Do Liberals Hope For?', *New Republic*, lxix (11 February 1932) 345–8.

——, 'Equity for Americans', *New Republic*, lxx (30 March 1932) 185–6.

——, 'The Literary Class War: II', *New Republic*, lxx (11 May 1932) 347–9.

——, 'Marxist History', *New Republic*, lxxiii (12 October 1932) 226–8.

——, 'Art, the Proletariat and Marx', *New Republic*, lxxii (23 August 1933) 41–5.

——, *Travels in Two Democracies* (New York: Harcourt Brace, 1936).

——, *To the Finland Station: A Study in the Writing and Acting of History* (New York: Harcourt Brace, 1940; London: Martin Secker, [1940]).

——, *Memoirs of Hecate County* (Garden City, New York: Doubleday and Co., 1946; London: W. H. Allen, 1951).

——, *The Shores of Light: A Literary Chronicle of the Twenties and Thirties* (New York: Farrar, Straus and Young, 1952; reissued Vintage Books, Random House, 1961).

——, *The Triple Thinkers* (London: John Lehmann, 1952; first published 1938).

——, *Red, Black, Blond and Olive: Studies in Four Civilizations* (London: W. H. Allen, 1956).

——, *The Twenties: From Notebooks and Diaries of the Period*, ed. Leon Edel (New York: Farrar, Straus & Giroux, 1975).

——, *Letters on Literature and Politics, 1912–1972*, selected and edited by Elena Wilson (London: Routledge & Kegan Paul, 1977).

——, *The Thirties: From Notebooks and Diaries of the Period*, ed. Leon Edel (London: Macmillan, 1980).

Yvor Winters, 'The Objectivists', *Hound and Horn*, vi (October–December 1932) 158–60.

Bertram D. Wolfe, *A Life in Two Centuries*, with an Introduction by Leonard Schapiro (New York: Stein and Day, 1981).

Richard Wright, *Black Boy* (New York: Harper & Row, 1945).

——, *American Hunger*, Afterword by Michel Fabre (New York: Harper & Row, 1977).

Avrahm Yassour, 'Bogdanov et son oeuvre', *Cahiers du monde russe et soviétique*, x (Juillet–Decembre 1969) 546–84.

John Nicholas Beffel, ed., *Art Young: His Life and Times* (New York: Sheridan House, 1939).

Igor Zhuravlev, 'The Relationships between Socialist Poetry in the U.S.A. at the Beginning of the Twentieth Century and the Graphic Arts of the Socialist Press', *Zeitschrift für Anglistik und Amerikanstik*, xviii (1970) 168–82.

Louis Zukofsky, ed., *An 'Objectivists' Anthology* (Le Beausset, Var: To, 1932).

Louis Zukofsky, *Prepositions: The Collected Essays of Louis Zukofsky* (London: Rapp and Carroll, 1967).
——, 'Sincerity and Objectification: with Special Reference to the Work of Charles Reznikoff', *Poetry*, xxxvii (February 1931) 272–85.

Index